Children's Daily Prayer

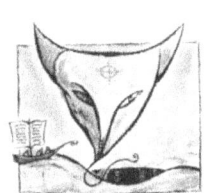  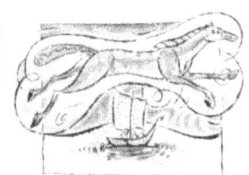  

Under the Southern Cross
2019

Margaret Smith sgs

and Associates

adapted from *Children's Daily Prayer*

by Elizabeth McMahon Jeep

A Liturgy of the Hours for the classroom:
an Order of Prayer for each school day
that reflects the spirit of the Church's Seasons and Feasts

Contents

CONTENTS
Title page	i
Contents	ii-iii
Publication Details	iv
Before you use *Children's Daily Prayer Under the Southern Cross*	v-vii
Hymn chart	viii-ix
About the Art	x

FEBRUARY ~ ORDINARY TIME   1
Looking Ahead	2-3
A Psalm for February	4
Daily Prayer	5-29
Psalms are prayers	*30*

EARLY LENT   31
Looking Ahead	32-33
A Psalm for Early Lent	34
A Blessing of Ashes	35
Daily Prayer	36-53
Psalms are poems	*54*

LATE LENT   55
Looking Ahead	56-57
A Psalm for Late Lent	58
Daily Prayer	59-68

EARLY EASTERTIME   69
Looking Ahead	70-71
A Psalm for Early Eastertime	72
Daily Prayer	73-87
Psalms are shouts	*88*

LATE EASTERTIME   89
Looking Ahead	90-91
A Psalm for Late Eastertime	92
Daily Prayer	93-107
Psalms are cries	*108*

JUNE ~ ORDINARY TIME   109
Looking Ahead	110-111
A Psalm for June	112
Daily Prayer	113-126

JULY ~ ORDINARY TIME   127
Looking Ahead	128-129
A Psalm for July	130
Daily Prayer	131-143
Psalms are cosmic chants	*144*

AUGUST ~ ORDINARY TIME   145
Looking Ahead	146-147
A Psalm for August	148
Daily Prayer	149-170

SEPTEMBER ∽ ORDINARY TIME   171

Looking Ahead	172-173
A Psalm for September	174
Daily Prayer	175-194

OCTOBER ∽ ORDINARY TIME   195

Looking Ahead	196-197
A Psalm for October	198
Daily Prayer	199-212

NOVEMBER ∽ ORDINARY TIME   213

Looking Ahead	214-215
A Psalm for November	216
Daily Prayer	217-236

ADVENT   237

Looking Ahead	238-239
A Psalm for Advent	240
Daily Prayer	241-255
Helpful Resources	256
Subject Index	257-258

Spectrum Publications Pty Ltd
PO Box 75, Richmond VIC 3121
www.spectrumpublications.com.au
in conjunction with
Sisters of the Good Samaritan
PO Box 1076
Glebe NSW 2037
www.goodsams.org.au

Children's Daily Prayer - under the Southern Cross 2019
Margaret Smith sgs and Associates
© Trustees of the Sisters of the Good Samaritan

Adapted from *Children's Daily Prayer* by Elizabeth McMahon Jeep, © copyright Archdiocese of Chicago: Liturgy Training Publications, 1800 North Hermitage Avenue, Chicago, IL 60622-1101, United States of America.

Psalms and scripture quotations are from the *Contemporary English Version of the Bible*, © American Bible Society 1991, 1995. Used by permission of the Bible Society of Australia Inc.

Excerpts from the English translation of the *Book of Blessings* copyright © 1988 ICEL. All rights reserved.

Nihil Obstat: Reverend Monsignor Peter J Kenny STD
Imprimatur: Monsignor Greg Bennet, Vicar General
The Nihil Obstat and Imprimatur are official declarations that a book, pamphlet or prayer card is free of doctrinal or moral error. No implication is contained therein that those who have granted the Nihil Obstat and Imprimatur agree with the contents, opinions or statements expressed. They do not necessarily signify that the work is approved as a basic text for catechetical instruction.

ISBN: 978-0-86786-030-6

Design by Sandra Nobes
Typesetting by Spectrum Publications Melbourne
Illustrations by Shane Nagle
Printed by Openbook Howden Adelaide

Before you use this book

What is this book and who is it for?
An annual liturgical prayer resource:
- containing day by day prayer, Monday – Friday, for the current school year.
- for students in parish schools, in parish religious education/sacramental classes or in religious education classes in government schools

What is special about the 2019 edition?
As in 2017 and 2018 it is simpler and shorter than previous editions because:
- it provides a single prayer service for each day
- it looks ahead to the Sunday gospel each Friday
- it contains five short introductions to the psalms:
  - *Psalms are Prayers*
  - *Psalms are Poems*
  - *Psalms are Shouts*
  - *Psalms are Cries*
  - *Psalms are Cosmic Chants*

What is unique about this prayer resource?
It is based on the church's long tradition of praying at certain times of the day – the Liturgy of the Hours. It uses:
- hymns
- psalms
- scripture readings
- reflection on the scriptures
- intercessions (At the beginning of the year, encourage children to write in names on their birth dates and names of deceased relatives and friends on anniversary dates.)

Why use this book?
Children's Daily Prayer Under the Southern Cross:
- is 'all there' and hence, user-friendly
- is led by students
- helps students to pray with the scriptures
- builds familiarity with the saints of our tradition, as well as 'prophets and peace-makers' of our own time
- broadens students' horizons by reference to the important celebrations of other faiths
- enables students to bring together prayer and daily life
- introduces students to a way of praying which might sustain them throughout their lives
- helps students to pray with the mind and heart of the church

Why a new book each year?
Children's Daily Prayer Under the Southern Cross is like a new diary. **Right** there on the **right day** and the **right date** and on the **right page** are the prayers and readings for every day of the school year.

Why a book for each CLASSROOM?
- students can participate in ritual action
- students can take regular turns in leading class prayer
- students can voice their own individual concerns in prayer
- classes can choose their own hymns

Who else might use this book?
This book can be used:
- to begin staff prayer and other school-based meetings
- by students in any Christian schools
- to begin parish meetings
- by RCIA groups
- by ministers on their visits to the sick
- as a resource for family prayer

Organisation and Content

How is the book arranged?
The book is arranged by:
- months (from February)
- the liturgical seasons
- for each month or liturgical season there is an introduction called **Looking Ahead** and a psalm for the month or season

Why are there some gaps?
Due to overlapping school holidays throughout Australia, there are three gaps in *Children's Daily Prayer*, arranged so that no state misses more than one week during these times. The gaps are from Monday April 15 – Friday April 26, Monday July 1 – Friday July 12, and Monday September 30 – Friday October 11. Schools that are in session during these periods can follow the instructions for prayer provided in the Looking Ahead pages for Early Eastertime (p. 71), June (p. 111) and October (p. 196).

What is the pattern for Daily Prayer?
The pattern for Daily Prayer is:
- An **Introduction** to help focus the prayer for the day
- A **Psalm** for the month or season
- A **Scripture Reading**
- A **Reflection** on the scripture reading
- A time for **Prayers of Intercession**
- A **Closing Prayer**

How are the Scriptures organised?
- Daily Prayer for Monday to Thursday has its own schema of readings. This schema:
  - is designed to introduce students to the great figures, epic stories and major themes of the bible
  - is not linked to the daily mass readings although, over some weeks, readings about the public ministry of Jesus from the gospel writer for the current Sunday cycle have been selected
  - spreads longer readings and stories from particular books of the Bible over a number of days or weeks [**Note:** To gain maximum benefit and to keep the continuity of these stories, the **full sequence needs to be read** on the indicated days.]
  - uses the same scripture translation as the *Lectionary for Masses with Children*.
- The readings for Friday will normally anticipate the Gospel reading for the following Sunday. This keeps a connection with the whole church hearing the same gospel on the actual Sunday.

For the Teacher or Catechist

What is the best way to use the book?
- One book for each classroom, shared by the leader and reader
- Copies of the **Psalm** for the month or season for each student. (Do these copies in seasonal colours and have students insert them into prayer folders, which they might make at the beginning of the year)
- **Student leadership** – leader and reader
- Familiarity with the **Looking Ahead** pages
- Regular use

For the Student Leader and Reader

When leading or reading:
- **Stand up straight.** This gives the prayer dignity and establishes a student's ministerial role
- **Slow everything down** – the pace of reading, walking, lighting the candle
- **Exaggerate everything a bit** – reading, bowing, signing, blessing

Instructions for the Leader
- **Find the page** with the correct date and mark it with a ribbon of the seasonal colour.
- **Turn to the Psalm.** There is always a page reference that tells you where to find it. Mark it also with a ribbon.
- **Practise** the Introduction and the Closing.
- **Check with the teacher** to see if you will read and discuss all or particular Reflection questions.
- **Practise** the parts of the Psalm marked 'Leader' and 'Side A'.
- **To begin,** announce the hymn if there is to be one, and any acclamations, and say where they will be sung. Then start with the Introduction.
- **Practise** giving blessings.

Instructions for the Reader
- **Find the page** with the correct date.
- **Practise** the reading on that page.
- **Turn to the Psalm.** You will lead the parts marked 'Side B'.
- **Practise** the parts of the Closing in heavier print. You will lead them.
- **Indicate** to the class with your arm when to say the parts in heavier print.

What about music?

Sung prayer is at the heart of our Christian tradition. Children's Daily Prayer will be enhanced when song is an integral part of it – hymns, chants, short refrains. A hymn can be sung at the beginning of the prayer. An 'Alleluia' can always conclude the prayer except during Lent. Settings of 'Lord, have mercy' or 'Kyrie eleison' are suitable for Lent.

Below is a chart with some suggested hymns. They are mainly from the collections As One Voice *(AOV) which is readily available, and* Gather Australia *(GA). Many will also be found in the recent compilation,* Catholic Worship Book II *(CWB2). You will note that the suggestions are usually hymns of praise or suited to the seasons and feasts of the church year, rather than Eucharistic hymns. The church's Daily Prayer is of a different form from Eucharist. The basis of selection is the liturgical season, suitability for students and what they are likely to hear in their parish Sunday assemblies.*

AOV   As One Voice *(Vol 1 & 2)*. Combined People's Edition. Manly Vale, NSW: Willow Publishing Pty Ltd.
GA   Gather Australia. NLMC Publications, Australia.
CWB2   Catholic Worship Book II. Northcote, Vic., Morning Star Publishing.
For other useful collections of music for the liturgy, see the 'Helpful Resources' (p. 256).

	AOV	GA		AOV	GA
ADVENT			**EASTER**		
Advent Litany		279	Alleluia, alleluia, give thanks to the risen Lord		360
Advent Song		281	Celtic Alleluia	1-013	141
O come, O come, Emmanuel	1-174	285	Christ be our light	2-003	404
Prepare the way		284	Easter Alleluia		358
A voice cries out		278	Halle, Halle,	2-046	107
A voice in the wilderness	1-062		Jesus lives	2-029	
			O sons and daughters		359
LENT			Out of Darkness	1-134	504
(Alleluia is not sung during Lent)			This day was made by the Lord	1-183	
A trusting psalm	1-115	455	This day was made by the Lord		356
Amazing Grace	1-29	437	We walk by faith	1-063	447
Ashes	2-016	209	***Leading up to Pentecost***		
Behold the Wood		333	Alleluia! Sing to Jesus	1-191	370
Come as you are	1-031	212	Come, Holy Spirit		377
Come to set us free	1-039	277	Enemy of apathy	2-075	372
Grant to us, O Lord, a heart renewed		303	O breathe on me, breath of God		342
Hosea	1-030	213	Send down the fire	1-164	475
Jesus, remember me	1-152	308	Take Christ to the world		369
Lord, Have mercy OR Kyrie eleison			Veni, Sancte Spiritus		268
	Any known settings		Warm our hearts	1-043	
Return to God		304			
Shepherd me O God	1-033	24			
Tree of life *(has general verses for Lent and then specific verses for the Sundays of Year A)*		307			
Ubi caritas		319			
Will you love me	1-040	505			

ORDINARY TIME
Alleluia settings:

Celtic Alleluia	1-013	141
Easter Alleluia		358
Halle, Halle, Halle	2-046	107

Hymns

All creatures of our God and King		395
All the earth	1-184	534
Bless the Lord	1-083	
Clap your hands, all you nations	2-001	
Companions on the journey	1-188	
For the fruits of this creation		426
Glory and praise to our God	1-016	417
God beyond all names	2-023	393
Holy is God	1-145	
Laudate Dominum		418
Let all the peoples	2-056	60
Morning has broken	1-135	537
One great family		396
Praise to you O Christ	1-028	407
Prayer of St Francis	2-126	490
Sing a new song	1-080	
Sing of the Lord's goodness	1-131	413
Sing praises to the Lord	1-032	
Sing to the Lord	1-046	
Strong and Constant	1-110	
This day God gives me		356
Though the mountains may fall	1-182	452

NOVEMBER
The Church's month for the deceased

Blest are they	1-055	477
The Beatitudes	1-163	489
May God bless and keep you	1-177	441
I shall dwell in the Lord's house	2-069	
Keep in mind	1-080	391
Like a child rests	1-085	
O God, nothing can take us from your love	1-139	
On eagle's wings	1-153	452
We will rise again	1-136	
We walk by faith	1-163	447

FEASTS OF THE LORD DURING ORDINARY TIME

Holy Trinity

Praise with joy the world's creator		379
Father in heaven		381

Body and Blood of Christ

Taste and see God's love for us		203
Come to the Feast	1-140	

Sacred Heart

I heard the voice of Jesus say	1-1542	
Jesus Christ is waiting	2-008	

Transfiguration

Christ be our light		404
The Lord is my light and my salvation (Refrain II)		28

Exaltation of the Cross

Processional song of the Cross		337
Adoramus te Christe		305

Feast of Christ the King

All the ends of the earth		420
Like a Shepherd	1-160	

FEASTS OF MARY

Hail Mary: Gentle Woman		544
Immaculate Mary		549
Magnificat		545
My soul rejoices		250
O God, hear us	1-022	
O holy Mary	1-141	
Oh Mary, we ask you – Michael Mangan, *My Spirit Sings*		
There is nothing told about this woman		548

About the Art

Water is all around us, gentle and powerful,
meeting us
as waves nibbling at our sandy toes,
a cool drink running down our thirsty throats,
showers and baths for washing and for splashing,
greening rain falling on dry land and gardens,
life-giving and life-saving.

From our baptism,
water carries us
into the life of Christ
and into God's wonderful world.

Like small boats, we sail along
through days and seasons:
some bright and happy,
some stormy, even fearful,
sometimes seeing many wonders,
sometimes missing everything
as we reach new shores.

Prayer raises our sails,
catches the Spirit-wind,
and blows us on our journey
towards God and other people.

On our voyage, upstream, downstream,
we meet other sailors and companions:
perhaps a pet or playmate,
perhaps an angel messenger,
young, little people,
and old ancestors,
who share our voyage and our prayer.

And the Southern Cross of stars is like a compass,
pointing us towards the home
God has prepared for us.

February

Wednesday, January 30

to Tuesday, March 5

Ordinary Time ~ February 2019
Looking Ahead

About the Month

For students, teachers and all concerned with education, February means 'back to school'. While summer holidays are over, summer continues. Days are hot and daylight hours long and still call us to beaches, rivers and pools. The weather is still warm enough for us to eat outside and to enjoy barbeques. In some parts of the country, trees are starting to look tired and are beginning to lose their leaves. This term lasts right through to the middle of Autumn.

At the beginning of this new school year, you may feel excited or perhaps a little bit anxious. You will be in a higher year. Are there new teachers? New students? New buildings or new things in the building? Do you have new things for school—uniforms, books? Who made sure you got those new things and made sure you were ready for the new school year? Those people deserve your thanks.

Going back to school is a time of hard work and preparation for your teachers. They might also be a little bit anxious and wonder what their new classes will be like. Teachers also deserve our thanks.

Someone else deserves our thanks. God has provided the wonderful months of summer and the holidays that summer brings. God has also protected us over this time. It is good to give God thanks and praise for all the love poured out on us and for all the good days to come.

During February, there is still a feeling of 'New Year' in the air. The church's 'New Year' began in Advent last year. The season of Christmas followed and closed on January 7. Until Lent begins we are in the first part of Ordinary Time; the second part will begin after Pentecost. This does not mean that the season is 'ordinary' but simply that each week will be counted in order, beginning with the first week of Ordinary Time. This year there are four or five school weeks of Ordinary Time before Lent.

Children's Daily Prayer Under the Southern Cross 2019 is one of our new books. It is a guide for your prayer for every day of the school year. Some prayers change each day. Some stay the same. This is the way the church prays.

Directions for using this book for prayer are on pages v-vii of the Introduction. When it is your turn to lead the prayer, you can read those instructions again. Attach ribbons to the book to mark your place—different colours for different liturgical seasons.

Readings

During the first week of February, our readings for Daily Prayer remind us that God has created us and loves us and is always present with us. The readings urge us to always turn to God in prayer.

Each year in Ordinary Time we read in turn from one of three gospels: Matthew, Mark and Luke. In this three year cycle, 2019 is Year C so this year we will be reading mostly from Luke. Our readings will give us Luke's story of the life and work of Jesus. The gospel of Matthew will be read in Year A and the gospel of Mark in Year B.

Our readings for each Friday will normally look ahead to the following Sunday's gospel. This keeps us connected with the whole church who will hear the same gospel on the actual Sunday.

Learn the correct responses to the readings. After a gospel reading, the reader says, 'The gospel of the Lord' and everyone responds, 'Praise to you, Lord Jesus Christ.' If the reading is not from one of the gospel writers, then the reader says, 'The word of the Lord' and everyone responds, 'Thanks be to God.'

Feasts and Other Commemorations

An important feast, normally observed on February 2 but here on January 31, is the Presentation of the Lord. Mary and Joseph brought Jesus to the temple 40 days after he was born. Jesus was greeted there by the prophets Simeon and Anna. They knew that he was the Messiah, the light of the world.

We also remember that Chinese New Year is celebrated on Tuesday, February 5.

Preparation for February

Children's Daily Prayer Under the Southern Cross includes a Psalm to be prayed each day. The psalms will change each month or season. Psalms are very ancient songs from the Bible. Often they are psalms of praise but there are also psalms of thanksgiving or psalms when we can bring our worries to God.
The Psalm for February, Psalm 145, is on page 4. We praise God who is patient and loving and who cares for all of creation. Students will need their own copies for each day. Make special 2019 prayer folders in which to keep them. You can add to these as the year goes on.

The Closing for Daily Prayer includes prayer for special intentions. Intentions are things to pray about. Students celebrating birthdays can be remembered in the intentions. Then there are other happy or sad events that happen--the birth of a new brother or sister, the sickness or death of a family member of a student or teacher. It is good to remember these in the intentions.

Encourage children to simply name the person or group for whom they wish to pray rather than enter into long stories. Examples might be: 'For Sam on his birthday'; 'For people who have died in the earthquake,' 'For N. who is sick'.

Suggested Hymns

See the hymn chart on pages viii-ix. Throughout the year, sing a hymn to begin Daily Prayer.

In February, Daily Prayer concludes with an 'Alleluia'. Sing this until Ash Wednesday.

A Psalm for February

Psalm 145:1-2, 8-9, 13-14, 17-18

LEADER
Sing and shout praises to the Lord our God!
ALL
Sing praise to the Lord for as long as you live.

SIDE A
You are merciful, Lord!
You are kind and patient and always loving.
You are good to everyone,
and you take care of all your creation.

SIDE B
Our Lord, you keep your word
and do everything you say.
When someone stumbles or falls,
you give a helping hand.

SIDE A
Our Lord, everything you do
is kind and thoughtful.

SIDE B
And you are near to everyone
whose prayers come from the heart.

LEADER
Sing and shout praises to the Lord our God!
ALL
Sing praise to the Lord for as long as you live.
Glory be to the Father, and to the Son,
and to the Holy Spirit:
as it was in the beginning, is now,
and ever shall be
world without end. **Amen**. Alleluia.

[Turn back to Daily Prayer for today.]

Wednesday Daily Prayer

[Reminder: The Psalm for February is on page 4. Make a copy for each member of the class.]

Introduction

As we begin a new school year, we think about how we want to be friends – friends with each other and friends with God. In today's reading from his first letter, John reminds us that God wants us to love each other as much as he loves us. This is not always easy. At school we are often in class with others who are not yet our friends. Perhaps we can make John's teaching our motto as we begin our new school year!

✞ All make the Sign of the Cross.

Hymn

A Psalm for February

[Turn to page 4.]

Reading   1 John 4:7-8, 16, 19-21

Listen to the words of the first letter of John:

My dear friends, we must love each other. Love comes from God, and when we love each other, it shows that we have been given new life. We are now God's children and we know him. God is love, and anyone who doesn't love others has never known him.

God is love. If we keep on loving others, we will stay one in our hearts with God and he will say one with us.

We love because God loves us first. But if we say we love God and don't love each other, we are liars. We cannot see God. So how can we love God, if we don't love the people we can see?

The commandment that God has given us is: "Love God and love each other!"

The word of the Lord.

Reflection

How do you feel about being in a new class? Are you ready to be loving to everyone? Are there any new students here who might be feeling lonely? How can I love them?

Closing

Blessed be God, Creator of days and seasons.

Let us all say: Blessed be God for ever!
Blessed be God for ever!

Let us bring our hopes and needs to God, as we pray: **God, our companion, hear our prayer.**

Let us pray with the words that Jesus taught us:

Our Father …

Loving God, you give us this new school year
and new friends with whom to share it.
Bless all who pray
and work and learn together.
May this year bring peace and harmony
throughout the world.
We ask this through Christ our Lord. **Amen.**

[Sing 'alleluia'.]

✞ All make the Sign of the Cross.

January 30, 2019

Thursday Daily Prayer

Introduction

On Saturday the church celebrates the feast of the Presentation of the Lord. We remember it today. It was an ancient Jewish custom to bring a first son to the temple forty days after he was born. When Mary and Joseph did this, Jesus was greeted in the temple by the prophets Simeon and Anna. They knew that he was the Messiah, the light of the world.

✞ All make the Sign of the Cross.

Hymn

A Psalm for February

[Turn to page 4.]

Reading   Luke 2:25-27, 27-32

Listen to the words of the holy gospel according to Luke:

Simeon (*SIM-ee-un*) was a good man. He loved God and was waiting for God to save the people of Israel. God's Spirit came to him and told him that he would not die until he had seen Christ the Lord.
  When Mary and Joseph brought Jesus to the temple, the Spirit told Simeon to go into the temple. Simeon took the baby Jesus in his arms and praised God,
"Lord, I am your servant,
  and now I can die in peace,
  because you have kept your promise to me.
With my own eyes I have seen
  what you have done to save your people,
  and foreign nations will also see this.
Your mighty power is a light for all nations,
  and it will bring honour to your people Israel."

The gospel of the Lord.

Reflection

Simeon shows us how to wait with hope for God. Can you see signs of God's goodness in your life? Are you ready to learn more about God this year? What good things are you looking forward to?

Closing

Let us all repeat:
The Lord is my light and my salvation;
of whom should I be afraid?
**The Lord is my light and my salvation;
of whom should I be afraid?**

Let us bring our hopes and needs to God, as we pray: **God, our companion, hear our prayer.**

Let us pray with the words that Jesus taught us:

Our Father …

Loving God, you gave us your Son Jesus
to be the light of the world.
When the way seems dark,
let his light shine upon us
and lead all people safely to you.

We ask this through Christ our Lord. **Amen.**

[Sing 'alleluia'.]

✞ All make the Sign of the Cross.

January 31, 2019

Friday Daily Prayer

Introduction

Our Friday readings are usually taken from the gospel at next Sunday's Mass. Every week we listen again to the good news and let it teach us how to live. This year we will hear most often from the gospel of Luke.

Today we hear how the mission of Jesus begins. Jesus goes back to his home town of Nazareth and meets with others on the Sabbath day to listen to the scriptures. He reads out a message from the prophet Isaiah and tells everyone that it has now come true.

✞ All make the Sign of the Cross.

Hymn

A Psalm for February

[Turn to page 4.]

Reading   Luke 4:16-19

Listen to the words of the holy gospel according to Luke:

Jesus went back to Nazareth, where he had been brought up, and as usual he went to the meeting place on the Sabbath. When he stood up to read from the Scriptures, he was given the book of Isaiah the prophet. He opened it and read,
"The Lord's Spirit has come to me,
because he has chosen me
   to tell the good news to the poor.
The Lord has sent me
to announce freedom for prisoners,
   to give sight to the blind,
to free everyone who suffers,
   and to say, 'This is the year the Lord has chosen.'"
Then Jesus said to them, "What you have just heard me read has come true today."

The gospel of the Lord.

Reflection

What does this tell us about the mission of Jesus? What kind of person was he? What did God's Spirit give him the power to do? How can we share in Jesus' work?

Closing

Blessed be God, Creator of days and seasons.

Let us all say: Blessed be God for ever!
Blessed be God for ever!

Let us bring our hopes and needs to God, as we pray: **God, our companion, hear our prayer.**

Let us pray with the words that Jesus taught us:

Our Father …

Loving God, you give us this new school year
and new friends with whom to share it.
Bless all who pray
and work and learn together.
May this year bring peace and harmony
throughout the world.
We ask this through Christ our Lord. **Amen.**

[Sing 'alleluia'.]

✞ All make the Sign of the Cross.

February 1, 2019

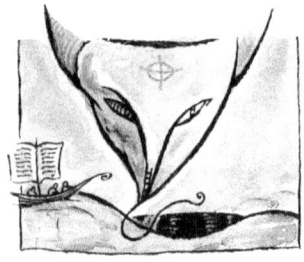

Monday Daily Prayer

Introduction

While the new school year is still getting under way, we think about how to pray well together. When we pray, we pay attention to God who is here with us. We listen to God's word, and share with God our thoughts, hopes and fears. We begin by trying to become still and ready, so that we can listen and speak with our heart.

The reading today tells how Elijah (*ee-LYE-juh*) made himself ready. He listened for the voice of God, and it came, not in loud thunder but in silence.

✞ All make the Sign of the Cross.

Hymn

A Psalm for February

[Turn to page 4.]

Reading   1 Kings 19:11-13

Listen to the words of the first book of Kings:

While Elijah (*ee-LYE-juh*) was on Mount Sinai (*SYE-nye*), the LORD said, "Go out and stand on the mountain. I want you to see me when I pass by."

All at once, a strong wind shook the mountain and shattered the rocks. But the LORD was not in the wind. Next, there was an earthquake, but the LORD was not in the earthquake. Then there was a fire, but the LORD was not in the fire. Finally, there was a gentle breeze, and when Elijah heard it, he covered his face with his coat. He went out and stood at the entrance of the cave.

The LORD asked, "Elijah, why are you here?"

The word of the Lord.

Reflection

As we pray at the beginning of the year, God asks: "Why are you here?" What do we want to happen this year? How are we going to help make this year good for others?

Closing

Blessed be God, Creator of days and seasons.

Let us all say: Blessed be God for ever!
Blessed be God for ever!

Let us bring our hopes and needs to God, as we pray: **God, our companion, hear our prayer.**

Let us pray with the words that Jesus taught us:

Our Father …

Loving God, you give us this new school year
and new friends with whom to share it.
Bless all who pray
and work and learn together.
May this year bring peace and harmony
throughout the world.
We ask this through Christ our Lord. **Amen.**

[Sing 'alleluia'.]

✞ All make the Sign of the Cross.

February 4, 2019

Tuesday Daily Prayer

Introduction

Today is the first day of the New Year for Chinese and other Asian people. It is a special day for them to come together with family and friends. They look ahead happily to the blessings of the year ahead. We can celebrate with them.

During these first days of the school year, our readings are about 'beginnings' and about prayer. After the reading we spend a few minutes in silence, letting the words of the Bible echo in our hearts. Today we hear some of what Jesus has to teach us about prayer. He wants us to be sure that God hears and answers our prayers.

✢ All make the Sign of the Cross.

Hymn

A Psalm for February

[Turn to page 4.]

Reading   *Matthew 7:7-11*

Listen to the words of the holy gospel according to Matthew:

Jesus said, "Ask, and you will receive. Search, and you will find. Knock, and the door will be opened for you. Everyone who asks will receive. Everyone who searches will find. And the door will be opened for everyone who knocks.
  "Would any of you give your hungry child a stone, if the child asked for some bread? Would you give your child a snake if the child asked for a fish? As bad as you are, you still know how to give good gifts to your children. But your heavenly Father is even more ready to give good things to people who ask."

The gospel of the Lord.

Reflection

Do I pray even when it seems that God is not listening? Am I able to be still and peaceful sometimes, remembering that God is with me? Is there someone for whom I often pray?

Closing

Blessed be God, Creator of days and seasons.

Let us all say: Blessed be God for ever!
Blessed be God for ever!

Let us bring our hopes and needs to God, as we pray: **God, our companion, hear our prayer.**

Let us pray with the words that Jesus taught us:

Our Father …

Loving God, you give us this new school year
and new friends with whom to share it.
Bless all who pray
and work and learn together.
May this year bring peace and harmony
throughout the world.
We ask this through Christ our Lord. **Amen.**

[Sing 'alleluia'.]

✢ All make the Sign of the Cross.

February 5, 2019

Wednesday Daily Prayer

Introduction

Today is Waitangi (*WHY-tongue-ee*) Day in New Zealand, the land called Aotearoa (*Owe-tee-uh-ro-uh*) by the Maori people. Waitangi Day commemorates the treaty made with them in 1840. In the world many countries have worked hard to become better places for different peoples to live in. Often they will sign promises, agreements or treaties which make it possible to develop a deeper understanding of how all people can live together in harmony. The Treaty of Waitangi – Te Tiriti O Waitangi – is one of these.

Prayer is possible because God is near to us. God is near when we celebrate the eucharist and when we bless food before we eat it. God is near when we are playing outside or when we are with our friends. God is near when we are frightened or lonely or full of joy. This is good news for all of us who love God and want to share ourselves with God in prayer.

✞ All make the Sign of the Cross.

Hymn

A Psalm for February

[Turn to page 4.]

Reading   Isaiah 43:1-3

Listen to the words of the prophet Isaiah (*eye-ZAY-uh*):

Descendants of Jacob, I, the LORD, created you
    and formed your nation.
Israel, don't be afraid. I have rescued you.
    I have called you by name; now you belong to me.
When you cross deep rivers, I will be with you,
    and you won't drown.
When you walk through fire, you won't be burned
    or scorched by the flames.
I am the LORD, your God,
the Holy One of Israel,
    the God who saves you.

The word of the Lord.

Reflection

Is it hard to talk to someone we are still getting to know? How does Isaiah introduce God to us? How would I introduce myself to God? What do we want to ask of God at the beginning of the school year?

Closing

Blessed be God, Creator of days and seasons.

Let us all say: Blessed be God for ever!
Blessed be God for ever!

Let us bring our hopes and needs to God, as we pray: **God, our companion, hear our prayer.**

Let us pray with the words that Jesus taught us:

Our Father …

Loving God, you give us this new school year
and new friends with whom to share it.
Bless all who pray
and work and learn together.
May this year bring peace and harmony
throughout the world.
We ask this through Christ our Lord. **Amen.**

[Sing 'alleluia'.]

✞ All make the Sign of the Cross.

February 6, 2019

Thursday Daily Prayer

Introduction

Today we remember St Josephine Bakhita, the first person from the Sudan to become a saint. Born in 1869, she was sold into slavery as a child and through the years, she belonged to various owners. Finally an Italian family took Josephine to Italy. It was there that she gained her freedom, was educated in the Catholic faith and eventually baptised.

She joined the religious order of the Canossian (*can-OSH-un*) Sisters and for fifty years served the poorest of the poor. Her life is an inspiration to work to free girls and women from violence and trafficking. She died in 1947.

The school year is still young. We do not know what lies ahead, so we can be very hopeful and a little anxious at the same time. This is exactly how the Christians of Thessalonica (*Thess-uh-LON-i-ka*) felt two thousand years ago. Paul's words of encouragement to them can still inspire us today.

☩ All make the Sign of the Cross.

Hymn

A Psalm for February

[Turn to page 4.]

Reading   1 Thessalonians 5:10-11, 16-18, 23-24

Listen to the words of the apostle Paul:

Christ died for us, so that we could live with him, whether we are alive or dead when he comes. That is why you must encourage and help one other, just as you are already doing.
  Always be joyful and never stop praying. Whatever happens, keep thanking God because of Jesus Christ. This is what God wants you to do.

  I pray that God, who gives peace, will make you completely holy. And may your spirit, soul, and body be kept healthy and faultless until our Lord Jesus Christ returns. The one who chose you can be trusted, and he will do this.

The word of the Lord.

Reflection

Paul's message is very upbeat. Does it encourage you? Are you positive and hopeful about this new year at school? How can you support and help others who may not be as confident?

Closing

Blessed be God, Creator of days and seasons.

Let us all say: Blessed be God for ever!
Blessed be God for ever!

Let us bring our hopes and needs to God, as we pray: **God, our companion, hear our prayer.**

Let us pray with the words that Jesus taught us:

Our Father …

Loving God, you give us this new school year
and new friends with whom to share it.
Bless all who pray
and work and learn together.
May this year bring peace and harmony
throughout the world.
We ask this through Christ our Lord. **Amen.**

[Sing 'alleluia'.]

☩ All make the Sign of the Cross.

Friday Daily Prayer

Introduction

On the Sundays of Ordinary Time this year the church reads from Luke's gospel. We hear Luke's story of the work of Jesus. In today's reading, Simon Peter and his fellow-workers listen to the teaching of Jesus. They see his wonderful works and are ready to follow him. When we hear the voice of God in our hearts and in the scriptures, something like that can happen to us.

✿ All make the Sign of the Cross.

Hymn

A Psalm for February

[Turn to page 4.]

Reading   Luke 5:1-6, 8, 10-11

Listen to the words of the holy gospel according to Luke:

Jesus was standing on the shore, teaching the people as they crowded around him to hear God's message. Near the shore he saw two boats left there by some fishermen who had gone to wash their nets. Jesus got into the boat that belonged to Simon and asked him to row it out a little way from the shore. Then Jesus sat down in the boat to teach the crowd.

When Jesus had finished speaking, he told Simon, "Row your boat out into the deep water and let your nets down to catch some fish."

"Master," Simon answered, "we have worked hard all night long and have not caught a thing. But if you tell me to, I will let the nets down." They did it and caught so many fish that their nets began ripping apart.

When Simon Peter saw this happen, he knelt down in front of Jesus and said, "Lord, don't come near me! I am a sinner."

Jesus told Simon, "Don't be afraid! From now on you will bring in people instead of fish." The men pulled their boats up on the shore. Then they left everything and went with Jesus.

The gospel of the Lord.

Reflection

Simon was a fisherman, so Jesus used fishing as a symbol of the work Simon would do for God. What does Jesus call us to do as students and teachers? How do we share the good news with others?

Closing

Blessed be God, Creator of days and seasons.

Let us all say: Blessed be God for ever!
Blessed be God for ever!

Let us bring our hopes and needs to God, as we pray: **God, our companion, hear our prayer.**

Let us pray with the words that Jesus taught us:

Our Father …

God of love,
your son Jesus is the light of the world.
He is a light that no darkness can overpower.
Teach us to walk in the light.
Keep us safe throughout the year
and turn our hearts to you
that we may be light for our world.
We ask this through Christ our Lord. **Amen.**

[Sing 'alleluia'.]

✿ All make the Sign of the Cross.

February 8, 2019

Monday Daily Prayer

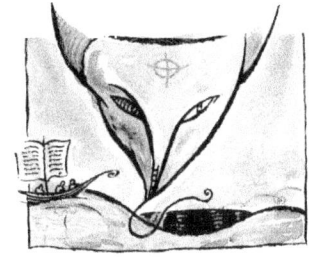

Introduction

Today is a special day of Prayer for the Sick around the world. This day reminds us to pray all the year round for those who are sick. We ask God to be with them to give them strength and courage. Jesus made many sick people well again.

Just over a week ago we heard the gospel writer Luke tell us how Jesus' mission began. We hear this reading again today, to prepare us for hearing more of the story over the next two days. It all began well, but as we shall see, Jesus' first success didn't last.

✛ All make the Sign of the Cross.

Hymn

A Psalm for February

[Turn to page 4.]

Reading   Luke 4:16-21

Listen to the words of the holy gospel according to Luke:

Jesus went to the meeting place on the Sabbath. When he stood up to read from the Scriptures, he was given the book of Isaiah (*eye-ZAY-uh*) the prophet. He opened it and read,
   "The Lord's Spirit has come to me,
   because he has chosen me
   to tell the good news to the poor.
   The Lord has sent me
   to announce freedom for prisoners,
   to give sight to the blind,
   to free everyone who suffers,
   and to say, 'This is the year the Lord has chosen.'"
Jesus closed the book, then handed it back to the man in charge and sat down. Everyone in the meeting place looked straight at Jesus.
   Then Jesus said to them, "What you have just heard me read has come true today."

The gospel of the Lord.

Reflection

A 'mission statement' tells the goals of a person or group. Jesus took Isaiah's words as his mission statement. What do these words tell us about Jesus? What are our mission goals for this year?

Closing

Blessed be God, Creator of days and seasons.

Let us all say: Blessed be God for ever!
Blessed be for ever!

Let us bring our hopes and needs to God, as we pray: **God, our companion, hear our prayer.**

Let us pray with the words that Jesus taught us:

Our Father ...

God of love,
your son Jesus is the light of the world.
He is a light that no darkness can overpower.
Teach us to walk in the light.
Keep us safe throughout the year
and turn our hearts to you
that we may be light for our world.
We ask this through Christ our Lord. **Amen.**

[Sing 'alleluia'.]

✛ All make the Sign of the Cross.

February 11, 2019

Tuesday Daily Prayer

Introduction

We have heard how Jesus announced his mission to the people of his home town. At first they are impressed but then they begin to turn against him. They could not accept that someone they knew so well was a prophet of God. This story gives us a clue about how Jesus will be rejected in the end.

✝ All make the Sign of the Cross.

Hymn

A Psalm for February

[Turn to page 4.]

Reading   *Luke 4:22, 23, 24, 28-30*

Listen to the words of the holy gospel according to Luke:

All the people in the meeting place started talking about Jesus and were amazed at the wonderful things he said. They kept on asking, "Isn't he Joseph's son?"

Jesus answered, "You will tell me to do the same things here in my own hometown that you heard I did in Capernaum (ku-PER-num). But you can be sure that no prophets are liked by the people of their own hometown."

When the people in the meeting place heard Jesus say this, they became so angry that they got up and threw him out of town. They dragged him to the edge of the cliff on which the town was built, because they wanted to throw him down from there. But Jesus slipped through the crowd and got away.

The gospel of the Lord.

Reflection

Why did the people of Jesus' hometown turn against him? Do people ever surprise me with their talents or good ideas? Have I ever been jealous of someone when they did something well and got praised for it?

Closing

Blessed be God, Creator of days and seasons.

Let us all say: Blessed be God for ever!
Blessed be God for ever!

Let us bring our hopes and needs to God, as we pray: **God, our companion, hear our prayer.**

Let us pray with the words that Jesus taught us:

Our Father ...

God of love,
your son Jesus is the light of the world.
He is a light that no darkness can overpower.
Teach us to walk in the light.
Keep us safe throughout the year
and turn our hearts to you
that we may be light for our world.
We ask this through Christ our Lord. **Amen.**

[Sing 'alleluia'.]

✝ All make the Sign of the Cross.

February 12, 2019

Wednesday Daily Prayer

Introduction

Today's reading gives us a picture of Jesus' work. He does two great things. The first is to heal people. He reaches out to those who are sick in body, mind or spirit and makes them well again. The second thing he does is to go around telling everybody the good news that God is with them. That is what is meant by "God's kingdom." God is with us making the world new.

✝ All make the Sign of the Cross.

Hymn

A Psalm for February

[Turn to page 4.]

Reading   Luke 4:38-41

Listen to the words of the holy gospel according to Luke:

Jesus went to Simon's home. When Jesus got there, he was told that Simon's mother-in-law was sick with a high fever. So Jesus went over to her and ordered the fever to go away. Right then she was able to get up and serve them a meal.
  After the sun had set, people with all kinds of diseases were brought to Jesus. He put his hands on each one of them and healed them.
  The next morning Jesus went out to a place where he could be alone, and crowds came looking for him. When they found him, they tried to stop him from leaving. But Jesus said, "People in other towns must hear the good news about God's kingdom. That's why I was sent." So he kept on preaching in the Jewish meeting places in Judea (joo-DEE-uh).

The gospel of the Lord.

Reflection

Do I know people who care for those who are sick and troubled? What can I learn from them? Do I trust Jesus with my problems and difficulties?

Closing

Blessed be God, Creator of days and seasons.

Let us all say: Blessed be God for ever!
Blessed be God for ever!

Let us bring our hopes and needs to God, as we pray: **God, our companion, hear our prayer.**

Let us pray with the words that Jesus taught us:

Our Father …

God of love,
your son Jesus is the light of the world.
He is a light that no darkness can overpower.
Teach us to walk in the light.
Keep us safe throughout the year
and turn our hearts to you
that we may be light for our world.
We ask this through Christ our Lord. **Amen.**

[Sing 'alleluia'.]

✝ All make the Sign of the Cross.

February 13, 2019

Thursday Daily Prayer

Introduction

Today we remember Saint Valentine. He was a bishop who bravely died for his faith. His name means 'valiant' and 'brave'. This day is connected with love because of a legend that birds pick their mates on February 14. Secret notes of love and friendship sent on this day are called Saint Valentine's notes or valentines.

Let us be sure to show that we appreciate those people whose love is so much part of our lives.

Our reading tell us how tireless Jesus was in telling everyone about the kingdom of God. He was always on the move so he could share the good news all over the land.

✢ All make the Sign of the Cross.

Hymn

A Psalm for February

[Turn to page 4.]

Reading   Luke 4:42-44

Listen to the words of the holy gospel according to Luke:

The next morning Jesus went out to a place where he could be alone, and crowds came looking for him. When they found him, they tried to stop him from leaving. But Jesus said, "People in other towns must hear the good news about God's kingdom. That's why I was sent." So he kept on preaching in the Jewish meeting places in Judea.

The gospel of the Lord.

Reflection

What good news do you have to share? What can you tell others about God's love for them? Do you show that love in the way you help those around you?

Closing

Blessed be God, Creator of days and seasons.

Let us all say: Blessed be God for ever!
Blessed be God for ever!

Let us bring our hopes and needs to God, as we pray: **God, our companion, hear our prayer.**

Let us pray with the words that Jesus taught us:

Our Father …

God of love,
your son Jesus is the light of the world.
He is a light that no darkness can overpower.
Teach us to walk in the light.
Keep us safe throughout the year
and turn our hearts to you
that we may be light for our world.
We ask this through Christ our Lord. **Amen.**

[Sing 'alleluia'.]

✢ All make the Sign of the Cross.

February 14, 2019

Friday Daily Prayer

Introduction

As usual our gospel reading for today is what we will hear at Sunday Mass. Jesus says that it is a blessing to be poor, hungry, sad and oppressed. This reading has been a favourite of Christians in every age even though it is such a mystery. How can things that seem bad be a blessing? What can Jesus mean? Think about this mystery today.

✟ All make the Sign of the Cross.

Hymn

A Psalm for February

[Turn to page 4.]

Reading   Luke 6:17, 18, 20-23

Listen to the words of the holy gospel according to Luke:

Jesus and his apostles went down from the mountain and came to some flat, level ground. Many other disciples were there to meet him. These people had come to listen to Jesus and to be healed of their diseases.
   Jesus looked at his disciples and said:
"God will bless you people who are poor.
His kingdom belongs to you!
God will bless you hungry people.
You will have plenty to eat!
God will bless you people who are crying.
You will laugh!
God will bless you when others hate you
   and won't have anything to do with you.
God will bless you when people insult you
   and say cruel things about you,
all because you are a follower of the son of Man. When this happens to you, be happy and jump for joy! You will have a great reward in heaven."

The gospel of the Lord.

Reflection

Have I ever been really hungry? What kinds of things make me cry? Am I ever kept out because I do the right thing? How does God bless us when things seem to be going wrong?

Closing

Blessed be God, Creator of days and seasons.

Let us all say: Blessed be God for ever!
Blessed be God for ever!

Let us bring our hopes and needs to God, as we pray: **God, our companion, hear our prayer.**

Let us pray with the words that Jesus taught us:

Our Father ...

God of love,
your son Jesus is the light of the world.
He is a light that no darkness can overpower.
Teach us to walk in the light.
Keep us safe throughout the year
and turn our hearts to you
that we may be light for our world.
We ask this through Christ our Lord. **Amen.**

[Sing 'alleluia'.]

✟ All make the Sign of the Cross.

February 15, 2019

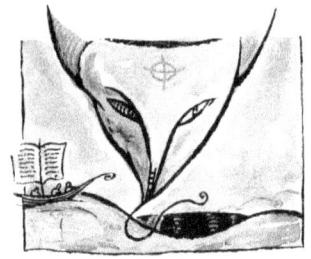

Monday Daily Prayer

Introduction

Today we remember Fred Hollows. His funeral was held on this day in Sydney in 1993.

Fred was born in New Zealand and became an eye surgeon. In 1969 he found that almost all Aboriginal people in Australian outback communities had eye diseases caused by poor living conditions. This led him to launch a national program to treat eye disease in indigenous people. Many people are known to have said: "Only for Fred Hollows, I wouldn't be able to see."

We hear more today about Jesus' work of healing and teaching. This makes him very popular with the people. But it doesn't make him proud or ambitious. Jesus knows that his power comes from God. That's why he always takes time out to pray.

✟ All make the Sign of the Cross.

Hymn

A Psalm for February

[Turn to page 4.]

Reading   Luke 5:12-16

Listen to the words of the holy gospel according to Luke:

Jesus came to a town where there was a man who had leprosy (*LEP-ruh-see*). When the man saw Jesus, he knelt down to the ground in front of Jesus and begged, "Lord, you have the power to make me well, if only you wanted to."

Jesus put his hand on him and said, "I do want to! Now you are well." At once the man's leprosy disappeared. Jesus told him, "Don't tell anyone about this, but go and show yourself to the priest. Then take a gift to the temple, just as Moses commanded, and everyone will know that you have been healed."

News about Jesus kept spreading. Large crowds came to listen to him teach, and to be healed of their diseases. But Jesus would often go to some place where he could be alone and pray.

The gospel of the Lord.

Reflection

Leprosy was often used as a symbol for sin. What new meanings does this give to the story? How can we help Jesus heal the sick? Do I find quiet times to pray, as Jesus did?

Closing

Blessed be God, Creator of days and seasons.

Let us all say: Blessed be God for ever!
Blessed be God for ever!

Let us bring our hopes and needs to God, as we pray: **God, our companion, hear our prayer.**

Let us pray with the words that Jesus taught us:

Our Father …

God of love,
your son Jesus is the light of the world.
He is a light that no darkness can overpower.
Teach us to walk in the light.
Keep us safe throughout the year
and turn our hearts to you
that we may be light for our world.
We ask this through Christ our Lord. **Amen.**

[Sing 'alleluia'.]

✟ All make the Sign of the Cross.

February 18, 2019

Tuesday Daily Prayer

Introduction

We have heard how Jesus healed people whose bodies were sick or had some disease. Now we hear a story about a deeper kind of healing. It's called forgiveness. This is healing for our hearts and minds. When we turn away from God and others, we need a healing that goes deep inside us and brings us back to a life of love. We need to have our sins forgiven and that is what Jesus offers us.

✞ All make the Sign of the Cross.

Hymn

A Psalm for February

[Turn to page 4.]

Reading   Luke 5:18-22, 23-25

Listen to the words of the holy gospel according to Luke:

Some people came to the house where Jesus was staying, carrying a crippled man on a mat. They tried to take him inside the house and put him in front of Jesus. But because of the crowd, they could not get him to Jesus. So they went up on the roof, where they removed some tiles and let the mat down in the middle of the room.

When Jesus saw how much faith they had, he said to the crippled man, "My friend, your sins are forgiven." Some people began arguing, "Jesus must think that he is God! Only God can forgive sins." Jesus said, "Is it easier for me to tell this crippled man that his sins are forgiven or to tell him to get up and walk? But now you will see that the Son of man has the right to forgive sins here on earth." Jesus then said to the man, "Get up! Pick up your mat and walk home."

At once the man stood up in front of everyone. He picked up his mat and went home, giving thanks to God.

The gospel of the Lord.

Reflection

Jesus' power to forgive sin is good news for us all. Where does Jesus get this power? In what ways can sin sometimes paralyse us and keep us from making the right moves? How can I be forgiven?

Closing

Blessed be God, Creator of days and seasons.

Let us all say: Blessed be God for ever!
Blessed be God for ever!

Let us bring our hopes and needs to God, as we pray: **God, our companion, hear our prayer.**

Let us pray with the words that Jesus taught us:

Our Father …

God of love,
your son Jesus is the light of the world.
He is a light that no darkness can overpower.
Teach us to walk in the light.
Keep us safe throughout the year
and turn our hearts to you
that we may be light for our world.
We ask this through Christ our Lord. **Amen.**

[Sing 'alleluia'.]

✞ All make the Sign of the Cross.

February 19, 2019

Wednesday Daily Prayer

Introduction

Not everyone was pleased with the way Jesus went about healing and teaching. The religious leaders were upset because Jesus was different from them. They put a lot of effort into obeying religious law, but Jesus was more concerned about the importance of love. The law that Jesus followed was the law of love, love for God and love for others. This made the authorities angry with him.

✟ All make the Sign of the Cross.

Hymn

A Psalm for February

[Turn to page 4.]

Reading *Luke 6:6-10*

Listen to the words of the holy gospel according to Luke:

Jesus was teaching in a Jewish meeting place, and a man with a crippled right hand was there. Some teachers of the Law of Moses kept watching Jesus to see if he would heal the man. They did this because they wanted to accuse Jesus of doing something wrong.

Jesus knew what they were thinking. So he told the man to stand up where everyone could see him. And the man stood up. Then Jesus asked, "On the Sabbath should we do good deeds or evil deeds? Should we save someone's life or destroy it?"

After he had looked around at everyone, he told the man, "Stretch out your hand." He did, and his bad hand became completely well.

The gospel of the Lord.

Reflection

People tried to stop Jesus from curing the man with a crippled hand. Has anyone ever tried to stop me from doing the right thing? How do I encourage my friends to do good things?

Closing

Blessed be God, Creator of days and seasons.

Let us all say: Blessed be God for ever!
Blessed be God for ever!

Let us bring our hopes and needs to God, as we pray: **God, our companion, hear our prayer.**

Let us pray with the words that Jesus taught us:

Our Father …

God of love,
your son Jesus is the light of the world.
He is a light that no darkness can overpower.
Teach us to walk in the light.
Keep us safe throughout the year
and turn our hearts to you
that we may be light for our world.
We ask this through Christ our Lord. **Amen.**

[Sing 'alleluia'.]

✟ All make the Sign of the Cross.

February 20, 2019

Thursday Daily Prayer

Introduction

Tomorrow's feast has an interesting name. It is called the Chair of Peter. Why does the church have a feast for a piece of furniture? At one time there was only one chair at official meetings. It was the bench of the judge, the throne of a queen, or the bishop's chair called the cathedra (*KATH-eh-druh*). Whoever guided the meeting sat in this important chair. The chair was a sign of the person in charge. Perhaps you have been a chairperson.

This feast is really about the unity of the church. We are all gathered around the chair of Saint Peter, who became the bishop of Rome and the leader among the bishops of the church. The person who is the bishop of Rome now is Pope Francis. Let us pray for him today.

In today's reading Jesus asks his disciples who people thought he was. In Peter's response we find the most basic belief of every Christian. One day he would die for that faith.

✞ All make the Sign of the Cross.

Hymn

A Psalm for February

[Turn to page 4.]

Reading *Luke 9:18-20*

Listen to the words of the holy gospel according to Luke:

When Jesus was alone praying, his disciples came to him, and he asked them, "What do people say about me?"

They answered, "Some say that you are John the Baptist or Elijah (*ee-LYE-juh*) or a prophet from long ago who has come back to life."

Jesus then asked them, "But who do you say I am?"

Peter answered, "You are the Messiah sent from God."

The gospel of the Lord.

Reflection

What does it mean to call Jesus our Messiah? How does the church express its faith in Jesus? How do we show our faith? What difference has the coming of Jesus made to our world?

Closing

Blessed be God, Creator of days and seasons.

Let us all say: Blessed be God for ever!
Blessed be God for ever!

Let us bring our hopes and needs to God, as we pray: **God, our companion, hear our prayer.**

Let us pray with the words that Jesus taught us:

Our Father …

Gracious God,
through the gift of your Spirit
and the teaching of your apostles,
we can proclaim with your church
that Jesus is the Messiah you sent to us.
Strengthen and deepen this gift of faith.
We ask this through Christ our Lord. **Amen**

[Sing 'alleluia'.]

✞ All make the Sign of the Cross.

February 21, 2019

Friday Daily Prayer

Introduction

In today's reading from the Sunday gospel Jesus calls us to be people of love. Does that mean we should love our friends? Yes! Does it mean that we should love the people in our families? Yes! But it means more than that. Jesus wants us to love everyone, even people who don't love us. Jesus often reminds us of this message of love.

✛ All make the Sign of the Cross.

Hymn

A Psalm for February

[Turn to page 4.]

Reading *Luke 6:27-28, 32-33, 35*

Listen to the words of the holy gospel according to Luke:

Jesus told everyone who would listen, "Love your enemies, and be good to everyone who hates you. Ask God to bless anyone who curses you, and pray for everyone who is cruel to you. Treat others just as you want to be treated.
  "If you love only someone who loves you, will God praise you for that? Even sinners love people who love them. If you are kind only to someone who is kind to you, will God be pleased with you for that? Even sinners are kind to people who are kind to them.
  "But love your enemies and be good to them. Lend without expecting to be paid back. Then you will get a great reward, and you will be the true children of God in heaven."

The gospel of the Lord.

Reflection

Jesus knows that it is not easy to be good to people who are not good to us. How can we love those who don't love us? What would it be like if everyone were really good to everyone else?

Closing

Blessed be God, Creator of days and seasons.

Let us all say: Blessed be God for ever!
Blessed be God for ever!

Let us bring our hopes and needs to God, as we pray: **God, our companion, hear our prayer.**

Let us pray with the words that Jesus taught us:

Our Father …

God of kindness and love,
you forgive us with all your heart
for the wrong we do.
Help us to love even our enemies
and to forgive those who do harm to us.
Help us to live together in peace.
We ask this through Christ our Lord. **Amen.**

[Sing 'alleluia'.]

✛ All make the Sign of the Cross.

February 22, 2019

Monday Daily Prayer

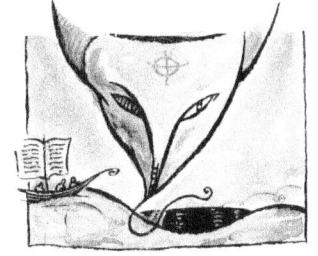

Introduction

Whenever Jesus had to make a big decision, he first spent time in prayer, sometimes for a whole night. That's what he did before he chose twelve of his followers to be his co-workers. They came to be called apostles. Just as God's people had been made up of twelve tribes, so Jesus called twelve disciples to be his companions. They were a sign of the new people of God that was coming into being.

☩ All make the Sign of the Cross.

Hymn

A Psalm for February

[Turn to page 4.]

Reading   *Luke 6:12-16*

Listen to the words of the holy gospel according to Luke:

Jesus went off to a mountain to pray, and he spent the whole night there. The next morning he called his disciples together and chose twelve of them to be his apostles. One was Simon, and Jesus named him Peter. Another was Andrew, Peter's brother. There were also James, John, Philip, Bartholomew (*bar-THOL-uh-mew*), Matthew, Thomas, and James the son of Alphaeus (*AL-fee-us*). The rest of the apostles were Simon, known as the Eager One, Jude, who was the son of James, and Judas Iscariot (*iss-KA-ree-ut*), who later betrayed Jesus.

The gospel of the Lord.

Reflection

The word 'apostle' means 'someone sent on a mission.' Do you have a favourite apostle? Today Jesus sends many people to speak for him and to do good things in his name. Can we name any of these people?

Closing

Blessed be God, Creator of days and seasons.

Let us all say: Blessed be God for ever!
Blessed be God for ever!

Let us bring our hopes and needs to God, as we pray: **God, our companion, hear our prayer.**

Let us pray with the words that Jesus taught us:

Our Father ...

Lord God,
we thank you for sending apostles
to the whole world.
May we always welcome
those who bring your good news.
Help us to listen to their teaching.
Call on us, one day, to become apostles, too.
We ask this through Christ our Lord. **Amen.**

[Sing 'alleluia'.]

☩ All make the Sign of the Cross.

February 25, 2019

Tuesday Daily Prayer

Introduction

The time Jesus spent in prayer gave him energy to continue his mission. He drew power from his loving relationship with God and used that power to heal people in body, mind and spirit. He did not hide away from the crowds to have peace and quiet for himself. He went out to meet them. He wanted them to be blessed with life.

☦ All make the Sign of the Cross.

Hymn

A Psalm for February

[Turn to page 4.]

Reading   *Luke 6:17-19*

Listen to the words of the holy gospel according to Luke:

Jesus and his apostles went down from the mountain and came to some flat, level ground. Many other disciples were there to meet him. Large crowds of people from all over Judea, Jerusalem, and the coastal cities of Tyre and Sidon were there too. These people had come to listen to Jesus and to be healed of their diseases. All who were troubled by evil spirits were also healed. Everyone was trying to touch Jesus, because power was going out from him and healing them all.

The gospel of the Lord.

Reflection

In what way can we reach out to those who are sick or troubled? Can our loving care help them find healing? Do we ask God in prayer for the power of love?

Closing

Blessed be God, Creator of days and seasons.

Let us all say: Blessed be God for ever!
Blessed be God for ever!

Let us bring our hopes and needs to God, as we pray: **God, our companion, hear our prayer.**

Let us pray with the words that Jesus taught us:

Our Father ...

Loving God,
through your son Jesus,
you bring your love and healing touch
to all your suffering people.
Bless, protect, and guide them.
Make us truly grateful
for your love and care of us.
We ask this through Christ our Lord. **Amen.**

[Sing 'alleluia'.]

☦ All make the Sign of the Cross.

February 26, 2019

Wednesday Daily Prayer

Introduction

Today's reading is one of the most famous in the gospels. It's Jesus' teaching about those who are blessed by God. This list of blessings is called the Beatitudes (*bee-AT-it-tewds*). The list in Matthew's gospel is better known, but Luke's is very similar. At first sight what Jesus says is very strange. It takes time to understand how those who are poor or hungry or hated can be called blessed.

☩ All make the Sign of the Cross.

Hymn

A Psalm for February

[Turn to page 4.]

Reading *Luke 6:20-23*

Jesus looked at his disciples and said:
  "God will bless you people who are poor.
  His kingdom belongs to you!
  God will bless you hungry people.
  You will have plenty to eat!
  God will bless you people who are crying.
  You will laugh!
God will bless you when others hate you
    and won't have anything to do with you.
  God will bless you when people insult you
    and say cruel things about you,
  all because you are a follower of the Son of Man.
  When this happens to you, be happy and jump for joy!
  You will have a great reward in heaven."

The gospel of the Lord.

Reflection

Jesus seems to be telling us to be patient in times of trouble. When do I find it hard to be patient? How can we believe that God makes things come out right in the end?

Closing

Blessed be God, Creator of days and seasons.

Let us all say: Blessed be God for ever!
Blessed be God for ever!

Let us bring our hopes and needs to God, as we pray: **God, our companion, hear our prayer.**

Let us pray with the words that Jesus taught us:

Our Father ...

God of all nations and Creator of all peoples,
heal all that divides us.
Teach us to live together in peace.
Give us one heart and one vision.
and make us one body in Jesus Christ.
We ask this through Christ our Lord. **Amen.**

[Sing 'alleluia'.]

☩ All make the Sign of the Cross.

February 27, 2019

Thursday Daily Prayer

Introduction

Today we hear one of the hardest things that Jesus teaches. He says we should love our enemies. This may sound impossible. It can be difficult to keep loving even our families and friends. How can we love those who turn against us? It is only possible when we know deep in our hearts how much God loves every person, no matter what. God's mercy has no limits.

The great religions of the world all teach the Golden Rule. This means that we should treat others as we would like them to treat us. If we want to be shown mercy, then we need to offer mercy to others. God always gives it to us.

✢ All make the Sign of the Cross.

Hymn

A Psalm for February

[Turn to page 4.]

Reading   Luke 6:20, 35-38

Listen to the words of the holy gospel according to Luke:

Jesus looked at his disciples and said: Love your enemies and be good to them. Lend without expecting to be paid back. Then you will get a great reward, and you will be the true children of God in heaven. He is good even to people who are unthankful and cruel. Have pity on others, just as your Father has pity on you.

Don't judge others, and God won't judge you. Don't be hard on others, and God won't be hard on you. Forgive others, and God will forgive you. If you give to others, you will be given a full amount in return. It will be packed down, shaken together, and spilling over into your lap. The way you treat others is the way you will be treated.

The gospel of the Lord.

Reflection

What does it mean to be "big-hearted"? Do you know some people that are "big-hearted"? Do you think you could be more like them?

Closing

Blessed be God, Creator of days and seasons.

Let us all say: Blessed be God for ever!
Blessed be God for ever!

Let us bring our hopes and needs to God, as we pray: **God, our companion, hear our prayer.**

Let us pray with the words that Jesus taught us:

Our Father …

God of kindness and love,
you forgive us with all your heart
   for the wrong we do.
Help us to love even our enemies
   and to forgive those who do harm to us.
Help us to live together in peace.
We ask this through Christ our Lord. **Amen.**

[Sing 'alleluia'.]

✢ All make the Sign of the Cross.

February 28, 2019

Friday Daily Prayer

Introduction

As he went around healing and teaching, Jesus became very popular with ordinary people. But he did not get carried away with his success, because he could see that the religious leaders were becoming more and more unhappy about his popularity. So he tried to warn his followers that things were going to turn out badly, but they did not understand what he was saying. This is what we hear in today's reading from the Sunday gospel.

✞ All make the Sign of the Cross.

Hymn

A Psalm for February

[Turn to page 4.]

Reading   Luke 9:43-45

Listen to the words of the holy gospel according to Luke:

While everyone was still amazed at what Jesus was doing, he said to his disciples, "Pay close attention to what I am telling you! The Son of Man will be handed over to his enemies." But the disciples did not know what he meant. The meaning was hidden from them. They could not understand it, and they were afraid to ask.

The gospel of the Lord.

Reflection

Sometimes we can be jealous of someone who is new and popular and successful. We can be angry with them and want them to fail. Does this help explain why the religious leaders turned against Jesus?

Closing

Blessed be God, Creator of days and seasons.

Let us all say: Blessed be God for ever!
Blessed be God for ever!

Let us bring our hopes and needs to God, as we pray: **God, our companion, hear our prayer.**

Let us pray with the words that Jesus taught us:

Our Father …

God of love,
your son Jesus is the light of the world.
He is a light that no darkness can overpower.
Teach us to walk in the light.
Keep us safe throughout the year
and turn our hearts to you
that we may be light for our world.
We ask this through Christ our Lord. **Amen.**

[Sing 'alleluia'.]

✞ All make the Sign of the Cross.

March 1, 2019

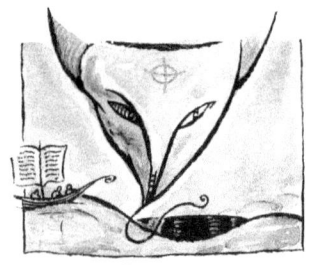

Monday Daily Prayer

Introduction

Jesus grew up in the countryside. He knew about the land and how things grow and how farmers worked. So in his teaching he often used simple examples from nature that people would understand. He used things they could see to teach them about hidden things. He wanted them to look into their own minds and hearts and to see how good or bad things came from them.

✠ All make the Sign of the Cross.

Hymn

A Psalm for February

[Turn to page 4.]

Reading *Luke 6:43-45*

Listen to the words of the holy gospel according to Luke:

A good tree cannot produce bad fruit, and a bad tree cannot produce good fruit. You can tell what a tree is like by the fruit it produces. You cannot pick figs or grapes from thornbushes. Good people do good things because of the good in their hearts. Bad people do bad things because of the evil in their hearts. Your words show what is in your heart.

The gospel of the Lord.

Reflection

If we have love in our hearts, then we will do loving things; if we have hate, we will do hateful things. This is Jesus' message. What can we do to keep love strong in our hearts? How can prayer help us?

March 4, 2019

Closing

Blessed be God, Creator of days and seasons.

Let us all say: Blessed be God for ever!
Blessed be God for ever!

Let us bring our hopes and needs to God, as we pray: **God, our companion, hear our prayer.**

Let us pray with the words that Jesus taught us:

Our Father …

O God,
you are good and generous,
giving plants for food
and flowers for our delight,
giving sunshine and rain
for the growth of all living things.
Make us always thankful
and free our hearts from endless desires.
We ask this through Christ our Lord. **Amen.**

[Sing 'alleluia'.]

✠ All make the Sign of the Cross.

Tuesday Daily Prayer

[Reminder: Tomorrow is Ash Wednesday. The Prayer for the Preparation of Ashes could replace today's Daily Prayer. The Psalm for Early Lent is on page 34. Make a copy for each member of the class.]

Introduction

Today is the day before Ash Wednesday. It is often called 'Pancake Tuesday' or 'Shrove Tuesday.' To prepare to fast during Lent, some people use up the extra food they have. One custom on this day is to 'feast' on pancakes. Today is a day to be happy and rejoice with food.

We will sing 'alleluia' for the last time until Easter Day. So at the end of today's prayer let us sing 'alleluia' with all our might.
In today's reading, the prophet Isaiah (*eye-ZAY-uh*) encourages the people with visions of feasts and festivals.

✠ All make the Sign of the Cross.

Hymn

A Psalm for February

[Turn to page 4.]

Reading   *Isaiah 25:6-9*

Listen to the words of the prophet Isaiah:

On this mountain the Lord All-Powerful
will prepare for all nations a feast
  of finest foods.
Choice wines and best meats will be served.
Here the Lord will strip away
  the burial clothes that cover the nations.
The Lord All-Powerful
will destroy the power of death
and wipe away all tears.

At that time, people will say,
  "The Lord has saved us!
Let's celebrate."

The word of the Lord.

Reflection

In what ways is a picnic on a mountain like the reign of God? What kinds of foods are served at our favourite celebrations? How will we help our families get ready for the season of Lent?

Closing

Blessed be God, Creator of days and seasons.

Let us all say: Blessed be God for ever!
Blessed be God for ever!

Let us bring our hopes and needs to God, as we pray: **God, our companion, hear our prayer.**

Let us pray with the words that Jesus taught us:

Our Father …

Loving God,
we thank you for the promise
that Easter will follow the hard work of Lent.
We thank you for days when we can rejoice together.
We thank you through Christ our Lord. **Amen.**

[Sing 'alleluia'.]

✠ All make the Sign of the Cross.

March 5, 2019

PSALMS ARE PRAYERS

Have you noticed? Every time you use Daily Prayer there's a psalm. After the hymn and introduction you pray some verses from one of the psalms. Each season and month has its own psalm (two for Lent and Easter). So just what is a psalm?

There are all sorts of ways of answering this question. Here's the first of five answers. The psalms are prayers. That's what we look at on this page. The other four answers are given later (see pp. 30, 54, 88, 108 and 144). They will tell us that the psalms are poems, shouts, cries and cosmic chants.

Right now let's explore the psalms as prayers. Prayers are the things that we want to say to God. In our prayers we talk to God. Sometimes we can do this without thinking of words – we just let our hearts speak for us. The psalms are prayers that have been written down. This means we can pray them together.

God's people have been praying these prayers for around three thousand years. Can you believe that? 3,000 years! They go back to God's first people, the Israelites, and to the time they settled in the Promised Land. They are the prayers that Jesus learnt when he was growing up. And they have been the prayers of Christian believers ever since. They are very old yet always new. They are both my prayers and everyone's prayers.

Here are a few samples of prayer from the psalms used in Daily Prayer:

"You are merciful, Lord! You are kind and patient and always loving. You are good to everyone, and you take care of all your creation … And you are near to everyone whose prayers come from the heart." *(Psalm 146, February)*

"My God, I lean on you, my shield, my rock, my champion, my defence … I love you, God my strength." *(Psalm 18, Lent)*

"You, Lord, are my shepherd. I will never be in need." *(Psalm 23, Easter)*

"Our God, be kind and bless us! Be pleased and smile." *(Psalm 67, November).*

Early Lent

Ash Wednesday, March 6, to Friday, March 29

Early Lent 2019
Looking Ahead

About the Season

In some ways, Lent is the most famous of all the church's seasons. People seem to know the most about Lent. It lasts for 40 days, counting from the First Sunday of Lent through to Holy Thursday. The four days from Ash Wednesday to the First Sunday of Lent are a kind of 'invitation' to keep the season.

Lent is a serious time when the Church prepares for the celebration of the great Easter mystery. It is not just a time for doing special things and saying special prayers for the sake of doing them. If our Lenten practices do not help us to understand God's word more clearly and to live according to that word more generously, then they are not useful. And so, with our families, we take this time to think about how much the gospel means to us and how well we are living up to God's law of love and to the promises of our baptism.

Lent has many traditions. We notice the purple colour in our churches and the absence of the 'Alleluia'. We will not sing or hear it again until Easter, when we will rejoice in the resurrection of Jesus. During Lent we frequently hear the call to pray, to fast, and to give alms. During Lent we try to become more prayerful, to make our lives simpler and to share what we have with those who are in need.

'Alms' are what we give to people in need. We give part of our pocket-money or baby-sitting money, non-perishable foods or clothes to help the poor. Project Compassion (Australia) and the Caritas Lenten Appeal (New Zealand) are great ways of doing this.

Readings

The readings for Ash Wednesday and the following two days emphasise the spirit of Lent. For the weeks of Early Lent the readings for Daily Prayer will be taken mainly from the writings of the prophets, Isaiah, Ezekiel and Jeremiah. They tell us that God is always loving and forgiving and will rescue us in time of trouble. We also read from the Book of Deuteronomy. We hear about God's law, how we are to be faithful to him, and how we are to love and care for those who are poor and to forgive one another.

Our readings for each Friday will normally anticipate the Sunday gospels of Lent. They are taken from Year C, the lectionary year that is shaped around the gospel of Luke.

On the first Sunday we hear about the forty days that Jesus spent in the desert before he began his public ministry. On the second Sunday we hear about his transfiguration. In the reading for the third Sunday we hear about a fig tree that does not produce any figs, but just as God is patient and gives the fig tree more time to grow, God always gives us every chance to grow in his love. On the fourth Sunday we listen to the well-known story of the wasteful son and his forgiving father.

Feasts and Other Commemorations

Three major feasts of the Church Year occur during the early weeks of Lent:
- March 18, St Patrick, the patron of Ireland, is honoured in Australia because of the many Irish people who brought the faith to Australia.
- March 19, St Joseph, was born of the royal house of David but worked as a carpenter. He was the husband of Mary and honoured as upright man.
- March 25, The Annunciation of the Lord. On this feast the Angel Gabriel announces to Mary that she was to be the mother of Jesus, the son of God.

At sunset on Wednesday, March 20, the Jewish feast of Purim begins. It is one of the most joyous and fun holidays on the Jewish calendar. Gifts are given to the poor and children celebrate with games and treats. Purim is a time to pray for hope. It commemorates a time when the Jewish people living in Persia – modern-day Iran – were saved from extermination.

Friday, March 21 is Harmony Day. This day calls all Australians to embrace cultural diversity and to share what we have in common.

Preparation for Lent

In the early weeks of Lent, we pray Psalm 18 (page 34). This psalm calls God a shelter and a rock on whom we can always depend. Students will need their own copies of each of these pages. Copy them on mauve paper, a Lenten colour.

On page 35 is a ritual for burning last year's palms to prepare ashes for Ash Wednesday. The afternoon before Ash Wednesday is a good time for this prayer.

Prepare the prayer space so that it looks like Lent. Place *Children's Daily Prayer Under the Southern Cross 2019* or a Bible on a purple drape – the Lenten colour. Place in this space a reminder of Lent – the class cross or crucifix, or a bowl of ashes to remind us of Ash Wednesday. A large Project Compassion box could also be placed in the prayer space, reminding us of our tradition to give alms during Lent. Some colourful autumn leaves could remind us that even though leaves fall and die, new life will spring forth, just as Jesus' death will lead to life.

Prayers of sorrow for sin are traditional during Lent. The class or the whole school may hold a penance service. It may include an opportunity for older students to celebrate the sacrament of reconciliation. This will take thoughtful and prayerful preparation. Another traditional prayer used during Lent is known as the 'Stations of the Cross'. This is a prayer in which we reflect on Jesus' suffering and death and the suffering and injustices of our world.

Suggested Hymns

See the hymn chart on pages viii-ix. It is good to have a 'Kyrie' or a 'Lord have mercy' in your Lenten repertoire.

A Psalm for Early Lent

Psalm 18:2-4, 7, 47

LEADER
Behold! Now is the acceptable time!
ALL
Now is the day of salvation!

LEADER
I love you, God my strength,
ALL
my rock, my shelter, my stronghold.

SIDE A
My God, I lean on you,
my shield, my rock,
my champion, my defence.

SIDE B
When I call for help,
I am safe from my enemies.

SIDE A
From the depths I cried out,
my plea reached the heavens.
God heard me.

SIDE B
The Lord lives!
Blessed be my rock,
the God who saves me.

LEADER
I love you, God my strength,
ALL
my rock, my shelter, my stronghold.

Glory be to the Father, and to the Son,
and to the Holy Spirit:
as it was in the beginning, is now,
and ever shall be,
world without end. Amen.

[Turn back to Daily Prayer for today.]

The Preparation of Ashes

Gather in an outdoor place away from the wind. Line a metal container with alfoil, and arrange dry palms on it. Bring matches, a poker to stir the fire, a bowl and pestle (or something for crushing the ashes) and a ceramic or terracotta container to hold the crushed ashes.

✞ All make the Sign of the Cross.

LEADER
Praised be the God of grace, mercy and peace.
Let us all say: Blessed be God for ever!
Blessed be God for ever!

LEADER
A year ago we held these palms and sang 'Hosanna' to Jesus our Messiah. We walked in procession to show that we would follow him. Today we burn these palms. Their ashes remind us that often we have not followed Jesus. When we are signed with these ashes we renew our promise to follow Christ our Lord.

READER   *Joel 2:12, 13, 15, 16, 17*

Listen to the words of the prophet Joel:

The Lord said, "It isn't too late.
you can still return to me with all your heart.
Turn back to me with broken hearts.
I am merciful, kind, and caring.

"Sound the trumpet on Zion!
Call the people together.
Bring adults, children, babies,
and even bring newlyweds from their festivities.

"Offer this prayer near the altar:
'Save your people, Lord God!'"

The word of the Lord.

[Light the fire. Wait in silence until the fire burns out.]

LEADER
Merciful God,
you called us forth from the dust of the earth.
You claimed us for Christ
in the waters of baptism.
Look upon us as we enter these Forty Days
bearing the mark of ashes.
Bless our journey through the desert of Lent
to the font of rebirth.
May our fasting be a hunger for justice;
   our alms, a making of peace;
   our prayer, the chant of humble and grateful hearts.
All that we do and pray is in the name of Jesus,
for in his cross you proclaim your love
   now and for ever. **Amen.**

Adapted from
Catholic Household Blessings and Prayers

✞ All make the Sign of the Cross.

To gather the ashes, crush them and pour them into the container.

Wednesday Daily Prayer

[Reminder: The Psalm for Early Lent is found on page 34. Make a copy for each member of the class.]

Introduction

Today, Ash Wednesday, many Christians receive a cross of ashes on their foreheads. This powerful sign has been used by God's people for hundreds of years. The cross of ashes reminds us, and tells friends and neighbours that we know we are not perfect.

We sometimes break the law of God. We hurt other people. We act selfishly. Today we tell God and each other that we are sorry. With the help of Jesus, we will try during Lent to become better. The cross of ashes means all of these things.

✞ All make the Sign of the Cross.

Hymn

A Psalm for Early Lent

[Turn to page 34.]

Reading   *Daniel 9:3-5, 9*

Listen to the words of the book of Daniel:

To show my sorrow, I went without eating and dressed in sackcloth and sat in ashes. I confessed my sins and earnestly prayed to the Lord my God: "Our Lord, you are a great and fearsome God, and you faithfully keep your agreement with those who love and obey you. But we have sinned terribly by rebelling against you and rejecting your laws and teachings. Lord God, you are merciful and forgiving."

The word of the Lord

Reflection

What do ashes remind us of? Why are ashes put on our foreheads in the Sign of the Cross? When I wear ashes today, people will know that I am a Christian. How does that make me feel?

Closing   *Adapted from the Byzantine Rite*

Receive Lent with gladness, O people!
Let us all say:
Be strong, and turn your life toward God.
Be strong, and turn your life toward God.

Let us bring our hopes and needs to God, as we pray: **God of mercy, hear our prayer.**

Let us pray with the words that Jesus taught us:

Our Father ...

Merciful God,
you called us forth from the dust of the earth;
you claimed us for Christ
    in the waters of baptism.
Look upon us as we enter these Forty Days
    bearing the mark of ashes.
Bless us on our journey
through the desert of Lent
to the font of rebirth.
May our fasting be hunger for justice;
    our alms, a making of peace;
    our prayer, the chant of humble
and grateful hearts.
All that we do and pray is in the name of Jesus,
for in his cross you proclaim your love
    now and for ever. **Amen**.

Adapted from
Catholic Household Blessings and Prayers

✞ All make the Sign of the Cross.

March 6, 2019

Thursday Daily Prayer

Introduction

This week we can bring to the classroom things that are symbols of Lent. We can place them on a table near the Bible or crucifix.

Wheat seeds can be planted in a ceramic or terracotta bowl. As they push through the earth the new shoots can remind us of our need to grow more like Jesus. The flowers of some native plants can remind us that God's Easter grace will bring us to life.

In many places tomorrow is observed as International Women's Day. It highlights the achievements of women around the world.

✞ All make the Sign of the Cross.

Hymn

A Psalm for Early Lent

[Turn to page 34.]

Reading   2 Corinthians 5:19, 20-6:2

Listen to the words of the apostle Paul:

God was in Christ, offering peace and forgiveness to the people of this world. We speak for Christ and sincerely ask you to make peace with God. Christ never sinned! But God treated him as a sinner, so that Christ could make us acceptable to God.

We work together with God, and we beg you to make good use of God's kindness to you. In the Scriptures God says, "When the time came, I listened to you, and when you needed help, I came to save you."

That time has come. This is the day for you to be saved.

The word of the Lord.

Reflection

How can we offer peace and forgiveness to each other? What does it mean 'to make good use of God's kindness'? Can we do that today?

Closing   Adapted from the *Byzantine Rite*

Receive Lent with gladness, O people!
Let us all say:
Be strong, and turn your life toward God.
Be strong, and turn your life toward God.

Let us bring our hopes and needs to God, as we pray: **God of mercy, hear our prayer.**

Let us pray with the words that Jesus taught us:

Our Father …

Merciful God,
as your loving children,
we are eager to do what is right.
Send your Holy Spirit to live with us
and to fill us with your light.
We ask this through Christ our Lord. **Amen.**

✞ All make the Sign of the Cross.

March 7, 2019

Friday Daily Prayer

Introduction

Lent is a time of change for the church. The ashes are a sign of repentance as we enter into the spirit of this Lenten season. For the next forty days, Christians will try to become better followers of Jesus. During Lent, let us make plans to pray more often and to listen to God's word with special care. We also want to become more generous and thoughtful towards each other at school, and in our families.

Lent is also a time when we remember those in need. We can use our Project Compassion boxes or the Caritas Lenten Appeal boxes for this.

The gospel for the first Sunday of Lent always tells about the time when Jesus spent forty days fasting and being tempted in the wilderness.

✞ All make the Sign of the Cross.

Hymn

A Psalm for Early Lent

[Turn to page 34.]

Reading   Luke 4:1-2, 3-6, 7-12

Listen to the words of the holy gospel according to Luke:

The Holy Spirit led Jesus into the desert. For forty days Jesus was tested by the devil, and during that time he went without eating. The devil said to Jesus, "If you are God's son, tell this stone to turn into bread." Jesus answered, "The scriptures say, 'No one can live only on food.'"

Then the devil led Jesus up to a high place and quickly showed him all the nations on earth. The devil said, "Just worship me, and you can have it all." Jesus answered, "The Scriptures say, 'Worship the Lord your God and serve only him!'"

Finally, the devil took Jesus to Jerusalem and had him stand on top of the temple. The devil said, "If you are God's Son, jump off. The Scriptures say, 'God will tell his angels to take care of you. They will catch you in their arms.'"

Jesus answered, "The Scriptures also say, 'Don't try to test the Lord your God!'"

The gospel of the Lord.

Reflection

Can we name the three ways Jesus was tempted? They may seem very different from our own temptations. Can we be tempted like that?

Closing   Adapted from the *Byzantine Rite*

Receive Lent with gladness, O people!
Let us all say:
Be strong, and turn your life toward God.
Be strong, and turn your life toward God.

Let us bring our hopes and needs to God, as we pray: **God of mercy, hear our prayer.**

Let us pray with the words that Jesus taught us:

Our Father …

Merciful God,
as your loving children,
we are eager to do what is right.
Send your Holy Spirit to live with us
and to fill us with your light.
We ask this through Christ our Lord. **Amen.**

✞ All make the Sign of the Cross.

March 8, 2019

Monday Daily Prayer

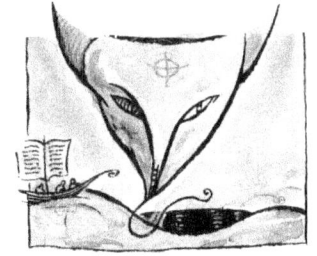

Introduction

During Lent the church asks adults to pray, fast and give alms. Alms are gifts to the poor. Fasting means eating less than usual. Catholics over the age of 14 are asked not to eat meat on Ash Wednesday and Good Friday.

Young people can share the spirit of fasting by giving up something they enjoy, like sweets or junk food or television. They can do good works like offering to do extra jobs around the house or by giving part of their pocket money to people in need. These are called sacrifices. They are good deeds, done in God's name, that show our love of God and sorrow for sins.

In today's reading, Isaiah (*eye-ZAY-uh*) tells us about the true spirit of Lenten sacrifice.

✠ All make the Sign of the Cross.

Hymn

A Psalm for Early Lent

[Turn to page 34.]

Reading   *Isaiah 58:5, 6-8*

Listen to the words of the prophet Isaiah:

The prophet said to the people of Israel:
Do you think the Lord wants you
to give up eating
or to dress in sackcloth and sit in ashes?
I'll tell you what it really means
to worship the Lord.
Remove the chains of prisoners
who are chained unjustly.
Free those who are abused!
Share your food with everyone who is hungry;
share your home with the poor and homeless.
Give clothes to those in need;
don't turn away your relatives.
Then your light will shine like the dawning sun,
and you will quickly be healed.

The word of the Lord.

Reflection

How will I share in the true spirit of Lent? How will my family keep Lent together? What can we do during Lent to make our school a more kind and loving place?

Closing   Adapted from the *Byzantine Rite*

Receive Lent with gladness, O people!
Let us all say:
Be strong, and turn your life toward God.
Be strong, and turn your life toward God.

Let us bring our hopes and needs to God, as we pray: **God of mercy, hear our prayer.**

Let us pray with the words that Jesus taught us:

Our Father ...

Merciful God,
as your loving children,
we are eager to do what is right.
Send your Holy Spirit to live with us
and to fill us with your light.
We ask this through Christ our Lord. **Amen.**

✠ All make the Sign of the Cross.

March 11, 2019

Tuesday Daily Prayer

Introduction

Many centuries before the coming of Jesus, the people of God were attacked by their enemies. The prophets told the people that they should not rely on their army alone to protect them. Their salvation was in the hands of God. The prophets urged them to take an honest look at their lives, and the life of their community, and see how far they had drifted from the law of God.

This was the message of Ezekiel (*ee-ZEE-kee-ul*), a prophet who was taken to Babylon in chains when Israel was defeated.

✞ All make the Sign of the Cross.

Hymn

A Psalm for Early Lent

[Turn to page 34.]

Reading   *Ezekiel 18:21-23, 30, 32*

Listen to the words of the prophet Ezekiel (*ee-ZEE-kee-ul*):

The Lord says this:
"Suppose wicked people stop sinning and start obeying my laws and doing right. All their sins will be forgiven, and they will live because they did right. I, the Lord God, don't like to see wicked people die. I enjoy seeing them turn from their sins and live.

"I will judge each of you for what you've done. So stop sinning, or else you will certainly be punished. I, the Lord God, don't want to see that happen to anyone. So stop sinning and live!"

The word of the Lord.

Reflection

All during Lent we hear the same message over and over: No matter what you have done, God will forgive you! No matter how mean or foolish you feel, God wants you to start again! Do I really believe this in my heart? Do we forgive others this way?

Closing   Adapted from the *Byzantine Rite*

Receive Lent with gladness, O people!
Let us all say:
Be strong, and turn your life toward God.
Be strong, and turn your life toward God.

Let us bring our hopes and needs to God, as we pray: **God of mercy, hear our prayer.**

Let us pray with the words that Jesus taught us:

Our Father ...

Merciful God,
as your loving children,
we are eager to do what is right.
Send your Holy Spirit to live with us
and to fill us with your light.
We ask this through Christ our Lord. **Amen.**

✞ All make the Sign of the Cross.

March 12, 2019

Wednesday Daily Prayer

Introduction

Lent invites us to spend some time looking into our hearts. We can see that sometimes we can be mean or selfish or avoid the truth. We can also see how much we have tried to be agreeable and to act with kindness toward others. When we look into our hearts, we can see both the good and the bad. In today's reading we hear how God promises to help us to be our best selves.

✞ All make the Sign of the Cross.

Hymn

A Psalm for Early Lent

[Turn to page 34.]

Reading   *Ezekiel 36:24-28, 37, 38*

Listen to the words of the prophet Ezekiel (*ee-ZEE-kee-ul*):

The Lord says this:
"I will gather you from the foreign nations and bring you home. I will sprinkle you with clean water, and you will be clean and acceptable to me.

"I will take away your stubborn heart and give you a new heart and a desire to be faithful. You will have only pure thoughts, because I will put my Spirit in you and make you eager to obey my laws and teachings. You will be my people, and I will be your God.

"I will once again answer your prayers, and I will let your nation grow until you are like a large flock of sheep. Then you will know that I am the Lord."

The word of the Lord.

Reflection

What can it mean to have a "stubborn heart" and a "new heart"? What other parts of the Bible speak of God's people as a "flock of sheep"? When I am discouraged, do I remember to pray with God's Spirit within me?

Closing   Adapted from the *Byzantine Rite*

Receive Lent with gladness, O people!
Let us all say:
Be strong, and turn your life toward God.
Be strong, and turn your life toward God.

Let us bring our hopes and needs to God, as we pray: **God of mercy, hear our prayer.**

Let us pray with the words that Jesus taught us:

Our Father ...

Merciful God,
as your loving children,
we are eager to do what is right.
Send your Holy Spirit to live with us
and to fill us with your light.
We ask this through Christ our Lord. **Amen.**

✞ All make the Sign of the Cross.

Thursday Daily Prayer

Introduction

Today we remember John Bede Polding, the first bishop of Australia, known as "The bishop of Botany Bay". Born in Liverpool, England, he came to Australia in 1835. The whole of Australia was his diocese. He travelled thousands of miles on horseback to look after the people of the early colony. He helped convicts, aborigines, poor people and the homeless, and, like the prophets, brought them hope.

In 1857, John Bede Polding founded an order of sisters called the Sisters of the Good Samaritan. He died in Sydney in 1877.

In today's reading God promises that we will be his people if we agree to obey his laws and teachings and to listen when he speaks to us.

✞ All make the Sign of the Cross.

Hymn

A Psalm for Early Lent

[Turn to page 34.]

Reading   Deuteronomy 26:16-18, 19

Listen to the words of the book of Deuteronomy (*dew-ter-ON-uh-mee*).

Moses said to Israel:
"Today the Lord your God has commanded you to obey these laws and teachings with all your heart and soul.

"In response, you have agreed that the Lord will be your God, that you will obey all his laws and teachings, and that you will listen when he speaks to you.

"Since you have agreed to obey the Lord, he has agreed that you will be his people and that you will belong to him, just as he promised. You will belong only to the Lord your God, just as he promised."

The word of the Lord.

Reflection

What are some of the "laws and teachings" that God has made known to us through the church? When did God adopt us as his special people? Can I find a way, during Lent, to renew my agreement to listen to God and obey God's teachings?

Closing   Adapted from the *Byzantine Rite*

Receive Lent with gladness, O people!
Let us all say:
Be strong, and turn your life toward God.
Be strong, and turn your life toward God.

Let us bring our hopes and needs to God, as we pray: **God of mercy, hear our prayer.**

Let us pray with the words that Jesus taught us:

Our Father …

Merciful God,
as your loving children,
we are eager to do what is right.
Send your Holy Spirit to live with us
and to fill us with your light.
We ask this through Christ our Lord. **Amen.**

✞ All make the Sign of the Cross.

March 14, 2019

Friday Daily Prayer

Introduction

The gospel reading for Sunday tells the story of a wonderful and mysterious event in Jesus' life. He takes his closest friends with him up a mountain. He prays there so deeply that he shines with God's glory. This is called the transfiguration (*trans-FIG-you-RAY-shun*) because Jesus looked so different. His friends did not know what to think.

☩ All make the Sign of the Cross.

Hymn

A Psalm for Early Lent

[Turn to page 34.]

Reading   *Luke 9:28-31, 33-36*

Listen to the words of the holy gospel according to Luke.

Jesus took Peter, John and James with him and went up on a mountain to pray. While he was praying, his face changed, and his clothes became shining white. Suddenly Moses and Elijah (*ee-LYE-juh*) were there speaking with him. They appeared in heavenly glory and talked about all that Jesus' death in Jerusalem would mean.
   Peter said to Jesus, "Master, it is good for us to be here! Let us make three shelters, one for you, one for Moses, and one for Elijah." While Peter was still speaking, a shadow from a cloud passed over them, and they were frightened as the cloud covered them. From the cloud a voice spoke, "This is my chosen son. Listen to what he says!"
   After the voice had spoken, Peter, John and James saw only Jesus.

The gospel of the Lord.

Reflection

This vision reminds us of the glory of Jesus' resurrection. Why does the church remind us of Easter at the beginning of Lent? How are apostles (Peter, John, James) and prophets (Moses and Elijah) important to us?

Closing   Adapted from the *Byzantine Rite*

Receive Lent with gladness, O people!
Let us all say:
Be strong, and turn your life toward God.
Be strong, and turn your life toward God.

Let us bring our hopes and needs to God, as we pray: **God of mercy, hear our prayer.**

Let us pray with the words that Jesus taught us:

Our Father ...

Merciful God,
as your loving children,
we are eager to do what is right.
Send your Holy Spirit to live with us
and to fill us with your light.
We ask this through Christ our Lord. **Amen.**

☩ All make the Sign of the Cross.

March 15, 2019

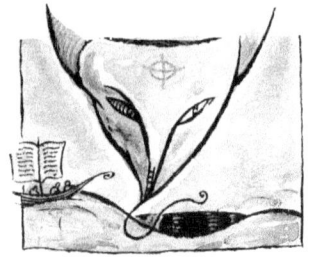

Monday Daily Prayer

Introduction

Today we remember Saint Patrick, the patron of Ireland. Patrick was actually British. He was kidnapped as a teenager and brought to Ireland as a slave. Later he escaped, returned to his family and his studies and became a priest. Years later he returned to Ireland as a missionary and bishop.

By the time Patrick died in 461, a great many Irish families had turned to Christ. Many Irish people came to Australia in the nineteenth century and helped the church to grow. The Closing for today is part of a long poem he may have written.

✢ All make the Sign of the Cross.

Hymn

A Psalm for Early Lent

[Turn to page 34.]

Reading   Luke 10:1-9

Listen to the words of the holy gospel according to Luke:

The Lord chose seventy-two followers and sent them out two by two to every town and village where he was about to go. He said to them, "A large crop is in the fields, but there are only a few workers. Ask the Lord in charge of the harvest to send out workers to bring it in.

"Now go, but remember, I am sending you like lambs into a pack of wolves. Don't take along a moneybag or a travelling bag or sandals. As soon as you enter a home, say, 'God bless this home with peace.' If the people living there are peace-loving, your prayer for peace will return to you. Stay with the same family, eating and drinking whatever they give you, because workers are worth what they earn.

"If the people of a town welcome you, eat whatever they offer. Heal their sick and say, 'God's kingdom will soon be here!' "

The gospel of the Lord.

Reflection

What harvest is Jesus talking about? How do we know when people are peace-loving? What are some of the signs that "God's kingdom" is here?

Closing

Let us bring our hopes and needs to God, as we pray: **God of peace, hear our prayer.**

Let us pray with the words that Jesus taught us:

Our Father …

I arise today
   through God's strength to pilot me,
   God's might to uphold me,
   God's wisdom to guide me,
   God's eye to look before me,
   God's ear to hear me,
   God's word to speak for me,
   God's hand to guard me,
   God's way to lie before me,
   God's shield to protect me.
I thank God through Christ our Lord. **Amen.**

✢ All make the Sign of the Cross.

March 18, 2019

Tuesday Daily Prayer

Introduction

Saint Joseph was the husband of Mary and the foster father of Jesus. We remember him today. Joseph was a descendant of the royal family of David, but he was not rich or famous. He worked as a carpenter in his home town of Nazareth.

In the reading we hear that Joseph had a dream. In the bible, a dream is a special way of receiving a message from God. Through his dream Joseph came to understand what had happened to Mary, and so he lovingly welcomed her as his wife.

Many parishes and schools are named after Saint Joseph. You may have friends named Joseph.

✝ All make the Sign of the Cross.

Hymn

A Psalm for Early Lent

[Turn to page 34.]

Reading   Matthew 1:18-21, 24

Listen to the words of the holy gospel according to Matthew:

A young woman named Mary was engaged to Joseph from King David's family. But before they were married, she learned that she was going to have a baby by God's Holy Spirit. Joseph was a good man and did not want to embarrass Mary in front of everyone. So he decided to call off the wedding quietly.

While Joseph was thinking about this, an angel from the Lord came to him in a dream. The angel said, "Joseph, the baby that Mary will have is from the Holy Spirit. Go ahead and marry her. Then after her baby is born, name him Jesus, because he will save his people from their sins."

After Joseph woke up, he and Mary were soon married, just as the Lord's angel had told him to do.

The gospel of the Lord.

Reflection

Why is Joseph a very special saint for the church? How did he show that he was a just and kind man? In what way are we called to be like Joseph?

Closing

Let us bring our hopes and needs to God, as we pray: **God of mercy, hear our prayer.**

Let us pray with the words that Jesus taught us:

Our Father ...

Loving God,
you put your Son, Jesus, in the care of Joseph.
Put us also in Joseph's care,
and may he always watch over
the whole church.
We ask this through Christ our Lord. **Amen.**

✝ All make the Sign of the Cross.

March 19, 2019

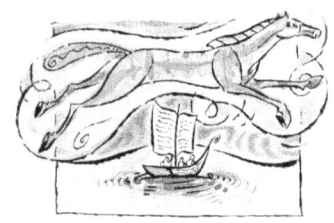

Wednesday Daily Prayer

Introduction

At sunset yesterday, the Jewish feast of Purim began. This feast honours Queen Esther who long ago saved the Jewish people from being killed by a wicked official in what is now Iran. During this feast Jews pray for religious freedom. Gifts are given to the poor and children celebrate with games and treats.

Today's reading reminds us again that we belong to God. God will protect, save and come to our rescue. It is like being held in the palm of God's hand. God will never forget his people. God is always there to protect us.

☩ All make the Sign of the Cross.

Hymn

A Psalm for Early Lent

[Turn to page 34.]

Reading   *Isaiah 41:13, 14, 17-20*

Listen to the words of the prophet Isaiah:

The Lord says this:
I am the Lord your God.
I am holding your hand,
so don't be afraid. I am here to help you.
I am the holy God of Israel, who saves
and protects you.
When the poor and needy are dying of thirst
and cannot find water,
I, the Lord God of Israel, will come to their rescue.
I won't forget them.
I will make rivers flow on mountain peaks.
I will send streams to fill the valleys.
Dry and barren land will flow with springs and become a lake.
I will fill the desert with all kinds of trees.
Everyone will see this and know that I,
the holy Lord God of Israel, created it all."

The word of the Lord.

Reflection

In what ways am I 'poor and needy' this Lent? Do I find it hard to really believe that God is always ready to help me? In what way do I ask God to help others? What do the symbols of desert and water mean?

Closing   Adapted from the *Byzantine Rite*

Receive Lent with gladness, O people!
Let us all say:
Be strong, and turn your life toward God.
Be strong, and turn your life toward God.

Let us bring our hopes and needs to God, as we pray: **God of mercy, hear our prayer.**

Let us pray with the words that Jesus taught us:

Our Father …

Merciful God,
as your loving children,
we are eager to do what is right.
Send your Holy Spirit to live with us
and to fill us with your light.
We ask this through Christ our Lord. **Amen.**

☩ All make the Sign of the Cross.

March 20, 2019

Thursday Daily Prayer

Introduction

Today is Harmony Day. It celebrates the many different cultures that are part of life in Australia. It's about including and respecting everyone and giving them a sense of belonging.

It's a day for all Australians to welcome cultural diversity and to share what we have in common. The message for Harmony Day is that 'everyone belongs.'

We have been hearing about God's law and how we are to love and forgive one another. As people who belong to God we are asked to agree that we will obey God's teachings and laws. In today's reading, God's laws are spoken of as the 'way of life'. We can choose to follow or not to follow this way.

✣ All make the Sign of the Cross.

Hymn

A Psalm for Early Lent

[Turn to page 34.]

Reading   *Deuteronomy 24:19-22*

Listen to the words of the book of Deuteronomy *(dew ter ON uh mee)*.

Moses said to Israel, "If you forget to bring in a stack of harvested grain, don't go back in the field to get it. Leave it for the poor, including foreigners, orphans, and widows, and the Lord will make you successful in everything you do. "When you harvest your olives, don't try to get them all for yourself, but leave some for the poor. And when you pick your grapes, go over the vines only once, then let the poor have what is left. You lived in poverty as slaves in Egypt until the Lord your God rescued you. That's why I am giving you these laws."

The word of the Lord.

Reflection

Who are people around me that I know are in need? Project Compassion is a way for all of us to help the poor. Am I sometimes tempted to keep good things for myself and forget those who do not have food, clothing and shelter?

Closing   Adapted from the *Byzantine Rite*

Receive Lent with gladness, O people!
Let us all say:
Be strong, and turn your life toward God.
Be strong, and turn your life toward God.

Let us bring our hopes and needs to God, as we pray: **God of mercy, hear our prayer.**

Let us pray with the words that Jesus taught us:

Our Father …

Merciful God,
as your loving children,
we are eager to do what is right.
Send your Holy Spirit to live with us
and to fill us with your light.
We ask this through Christ our Lord. **Amen.**

✣ All make the Sign of the Cross.

March 21, 2019

Friday Daily Prayer

Introduction

Jesus tells stories about things that were part of the life of the people he was teaching. He helps them to them think about the life of love and kindness that will last forever in heaven. Jesus is like the gardener that pleads for more time to look after the fig tree so that it will bear fruit in the future. Jesus doesn't give up on us, either, even when we don't do the right thing.

✞ All make the Sign of the Cross.

Hymn

A Psalm for Early Lent

[Turn to page 34.]

Reading
Luke 13:6-9

Listen to the words of the holy gospel according to Luke:

Jesus told this story:
A man had a fig tree growing in his vineyard. One day he went out to pick some figs, but he didn't find any. So he said to the gardener, "For three years I have come looking for figs on this tree, and I haven't found any yet. Chop it down! Why should it take up space?"

The gardener answered, "Master, leave it for another year. I'll dig around it and put some manure on it to make it grow. Maybe it will have figs on it next year. If it doesn't you can have it cut down."

The gospel of the Lord.

Reflection

If God is the gardener of the story, what could the fig tree represent? When the gardener asks that the tree be left for another year, how is this like Lent? Have my friends and I ever needed time to "bear fruit?"

Closing
Adapted from the *Byzantine Rite*

Receive Lent with gladness, O people!
Let us all say:
Be strong, and turn your life toward God.
Be strong, and turn your life toward God.

Let us bring our hopes and needs to God, as we pray: **God of mercy, hear our prayer.**

Let us pray with the words that Jesus taught us:

Our Father …

Merciful God,
as your loving children,
we are eager to do what is right.
Send your Holy Spirit to live with us
and to fill us with your light.
We ask this through Christ our Lord. **Amen.**

✞ All make the Sign of the Cross.

March 22, 2019

Monday Daily Prayer

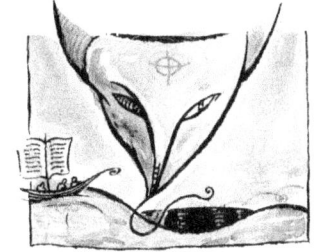

Introduction

Today we celebrate the Annunciation (*uh-nun-see-AY-shun*) of the Lord. We read in the gospel story that the angel Gabriel announced that Mary was to be the mother of Jesus. We are happy that the Son of God loved us enough to become one of us. We are happy that Mary said "yes" to God in a very special way. Many others have said their own "yes" to Jesus.

☦ All make the Sign of the Cross.

Hymn

A Psalm for Early Lent

[Turn to page 34.]

Reading   *Luke 1:26-32, 34-35, 38*

Listen to the words of the holy gospel according to Luke:

God sent the angel Gabriel to the town of Nazareth in Galilee with a message for a virgin named Mary. She was engaged to Joseph from the family of King David. The angel greeted Mary and said, "You are truly blessed! The Lord is with you."

Mary was confused by the angel's words and wondered what they meant. Then the angel told Mary, "Don't be afraid! God is pleased with you and you will have a son. His name will be Jesus. He will be great and will be called the Son of God Most High."

Mary asked the angel, "How can this happen? I am not married!"
The angel answered, "The Holy Spirit will come down to you, and God's power will come over you. So your child will be called the holy Son of God."

Mary said, "I am the Lord's servant! Let it happen as you have said."

The gospel of the Lord.

Reflection

The Annunciation is the beginning of the story of Jesus. How much do we remember about the life and work of Jesus? How do we accept Jesus into our lives?

Closing

Let us bring our hopes and needs to God, as we pray: **God of love and mercy, hear our prayer.**

Mary, Mother of Christ we are your children. **Pray for us.**

Let us all say:
**Hail Mary, full of grace,
the Lord is with you!
Blessed are you among women,
and blessed is the fruit
of your womb, Jesus.
Holy Mary, Mother of God,
prayer for us sinners,
now and at the hour of our death. Amen.**

☦ All make the Sign of the Cross.

March 25, 2019

Tuesday Daily Prayer

Introduction

In the Bible God is sometimes described as being angry, especially with those who turn away from him. This is a human way of describing how God feels about our bad choices. But his anger never lasts, in fact it turns to comfort. We can be confident that our strength comes from God and that God will save us. For this we can be truly thankful.

✞ All make the Sign of the Cross.

Hymn

A Psalm for Early Lent

[Turn to page 34.]

Reading
Isaiah 12:1-2, 4-6

Listen to the words of the prophet Isaiah:

At that time you will say, "I thank you, Lord! You were angry with me, but you stopped being angry and gave me comfort. I trust you to save me, Lord God, and I won't be afraid. My power and my strength come from you, and you have saved me."

At that time you will say, "Our Lord, we are thankful, and we worship only you. We will tell the nations how glorious you are and what you have done. Because of your wonderful deeds we will sing your praises everywhere on earth."

Sing, people of Zion! Celebrate the greatness of the holy Lord of Israel. God is here to help you.

The word of the Lord.

Reflection

Does thinking about God give me comfort and strength? Does it make me brave and joyful? Do I worry that God might be more interested in sins than in happiness? How do ideas like that spoil the way I see God's love in my life?

Closing

During this season of Lent,
let us acknowledge that we are sinners,
let us express our sorrow,
and ask God to forgive us.

Our responses to the following three petitions are 'Lord, have mercy,' then 'Christ, have mercy,' and then 'Lord, have mercy."

Lord, we ask your forgiveness for all our sins.
   Lord, have mercy.

Christ, we turn our hearts toward you.
   Christ, have mercy.

Lord, we ask your blessing on us during Lent.
   Lord, have mercy.

Let us also remember our other hopes and needs as we pray: **God of comfort, hear our prayer.**

Let us pray with the words that Jesus taught us:

Our Father …

✞ All make the Sign of the Cross.

March 26, 2019

Wednesday Daily Prayer

Introduction

We have been hearing about God's law and how we are to love and forgive one another. As people who belong to God we are asked to agree that we will obey God's teachings and laws. In today's reading, God's laws are spoken of as the 'way of life'. We can choose to follow or not to follow this way.

✢ All make the Sign of the Cross.

Hymn

A Psalm for Early Lent

[Turn to page 34.]

Reading   *Deuteronomy 30:15-17, 19-20*

Listen to the words of the book of Deuteronomy (*dew-ter-ON-uh-mee*):

Today I am giving you a choice. You can choose [between] life and success or death and disaster. I am commanding you to be loyal to the Lord, to live the way he has told you, and to obey his laws and teachings.
  Choose Life! Be completely faithful to the Lord your God, love him, and do whatever he tells you. The Lord is the only one who can give life, and he will let you live a long time in the land that he promised to your ancestors Abraham, Isaac, and Jacob.

The word of the Lord.

Reflection

Some people think we have more fun and a better life if we just don't worry about God's laws. Others think that the laws of God bring us a good life. What do you think of this?

Closing

My sisters and brothers,
during this season of Lent
let us express our sorrow for sin
and ask God to forgive us.

Our responses to the following three petitions are 'Lord, have mercy,' then 'Christ, have mercy,' and then 'Lord, have mercy.'

Lord, we ask your forgiveness for all our sins.
  Lord, have mercy.

Christ, we turn our hearts toward you.
  Christ, have mercy.

Lord, we ask your blessing on us during Lent.
  Lord, have mercy.

Let us also remember our other hopes and needs as we pray: **God of comfort, hear our prayer.**

Let us pray with the words that Jesus taught us:

Our Father …

✢ All make the Sign of the Cross.

March 27, 2019

Thursday Daily Prayer

Introduction

The prophets of Israel told the people to repent. "Remember God, and turn from your evil ways," they said. But they also brought a message of hope. "No matter how bad things seem to be, God has not forgotten you," they said. "God will be your Saviour."

When their country was at war and there was not enough to eat, the people remembered these promises. They prayed and waited for the Saviour. During Lent, we listen again to these messages of repentance and of hope.

✝ All make the Sign of the Cross.

Hymn

A Psalm for Early Lent

[Turn to page 34.]

Reading   Jeremiah 29:10-14

Listen to the words of the prophet Jeremiah (jer-uh-MY-uh):

The Lord says this:

"I will be kind and bring you back to Jerusalem, just as I have promised. I will bless you with a future filled with hope—a future of success, not of suffering. You will turn back to me and ask for help, and I will answer your prayers.

"You will worship me with all your heart, and I will be with you and accept your worship. I will gather you from the nations where I scattered you, and you will return to Jerusalem."

The word of the Lord.

Reflection

Are we surprised that God cares for us so much? Many people come to this country without friends or security. How hard would it be for me to move to a foreign country? How do I treat new people in my school or neighbourhood?

Closing

My sisters and brothers,
during this season of Lent
let us express our sorrow for sin
and ask God to forgive us.

Our responses to the following three petitions are 'Lord, have mercy,' then 'Christ, have mercy,' and then 'Lord, have mercy.'

Lord, we ask your forgiveness for all our sins.
   Lord, have mercy.
Christ, we turn our hearts toward you.
   Christ, have mercy.
Lord, we ask your blessing on us during Lent.
   Lord, have mercy.

Let us also remember our other hopes and needs as we pray: **God of comfort, hear our prayer.**

Let us pray with the words that Jesus taught us:

Our Father …

✝ All make the Sign of the Cross.

Friday Daily Prayer

[Reminder: The Psalm for Late Lent is found on page 58. Make a copy for each member of the class.]

Introduction

Today's reading from the Sunday gospel is another of the stories that Jesus told. It is a favourite of Christians everywhere, so you may know it by heart. Listen again to the story of the wasteful son and his forgiving father.

✞ All make the Sign of the Cross.

Hymn

A Psalm for Early Lent

[Turn to page 34.]

Reading   Luke 15:11-20, 22, 24

Listen to the words of the holy gospel according to Luke:

Jesus told this story: Once a man had two sons. The younger son said to his father, "Give me my share of the property." So the father divided his property between his two sons. The younger son packed up everything he owned and left for a foreign country. He had spent everything when a bad famine spread through that whole land. He went to work for a man in that country and the man sent him out to take care of his pigs. He would have been glad to eat what the pigs were eating, but no one gave him a thing.

Finally, he came to his senses and said, "My father's workers have plenty to eat, and here I am, starving to death! I will go to my father and say to him, 'Father, I have sinned against God in heaven and against you. I am no longer good enough to be called your son. Treat me like one of your workers.'"

The younger son got up and started back to his father. But when he was still a long way off, his father saw him and felt sorry for him. He ran to his son and hugged and kissed him. His father said to the servants. "Hurry and bring the best clothes and put them on him. Give him a ring for his finger and sandals for his feet. This son of mine was dead, but has now come back to life. He was lost and has now been found."

The gospel of the Lord.

Reflection

What does this story say to me? Why is this a good story for Lent? Would I be able to forgive someone the way the father forgave his son?

Closing

My sisters and brothers,
during this season of Lent
let us express our sorrow for sin
and ask God to forgive us.

Our responses to the following three petitions are 'Lord, have mercy,' then 'Christ, have mercy,' and then 'Lord, have mercy.'

Lord, we ask your forgiveness for all our sins.
   Lord, have mercy.
Christ, we turn our hearts toward you.
   Christ, have mercy.
Lord, we ask your blessing on us during Lent.
   Lord, have mercy.

Let us also remember our other hopes and needs as we pray. **Forgiving God, hear our prayer.**

Let us pray with the words that Jesus taught us:

Our Father …

Forgiving Lord,
even when we wander
you long for us to return to you.
Forgive us always and open your arms
   to welcome us.
We ask this through Christ our Lord. **Amen.**

✞ All make the Sign of the Cross.

March 29, 2019

PSALMS ARE POEMS

Can you imagine a desert turning into a garden? A mountain rocking with happiness? A valley of wheat singing for joy? Can you imagine God as a shepherd leading sheep to a running stream? Or as a solid rock on which to stand? Can you imagine God smiling?

This is what the psalms invite us to do – to use our imaginations. That's because they are poems. Poems open our eyes to see things in a new way. They open our minds to understand things differently. They open our hearts to new and deeper feelings.

God's first people, the Israelites, used all sorts of down-to-earth images to try and say something about the mystery of God. They knew God couldn't be pinned down with a name, so they spoke of God as a husband, a father, a shepherd, a king, a warrior, a creator, a rock, a shield and many other things.

Do you remember any of these images from the psalms we've already prayed?

"The stone that the builders tossed aside has now become the most important stone." (*Psalm 118, Easter*)

"You, Lord, are my shepherd … You let me rest in fields of green grass. You lead me to streams of peaceful water, and you refresh my life." (*Psalm 23, Easter*)

"Desert pastures blossom and mountains celebrate. Meadows are filled with sheep and goats. Valleys overflow with grain and echo with joyful songs." (*Psalm 65, July*).

In their prayer-poems, the psalms, the Israelites loved to say the same thing over and over again. Once they found something good to say, they repeated it, sometimes in reverse, sometimes by using slightly different words. They enjoyed this poetic play.

The psalms help us with their poetry. They remind us that God is not someone or something that can be captured and put in a box. God is always more than we can think or imagine.

The poetry of the psalms helps us in another way too. You can't rush through poetry. You need to take time with it, to let words sink in. The psalms invite us to take our time with God.

Late Lent

Monday, April 1,
to Friday, April 12

Late Lent 2019
Looking Ahead

About the Season

Has Lent begun to seem long? We are now halfway through the 40 days of Lent, and that is good news! That means we are halfway to Easter. We count the 40 days from the First Sunday of Lent through to Holy Thursday.

Our forty days are not over yet, so it is not too late to make a fresh start. Remember, Lent is not just a time for doing special things and saying special prayers for the sake of doing them. If our Lenten practices do not help us to understand God's word more clearly and to live according to that word more generously, then they are not useful.

The number 'forty' appears in the Bible many times. The most important '40' is the 40 years that the Hebrew people lived in the desert after their lives of slavery in Egypt and before they moved into the Promised Land. That certainly was a long time, but when they thought about it later, they decided that God had kept them in the desert for as long as it took to make them ready to hear God's word and to live as that word commanded.

Do you remember the story about Noah and his ark? In that story, the rain fell for 40 days and nights. Maybe the author meant that God kept Noah and his family away from their 'Promised Land' until they were ready to hear God's word and live by it.

Jesus spent 40 days and nights in the desert before he began his preaching. Maybe God was giving him a chance to become strong before his work began. Has God been making us strong during Lent?

During Lent, even though it seems strange, there is a joy about the season. Many people are listening to and turning to God. Many are preparing to be baptised at Easter. Many are helping one other, working for peace and carrying the good news of Jesus to every corner of the world.

Lent ends on the evening of Holy Thursday, April 18. Then the church celebrates the three holiest days of the year. We call these days the Paschal Triduum. 'Triduum' is a Latin word meaning 'three days.' And the word 'paschal' means 'Passover.' These three days, counted from sunset on Holy Thursday to sunset on Easter Sunday, are the Christian Passover feast.

Readings

During the last two weeks of Lent we will listen to two long readings from the Gospel of John. They are stories about conversion and new life.

We begin with the story of the Samaritan woman who comes to the well and meets Jesus. This gospel is often used on the third Sunday of Lent to prepare people for Easter baptism. At that time, Jews did not speak to Samaritans and men were not allowed to speak to women they do not know.

Then we will begin another powerful reading from the Gospel of John. The story tells about a blind man who receives sight from Jesus. But it is also about all of us who need to be healed by Jesus. He is truly the light of the world.

Preparation for Late Lent

The Psalm for Late Lent is Psalm 130 (page 58). In this psalm we ask God for forgiveness and mercy. Students will need their own copies of each of these pages.

Freshen up the prayer space during these days of Late Lent. If you used a bowl of ashes in Early Lent, you might replace this with a pot of bare branches. This could help us to be mindful that Lent is a time of pruning and of preparation for the flowering of Easter joy. Alternatively, some colourful autumn leaves could remind us that, even though leaves fall and die, new life will spring forth, just as Jesus' death will lead to new life.

For most states across Australia, first term concludes on the Friday before Palm Sunday. On Palm Sunday, palms are blessed in memory of Jesus peacefully entering Jerusalem on a donkey. This marks the beginning of Holy Week, the special days of preparing to remember the death and resurrection of Jesus. All schools are on holidays for Holy Week and the Paschal Triduum. That means many people will have the opportunity to take part in the most important ceremonies in the whole year: the Evening Mass on Holy Thursday, the Solemn Commemoration of the Lord's Passion on Good Friday afternoon, and the Easter Vigil on Saturday night. Most states are also on holidays for the first week of the Easter season. This year Anzac Day falls during this week.

Before you leave for the Easter break, put away Lenten decorations and clean the classroom. Then the room will be ready for the colourful decorations of Eastertime.

Suggested Hymns

See the hymn chart on pages viii-ix. Some of the hymns from Early Lent can still be sung in Late Lent. Choice of hymns might change as we approach Palm Sunday and Holy Week. During these weeks you might take some time to learn the music you will sing in church during the Paschal Triduum. The services in church are very beautiful. Maybe you can have someone talk about them with the class.

A Psalm for Late Lent

Psalm 130:1-6, 7-8

LEADER
Behold! Now is the acceptable time!
ALL
Now is the day of salvation!

LEADER
From a sea of troubles,
I call out to you, Lord.
ALL
Won't you please listen
as I beg for mercy?

SIDE A
If you kept record of our sins,
no one could last long.

SIDE B
But you forgive us,
and so we will worship you.

SIDE A
With all my heart,
I am waiting, Lord, for you!
I trust your promises.

SIDE B
I wait for you more eagerly
than a soldier on guard duty
waits for the dawn.

SIDE A
Israel, trust the Lord!
He is always merciful.

SIDE B
Israel, the Lord will save you
from all your sins.

LEADER
From a sea of troubles,
I call out to you, Lord.
ALL
Won't you please listen
as I beg for mercy?

Glory be to the Father, and to the Son,
and to the Holy Spirit:
as it was in the beginning, is now,
and ever shall be,
world without end. Amen.

[Turn back to Daily Prayer for today.]

Monday Daily Prayer

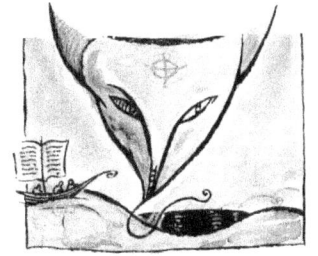

[Reminder: The Psalm for Late Lent is found on page 55. Make a copy for each member of the class.]

Introduction

Today we begin a long story from the gospel of John. It is often used on the third Sunday of Lent to prepare people for Easter baptism. It is a story about a Samaritan woman who meets Jesus. At that time Jews did not speak to Samaritans, and men were not allowed to speak to women they did not know.

✟ All make the Sign of the Cross.

Hymn

A Psalm for Late Lent

[Turn to page 55.]

Reading   *John 4:7-11, 13-14*

Listen to the words of the holy gospel according to John:

A Samaritan woman came to draw water from the well. Jesus asked her, "Would you please give me a drink of water?"

"You are a Jew," she replied, "and I am a Samaritan woman. How can you ask me for a drink of water when Jews and Samaritans won't have anything to do with each other?"

Jesus answered, "You don't know what God wants to give you, and you don't know who is asking you for a drink. If you did, you would ask me for water that gives life."

"Sir," the woman said, "you don't even have a bucket, and the well is deep. Where are you going to get this life-giving water?"

Jesus answered, "Everyone who drinks this water will get thirsty again. But no one who drinks the water I give will ever be thirsty again. The water I give is like a flowing fountain that gives eternal life."

The gospel of the Lord.

Reflection

How did Jesus deal with the hateful feelings between Jews and Samaritans? How can this be a model for us? What can Jesus mean by "life-giving water?"

Closing

During Lent,
God looks upon hearts that are parched with thirst,
and invites us to open our hearts to others.

Our responses to the following three petitions are 'Lord, have mercy,' then 'Christ, have mercy,' and then 'Lord, have mercy.'

Lord, be with those who thirst for you.
   Lord, have mercy.
Christ, be with those who believe in you.
   Christ, have mercy.
Lord, be with those
who hope in your resurrection.
   Lord, have mercy.

Let us bring our other hopes and needs to God, as we pray: **God of new life, hear our prayer.**

Let us pray with the words that Jesus taught us:

Our Father ...

✟ All make the Sign of the Cross.

April 1, 2019

Tuesday Daily Prayer

Introduction

Yesterday we began the story of the Samaritan woman who met Jesus at Jacob's well. Jesus was thirsty for water but he thirsted more for the woman's faith. The woman too was thirsty for water but she also thirsted for the truth. During Lent, people who are thirsty for the truth prepare to be baptised at Easter.

✢ All make the Sign of the Cross.

Hymn

A Psalm for Late Lent

[Turn to page 55.]

Reading *John 4:19-21, 23, 24*

Listen to the words of the holy gospel according to John:

The Samaritan woman said to Jesus, "Sir, I can see that you are a prophet, [so explain this to me]. My ancestors worshipped on this mountain, but you Jews say Jerusalem is the only place to worship."

Jesus said to her, "Believe me, the time is coming when you won't worship the Father either on this mountain or in Jerusalem. Even now the true worshippers are being led by the Spirit to worship the Father according to the truth. God is Spirit, and those who worship God must be led by the Spirit to worship him according to the truth."

The gospel of the Lord.

Reflection

We worship God each time we pray reverently. Have we learned to pray well in our class? What are some special times or places when I pray to God? What might it mean to worship God "in truth"?

Closing

During Lent,
God looks upon hearts that are parched with thirst,
and invites us to open our hearts to others.

Our responses to the following three petitions are 'Lord, have mercy,' then 'Christ, have mercy,' and then 'Lord, have mercy.'

Lord, be with those who thirst for you.
   Lord, have mercy.
Christ, be with those who believe in you.
   Christ, have mercy.
Lord, be with those
who hope in your resurrection.
   Lord, have mercy.

Let us bring our other hopes and needs to God, as we pray: **God of new life, hear our prayer.**

Let us pray with the words that Jesus taught us:

Our Father …

✢ All make the Sign of the Cross.

April 2, 2019

Wednesday Daily Prayer

Introduction

Today we continue the story of the Samaritan woman who met Jesus at Jacob's well. Jesus has led the woman step by step to understand that he was the Messiah she was longing for. She is so excited at what she has discovered that she wants to share it with all her neighbours.

✝ All make the Sign of the Cross.

Hymn

A Psalm for Late Lent

[Turn to page 55.]

Reading   John 4:25-26, 28-30, 39, 41-42

Listen to the words of the holy gospel according to John:

The Samaritan woman said, "I know that the Messiah will come. He is the one we call Christ. When he comes, he will explain everything to us."
    "I am that one," Jesus told her. The woman left her water jar and ran back into town. She said to the people, "Come and see a man who told me everything I have ever done! Could he be the Messiah?" Everyone in town went out to see Jesus. A lot of Samaritans in that town put their faith in Jesus because [of what] the woman had said. Many more Samaritans put their faith in Jesus because of what they heard him say. They told the woman, "We no longer have faith in Jesus just because of what you told us. We have heard him ourselves, and we are certain that he is the Saviour of the world!"

The gospel of the Lord.

Reflection

The woman brought others to Jesus. Who has brought me to believe in Jesus? How can we believe in Jesus 'for ourselves'? How can I share the good news of Jesus with others?

Closing

During Lent,
God looks upon hearts that are parched with thirst,
and invites us to open our hearts to others.

Our responses to the following three petitions are 'Lord, have mercy,' then 'Christ, have mercy,' and then 'Lord, have mercy.'

Lord, be with those who thirst for you.
    Lord, have mercy.
Christ, be with those who believe in you.
    Christ, have mercy.
Lord, be with those
who hope in your resurrection.
    Lord, have mercy.

Let us bring our other hopes and needs to God, as we pray: **God of new life, hear our prayer.**

Let us pray with the words that Jesus taught us:

Our Father …

✝ All make the Sign of the Cross.

April 3, 2019

Thursday Daily Prayer

Introduction

Today we will begin reading another powerful story from the gospel of John. The story tells about a blind man who receives sight from Jesus. But it is also about all of us who need to be healed by Jesus. He is truly the light of the world.

✞ All make the Sign of the Cross.

Hymn

A Psalm for Late Lent

[Turn to page 55.]

Reading   John 9:1-3, 5-7

Listen to the words of the holy gospel according to John:

As Jesus walked along, he saw a man who had been blind since birth. Jesus' disciples asked, "Teacher, why was this man born blind? Was it because he or his parents sinned?"

"No, it wasn't!" Jesus answered. "But you will see God work a miracle for him. While I am in the world, I am the light for the world." After Jesus said this, he spat on the ground. He made some mud and smeared it on the man's eyes. Then he said, "Go and wash off the mud in Siloam (SIL-oh-ahm) Pool." The man went and washed in Siloam. When he had washed off the mud, he could see.

The gospel of the Lord.

Reflection

What things has Jesus helped me to see this year? How has Jesus been a light for my family and me? Have I got any 'blindness' about certain things?

Closing

During Lent,
God invites us to seek Jesus,
the true light of the world,
and to renewed in our hearts and minds.

Our responses to the following three petitions are 'Lord, have mercy,' then 'Christ, have mercy,' and then 'Lord, have mercy.'

Lord, be with those who believe in you.
   Lord, have mercy.
Christ, be with those who take up their cross and follow you.
   Christ, have mercy.
Lord, be with those
who hope in your resurrection.
   Lord, have mercy.

Let us bring our other hopes and needs to God, as we pray: **God of light, hear our prayer.**

Let us pray with the words that Jesus taught us:

Our Father …

✞ All make the Sign of the Cross.

April 4, 2019

Friday Daily Prayer

Introduction

The end of Lent is not far off. But it is not too late to do something special. Lent is the time to try harder, to be more sensitive to others and to listen to the word that God speaks in our hearts.

After we listen to this reading from Sunday's gospel, we should sit quietly for a minute, to allow God's word to take root in us. The word of God deserves prayerful listening. It's good news!

✟ All make the Sign of the Cross.

Hymn

A Psalm for Late Lent

[Turn to page 55.]

Reading   John 8:3-7, 9-11

Listen to the words of the holy gospel according to John:

[The leaders brought a sinful woman to Jesus.] They made her stand in the middle of the crowd. Then they said, "Teacher, this woman was caught with a man who wasn't her husband. The Law of Moses teaches that a woman like this should be stoned to death! What do you say?"

Jesus simply bent over and started writing on the ground with his finger. Finally, he stood up and said, "If any of you has never sinned, then go ahead and throw the first stone at her!" The people left one by one, beginning with the oldest. Finally, Jesus and the woman were there alone.

Jesus stood up and asked her, "Where is everyone? Isn't there anyone left to accuse you?"

"No sir," the woman answered. Then Jesus told her, "I am not going to accuse you either. You may go now, but don't sin any more."

The gospel of the Lord.

Reflection

Why did the people leave instead of punishing the woman? What does this story teach us about judging others? And about forgiveness? How is this gospel like the sacrament of reconciliation?

Closing

Our responses to the following three petitions are 'Lord, have mercy,' then 'Christ, have mercy,' and then 'Lord, have mercy.'

Lord, be with those who believe in you.
   Lord, have mercy.
Christ, be with those who take up their cross and follow you.
   Christ, have mercy.
Lord, be with those
who hope in your resurrection.
   Lord, have mercy.

Let us bring our hopes and needs to God, as we pray: **Gentle God, hear our prayer.**

Let us pray with the words that Jesus taught us:

Our Father …

Forgiving Lord,
even when we wander
you long for us to return to you.
Forgive us always
and open your arms
   to welcome us.
We ask this through Christ our Lord. **Amen.**

✟ All make the Sign of the Cross.

April 5, 2019

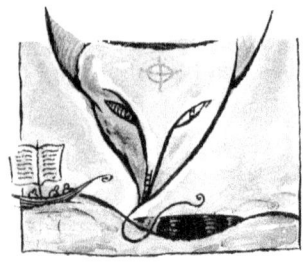

Monday Daily Prayer

Introduction

Today we continue to read about the man who received sight from Jesus. Things should be much easier for him now that he is able to see things for himself, but his neighbours do not understand what happened. They want him to explain it, but he is not able to tell them very much. Sometimes it takes a long time to understand the meaning of things that happen to us.

✝ All make the Sign of the Cross.

Hymn

A Psalm for Late Lent

[Turn to page 55.]

Reading *John 9:8-12*

Listen to the words of the holy gospel according to John:

The [neighbours of the man born blind], and the people who had seen him begging wondered if he really could be the same man. Some of them said he was the same beggar, while others said he only looked like him. But he told them, "I am that man."

"Then how can you see?" they asked.

He answered, "Someone named Jesus made some mud and smeared it on my eyes. He told me to go and wash it off in Siloam (*SIL-oh-ahm*) Pool. When I did, I could see."

"Where is he now?" they asked.

"I don't know," he answered.

The gospel of the Lord.

Reflection

Notice how the man gives straight and honest answers when he is questioned. If someone asked me about Jesus, what would I answer? How does learning more about Jesus open our eyes?

Closing

During Lent,
God invites us to seek Jesus,
the true light of the world,
and to renewed in our hearts and minds.

Our responses to the following three petitions are 'Lord, have mercy,' then 'Christ, have mercy,' and then 'Lord, have mercy.'

Lord, be with those who believe in you.
   Lord, have mercy.
Christ, be with those who take up their cross and follow you.
   Christ, have mercy.
Lord, be with those
who hope in your resurrection.
   Lord, have mercy.

Let us bring our other hopes and needs to God, as we pray: **God of light, hear our prayer.**

Let us pray with the words that Jesus taught us:

Our Father …

✝ All make the Sign of the Cross.

April 8, 2019

Tuesday Daily Prayer

Introduction

Today we hear the next part of the story about the man who received sight from Jesus. He was happy. His parents and his friends were also happy. But some people were not pleased. They knew that Jesus was working many signs that showed God's power. Some thought he was the Messiah, but others thought he was a fake. Many were just confused, and many were afraid.

✝ All make the Sign of the Cross.

Hymn

A Psalm for Late Lent

[Turn to page 55.]

Reading
John 9:13-16, 17

Listen to the words of the holy gospel according to John:

The day when Jesus made the mud and healed the man was a Sabbath. So the people took the man to the religious leaders. They asked him how he was able to see, and he answered, "Jesus made some mud and smeared it on my eyes. Then after I washed it off, I could see."

Some of the leaders said, "This man Jesus does not come from God. If he did, he would not break the law of the Sabbath."

Others asked, "How could someone who is a sinner work such a miracle?"

They asked the man, "What do you say about this one who healed your eyes?"

"He is a prophet!" the man told them.

The gospel of the Lord.

Reflection

What could the man cured from blindness see that some of the leaders could not? In what way are we like the man in this story? In what ways are we like the people who saw it all happening? In what ways are we like the leaders?

Closing

During Lent,
God invites us to seek Jesus,
the true light of the world,
and to renewed in our hearts and minds.

Our responses to the following three petitions are 'Lord, have mercy,' then 'Christ, have mercy,' and then 'Lord, have mercy.'

Lord, be with those who believe in you.
Lord, have mercy.
Christ, be with those who take up their cross and follow you.
Christ, have mercy.
Lord, be with those
who hope in your resurrection.
Lord, have mercy.

Let us bring our other hopes and needs to God, as we pray: **God of light, hear our prayer.**

Let us pray with the words that Jesus taught us:

Our Father …

✝ All make the Sign of the Cross.

April 9, 2019

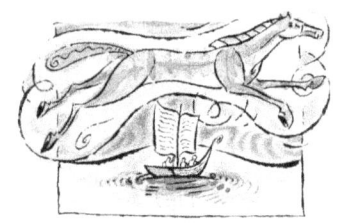

Wednesday Daily Prayer

Introduction

The story we are reading from the gospel of John tells about something that Jesus did long ago. But it also tells us what Jesus is doing today. Jesus is still active in the events of daily life.

We are like the man who had been blind. We know that Jesus has saved us. But we have to keep thinking about what this means for us.

✠ All make the Sign of the Cross.

Hymn

A Psalm for Late Lent

[Turn to page 55.]

Reading   John 9:23, 24-25, 28-29, 31, 33

Listen to the words of the holy gospel according to John:

The leaders would not believe that the man had once been blind. They had already agreed that no one was to have anything to do with anyone who said Jesus was the Messiah.

The leaders called the man back and said, "Swear by God to tell the truth! We know that Jesus is a sinner."

The man replied, "I don't know if he is a sinner or not. All I know is that I used to be blind but now I can see!"

The leaders insulted the man and said, "You are his follower! We are followers of Moses. We are sure that God spoke to Moses, but we don't even know where Jesus comes from."

The man replied, "We know that God listens only to people who love and obey him. Jesus could not do anything unless he came from God."

The gospel of the Lord.

Reflection

Why do some people today not believe in Jesus? What stops them? Why is it important to be able to talk about our faith with other people?

Closing

During Lent,
God invites us to seek Jesus,
the true light of the world,
and to renewed in our hearts and minds.

Our responses to the following three petitions are 'Lord, have mercy,' then 'Christ, have mercy,' and then 'Lord, have mercy.'

Lord, be with those who believe in you.
   Lord, have mercy.
Christ, be with those who take up their cross and follow you.
   Christ, have mercy.
Lord, be with those
who hope in your resurrection.
   Lord, have mercy.

Let us bring our other hopes and needs to God, as we pray: **God of light, hear our prayer.**

Let us pray with the words that Jesus taught us:

Our Father …

✠ All make the Sign of the Cross.

April 10, 2019

Thursday Daily Prayer

Introduction

In the story we have been reading, the blind man whom Jesus has cured makes his way step by step to another kind of sight. We call it faith. Today we reach the climax of the story when the man says to Jesus, "Lord, I put my faith in you!"

✞ All make the Sign of the Cross.

Hymn

A Psalm for Late Lent

[Turn to page 55.]

Reading   John 9:34-38

Listen to the words of the holy gospel according to John:

The leaders told the man [who was healed by Jesus], "You have been a sinner since the day you were born! Do you think you can teach us anything?" then they said, "You can never come back into any of our meeting places!"
When Jesus heard what had happened, he went and found the man. Then Jesus asked, "Do you have faith in the Son of Man?"
   He replied, "Sir, if you will tell me who [the Son of Man] is, I will put my faith in him."
   "You have already seen him," Jesus answered, "and right now he is talking with you!"
   The man said, "Lord, I put my faith in you!" Then he worshipped Jesus.

The gospel of the Lord.

Reflection

Did the man who had been cured see Jesus with his eyes or in some other way? How is it possible for us to 'see' Jesus? In what way is the man in this story like people who are preparing for baptism at Easter?

Closing

During Lent,
God invites us to seek Jesus,
the true light of the world,
and to renewed in our hearts and minds.

Our responses to the following three petitions are 'Lord, have mercy,' then 'Christ, have mercy,' and then 'Lord, have mercy.'

Lord, be with those who believe in you.
   Lord, have mercy.
Christ, be with those who take up their cross and follow you.
   Christ, have mercy.
Lord, be with those
who hope in your resurrection.
   Lord, have mercy.

Let us bring our other hopes and needs to God, as we pray: **God of light, hear our prayer.**

Let us pray with the words that Jesus taught us:

Our Father …

✞ All make the Sign of the Cross.

Friday Daily Prayer

Introduction

At Mass on this coming Sunday, palms are blessed, and we hear the reading of the passion (this means the suffering) of Jesus. So that is why it is called both 'Passion Sunday' and 'Palm Sunday.'

Carrying branches on the Sunday before Easter unites us with all people who have ever welcomed Jesus as the Messiah.

✠ All make the Sign of the Cross.

Hymn

A Psalm for Late Lent

[Turn to page 55.]

Reading   Luke 19:28, 29-38

Listen to the words of the holy gospel according to Luke:

Jesus went on toward Jerusalem. He sent two of his disciples on ahead. He told them, "Go into the next village, where you will find a young donkey that has never been ridden. Untie the donkey and bring it here. If anyone asks why you are doing that, just say, 'The Lord needs it.'"

They went off and found everything just as Jesus had said. While they were untying the donkey, its owners asked, "Why are you doing that?"

They answered, "The Lord needs it."

Then they led the donkey to Jesus. They put some of their clothes on its back and helped Jesus get on. And as he rode along, the people spread clothes on the road in front of him. When Jesus was starting down the Mount of Olives, his large crowd of disciples were happy and praised God because of all the miracles they had seen.

They shouted, "Blessed is the king who comes in the name of the Lord! Peace in heaven and glory to God."

The gospel of the Lord.

Reflection

Why did people put their coats on the ground before Jesus? They also shouted "Hosanna" to honour Jesus. When do we sing or say "Hosanna" at Mass? How do I show honour to Jesus?

Closing

As we prepare to keep the Three Days of Easter, let us all say:

Holy God: **Holy God!**
Holy mighty One: **Holy Mighty One!**
Holy immortal One, have mercy on us:
Holy immortal One, have mercy on us!

Let us bring our hopes and needs to God, as we pray: **Holy God, hear our prayer.**

O God,
grant us your forgiveness and mercy
as we celebrate the death, burial
and resurrection of Jesus.
We ask this through Christ our Lord. **Amen.**

Let us pray with the words that Jesus taught us:

Our Father ...

✠ All make the Sign of the Cross.

April 12, 2019

Early Eastertime

Monday, April 29,
to Friday, April 17

Early Eastertime 2019
Looking Ahead

Note: Because of overlapping school holidays throughout Australia, there is a two-week gap in Daily Prayer from Monday, 15 April, to Friday, 26 April

About the Season

Christ is risen! Alleluia! Lent has given way to Easter. We rejoice in the glory of Jesus and the share he has given us in his resurrection. And so we sing over and over, 'Alleluia.'

Easter is about new life. We rejoice in the new life of Jesus. We rejoice that members of our parish were baptised and confirmed at the Easter Vigil. We rejoice that all of us are nourished by the life of God whenever we share in the Easter sacrament of the Eucharist.

Easter is also about light overcoming darkness. At the Easter Vigil, the paschal candle was lit from the Easter fire and carried into the darkened church. The church sang 'The light of Christ' and responded, 'Thanks be to God.' This new paschal light will burn brightly for the 50 days of Easter. It is a symbol of the risen Jesus, the 'Light of the world', whose light was not put out with death but shines now for all believers to see.

There are many other times during the year when we speak of Jesus as the 'Light of the world.' During Advent we light candles on an Advent wreath to show that the Saviour brings God's light into the world's darkness. During Christmastime we read about Simeon who called Jesus the 'light of revelation,' and so we use lights and candles to celebrate the coming of Christ. We put lights on trees, inside and outside our homes.

The sun rises each morning, bright and strong, and is a constant reminder of the resurrection of Jesus. The sun has always been recognised as a sign of God's warmth, love and life-giving power. Even in these days of autumn as our days are getting shorter, we can still appreciate the warmth of the sun. Often during autumn we enjoy what we call an 'Indian Summer' with sunny days, clear blue skies and the crisp brightness of the stars at night.

Easter is not just one day. It is a whole season of 50 days, which will last until Pentecost. We take even longer to celebrate Easter than we took during Lent to prepare for it. During this time we are reminded over and over how close the risen Jesus is to us.

Readings

The message of Easter is new life. Our readings during the early days of Easter tell us how Jesus appeared to his disciples after he had risen from the dead. Jesus lives, and he shares his new life with us, just as he promised.

Our readings for each Friday will normally anticipate the Sunday gospels of Easter. On the Third Sunday of Easter, Jesus appears to the disciples on the shore of a lake. This gospel tells us how the risen Jesus strengthened their faith and spoke words of love, peace and forgiveness. On the Fourth Sunday, Jesus speaks of himself as the shepherd of God's people who will always stay close to them and protect them. Then on the Fifth Sunday of Easter we listen to the command of Jesus to love one another as he has loved us. If we do this, we too are bringers of life.

All of our readings proclaim that, in Christ, life has conquered death; light has triumphed over darkness.

In some Australian states, school resumes on 23 April. This is Tuesday of Easter week. Anzac Day falls on Thursday, 25 April. This leaves three days for Daily Prayer. Those who wish to pray can follow this simple pattern: This is how you can do it:

1. Begin with the Sign of the Cross
2. Pray the Psalm for Early Easter
3. Read one of these passages from Paul's Letter to the Ephesians:
    1:17-20
    3:14-19
    4:1-6
4. Reflect in silence after the reading
5. Pray intercessions in the usual way
6. Use the Closing Prayer for Early Easter

Feasts and Other Commemorations

During Easter we will celebrate the feasts of three apostles:
- May 3 (but relocated here to May 2), Sts Philip and James. Philip became a disciple of Jesus and later and apostle. James was one of the Twelve apostles and known as James the Less. He is known as the author of the Letter of James.
- May 14, St Matthias. He was chosen as an apostle to take the place of Judas who betrayed Jesus.

On May 7, Muslim communities, the followers of Islam, begin a special month of prayer and fasting, called Ramadan. Ramadan is the month in which the first verses of the sacred book, the Qur'an, were claimed to have been revealed to the prophet Mohammed.

On Thursday, May 9, we will remember and pray for our mothers and all who are mother to us.

Preparation for Early Eastertime

Make copies of the Psalm118 (page 72) for each member of the class. Copy them on bright yellow or gold paper. This is an Easter psalm in which we cry out our joy in the resurrection of Jesus.

The first thing to do after Easter break is to make our prayers ring with 'Alleluias'. This can be done with joyful singing and lots of music. Use some instruments when you sing your prayer such as guitars, rhythm sticks, finger cymbals, drums and tambourines.

Drape the table in the prayer space in festive gold or white. Two important Easter symbols are water and light. We can place a bowl of Easter water and a special Easter candle on the table. The water can be used for sprinkling and signing to remind us of our baptism. Perhaps some of your class celebrated the Easter sacraments of baptism, confirmation and eucharist. If so, it is important that we share in their joy. We can make special remembrance of them in our prayers of intercession.

Suggested Hymns

See the hymn chart on pages viii-ix. Sing hymns that ring with the joy of Easter. Sing 'alleluia' whenever you can. The 'Celtic Alleluia' and 'Halle, Halle, Halle' are both very joyful.

A Psalm For Early Easter

Psalm 118:1-2, 5, 14, 22-23

LEADER
Christ is risen like the sun, alleluia!
ALL
**The light of Christ shines
over the whole world, alleluia!**

[Light a candle, and then say:]
LEADER
This is the day the Lord made.
ALL
Let us rejoice and be glad.

SIDE A
Tell the Lord how thankful you are,
because he is kind and always merciful.
Let Israel shout, "God is always merciful!"

SIDE B
When I was really hurting
I prayed to the Lord.
The Lord answered my prayer
and took my worries away.

SIDE A
My power and my strength
come from the Lord
and he saved me.

SIDE B
The stone that the builders tossed aside
has now become the most important stone.
The Lord has done this,
and it is amazing to us.

LEADER
This is the day the Lord made.
ALL
Let us rejoice and be glad.

**Glory be to the Father, and to the Son
and to the Holy Spirit.
As it was in the beginning, is now,
and ever shall be
world without end. Amen. Alleluia.**

[Turn back to Daily Prayer for today.]

Monday Daily Prayer

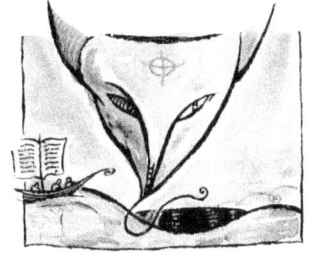

[Reminder: The Psalm for Early Easter is on p. 72. Make a copy for each member of the class.]

[Light the Easter candle]

Introduction

The most joyful season of our year began on Easter Sunday. This season lasts for fifty days, from Easter Sunday to Pentecost Sunday. Because we believe Jesus is with us as Risen Lord, this is a time of great rejoicing.

The message of Easter is new life. Our readings this week tell us how Jesus appeared to his disciples after he had risen from the dead. Jesus lives, and he shares his new life with us, just as he promised.

✞ All make the Sign of the Cross.

Hymn

A Psalm for Early Eastertime

[Turn to page 72.]

Reading   Matthew 28:1-3, 5-6, 7-8

Listen to the words of the holy gospel according to Matthew:

The Sabbath was over, and it was almost daybreak on Sunday when Mary Magdalene (MAG-duh-lin) and the other Mary went to see the tomb. Suddenly a strong earthquake struck, and the Lord's angel came down from heaven. He rolled away the stone and sat on it. The angel looked as bright as lightning, and his clothes were white as snow.

The angel said to the women, "Don't be afraid! I know you are looking for Jesus, who was nailed to a cross. He isn't here! God has raised him to life, just as Jesus said he would. Now hurry! Tell his disciples that he has been raised to life and is on his way to Galilee. Go there, and you will see him. That is what I came to tell you."

The women were frightened and yet very happy, as they hurried from the tomb and ran to tell his disciples.

The gospel of the Lord.

Reflection

Why were the women frightened when they went to the tomb? Why were they happy? Even though we did not see the empty tomb, why do we believe in the resurrection?

Closing

Let us bring our hopes and needs to God, as we pray: **God of new life, hear our prayer.**

Let us pray with the words that Jesus taught us:

Our Father ...

Gracious God,
through the announcement of the holy women,
you bring the good news of your love
to people everywhere.
Strengthen us to carry that good news
in our lives, in our hearts and in our words.
We ask this through Christ our Lord. **Amen.**

[Sing 'alleluia'.]

May we live in the light of Christ. **Amen.**

✞ All make the Sign of the Cross.

[Put out the candle.]

April 29, 2019

Tuesday Daily Prayer

[Light the Easter candle]

Introduction

In these early days of the Easter Season, our readings will tell us how different people reacted to the wonderful news of the resurrection. The resurrection of Jesus is the foundation of our faith. Jesus is truly risen and is with us still.

Today we see that the women are sent to share this good news with the other disciples. They are not only followers but also apostles.

✞ All make the Sign of the Cross.

Hymn

A Psalm for Early Eastertime

[Turn to page 72.]

Reading   Matthew 28:8-10

Listen to the words of the holy gospel according to Matthew:

The women were frightened and yet very happy, as they hurried from the tomb and ran to tell his disciples. Suddenly Jesus met them and greeted them. They went near him, held on to his feet, and worshipped him. Then Jesus said, "Don't be afraid! Tell my followers to go to Galilee. They will see me there."

The gospel of the Lord.

Reflection

Why did the women hold on to Jesus' feet? What did Jesus say to them? Can we say that the women were "apostles to the apostles"?

Closing

Let us bring our hopes and needs to God, as we pray: **God of new life, hear our prayer.**

Let us pray with the words that Jesus taught us:

Our Father …

Gracious God,
through the announcement of the holy women,
you bring the good news of your love
to people everywhere.
Strengthen us to carry that good news
in our lives, in our hearts and in our words.
We ask this through Christ our Lord. **Amen.**

[Sing 'alleluia'.]

May we live in the light of Christ. **Amen.**

✞ All make the Sign of the Cross.

[Put out the candle.]

April 30, 2019

Wednesday Daily Prayer

[Light the Easter candle]

Introduction

Today we remember Pierre Teilhard de Chardin (*TIE-yar de shar-DAN*) a priest, poet and scientist. He was born on this day in 1881. His great love for the earth and his ability to see God's energy in all parts of creation have inspired many people. Teilhard once said that he would like to die on the day of the resurrection and he did die on Easter Sunday in 1955.

Today's reading tells us that the soldiers who had been guarding the tomb went into the city and reported to the leaders that the tomb was empty. Let us listen to what happened!

✞ All make the Sign of the Cross.

Hymn

A Psalm for Early Eastertime

[Turn to page 72.]

Reading   Matthew 28:11-12, 12-15

Listen to the words of the holy gospel according to Matthew:

While the women were on their way, some soldiers who had been guarding the tomb went into the city. They told the leaders everything that had happened. So the leaders decided to bribe the soldiers with a lot of money. They said to the soldiers, "Tell everyone that Jesus' disciples came during the night and stole his body while you were asleep. If the governor hears about this, we will talk to him. You won't have anything to worry about."

The soldiers took the money and did what they were told. Some people still tell each other this story.

The gospel of the Lord.

Reflection

Why did the soldiers agree to tell a lie? What was the truth that they were trying to hide? How would you tell the story of what happened?

Closing

Let us bring our hopes and needs to God, as we pray: **God of new life, hear our prayer.**

Let us pray with the words that Jesus taught us:

Our Father ...

Loving and glorious God,
we praise you with Easter joy
because Christ is our redeemer.
Christ has broken the power of sin
and healed an injured world.
Christ has made us whole again.
Bless our celebrations and our joy.
We ask this through Christ our Lord. **Amen.**

[Sing 'alleluia'.]

May we live in the light of Christ. **Amen.**

✞ All make the Sign of the Cross.

[Put out the candle.]

May 1, 2019

Thursday Daily Prayer

[Light the Easter candle]

Introduction

Tomorrow is the feast of the apostles Philip and James. Apostles are important reminders that the church has received the true teaching of Jesus. This teaching has been handed down to us from the people who learned these teachings from Jesus himself. Today's gospel story tells us how Philip took another person to listen to Jesus.

We also remember the Jewish community today. Tonight they begin observing Yom Hashoah (*ha-SHOW-ah*), their day of remembrance for the six million Jewish people killed out of racial prejudice during the Second World War. We pray that we will never give such hatred a place in our hearts.

✞ All make the Sign of the Cross.

Hymn

A Psalm for Early Eastertime

[Turn to page 72.]

Reading   *John 1:43-46*

The next day Jesus decided to go to Galilee. There he met Philip, who was from Bethsaida, the hometown of Andrew and Peter. Jesus said to Philip, "Come with me."
   Philip then found Nathanael (*nuh-THAN-yell*) and said, "We have found the one that Moses and the Prophets wrote about. He is Jesus, the son of Joseph from Nazareth."
   Nathanael asked, "Can anything good come from Nazareth?"
   Philip answered, "Come and see."

The gospel of the Lord.

May 2, 2019

Reflection

Philip can't wait to share Jesus with Nathanael. What did he discover about Jesus? What did he want Nathanael to find? Do you share your discoveries with your friends?

Closing

Let us bring our hopes and needs to God, as we pray: **God of apostles, hear our prayer.**

Let us pray with the words that Jesus taught us:

Our Father ...

Loving and glorious God,
we praise you with Easter joy
because Christ is our redeemer.
We thank you
for sending apostles to preach the good news.
We welcome
and pray for all who preach the gospel.
Call on us one day, to become apostles too.
We ask this through Christ our Lord. **Amen.**

[Sing 'alleluia'.]

May we live in the light of Christ. **Amen.**

✞ All make the Sign of the Cross.

[Put out the candle.]

Friday Daily Prayer

[Light the Easter candle]

Introduction

Many stories in the gospels tell of Jesus appearing to the disciples after his resurrection, like this one from Sunday's gospel. Each visit strengthened the disciples' faith that Jesus had truly risen, and that he was truly the Messiah. Jesus is still present to his disciples today. He shares a meal with us and wants us to realise he is present with us.

✞ All make the Sign of the Cross.

Hymn

A Psalm for Early Eastertime

[Turn to page 72.]

Reading — John 21:3-6, 9, 12

Listen to the words of the holy gospel according to John:

Simon Peter said, "I'm going fishing!" The others said, "We'll go with you." They went out in their boat. But they didn't catch a thing that night.

Early the next morning Jesus stood on the shore, but the disciples did not realise who he was. Jesus shouted, "Friends, have you caught anything?" "No!" they answered. So he told them, "Let your net down on the right side of your boat, and you will catch some fish."

They did, and the net was so full of fish that they could not drag it up into the boat.

When the disciples got out of the boat, they saw some bread and a charcoal fire with fish on it. Jesus said, "Come and eat!" but none of the disciples dared ask who he was. They knew he was the Lord.

The gospel of the Lord.

Reflection

How did the disciples recognise that it was Jesus? How does Jesus feed his people today? Is there a special meal that Jesus calls us to?

Closing

Let us bring our hopes and needs to God, as we pray: **God of new life, hear our prayer.**

Let us pray with the words that Jesus taught us:

Our Father …

Loving and glorious God,
we praise you with Easter joy
because Christ is our redeemer.
Through the eucharist we live the risen life
and share the mission of your Son.
Keep us faithful to Jesus,
who is always with us.
We ask this through Christ our Lord. **Amen.**

[Sing 'alleluia'.]

May we live in the light of Christ. **Amen.**

✞ All make the Sign of the Cross.

[Put out the candle.]

May 3, 2019

Monday Daily Prayer

[Light the Easter candle]

Introduction

Tonight Muslim communities, the followers of Islam, begin their special month of fasting and prayer called Ramadan. It is the month in which the first verses of the Qur'an were claimed to have been revealed to the prophet Muhammad.

All of the gospels tell us that the women disciples were the first to discover that Jesus had risen. In today's reading Jesus appears to Mary Magdalene (MAG-duh-lin), a disciple of Jesus who was very close to him.

✞ All make the Sign of the Cross.

Hymn

A Psalm for Early Eastertime

[Turn to page 72.]

Reading   *John 20:11-16*

Listen to the words of the holy gospel according to John:

Mary Magdalene (MAG-duh-lin) stood crying outside the tomb. She was still weeping when she stooped down and saw two angels inside. They were dressed in white and were sitting where Jesus' body had been. One was at the head and the other was at the foot. The angels asked Mary, "Why are you crying?"

She answered, "They have taken away my Lord's body! I don't know where they have put him."

As soon as Mary said this, she turned around and saw Jesus standing there. But she did not know who he was. Jesus asked her, "Why are you crying? Who are you looking for?"

She thought he was the gardener and said, "Sir, if you have taken his body away, please tell me, so I can go and get him."

Then Jesus said to her, "Mary!"

She turned and said to him, "Teacher."

The gospel of the Lord.

Reflection

Why didn't Mary recognise Jesus at first? What helped her to realise that it was Jesus? Does Jesus call us by name?

Closing

Let us bring our hopes and needs to God, as we pray: **God of new life, hear our prayer.**

Let us pray with the words that Jesus taught us:

Our Father …

Gracious God,
through the announcement
of the holy women
and the preaching of the apostles,
you bring the good news of your love
to all the peoples of the earth.
Strengthen us to carry that good news
in our lives, in our hearts and in our words.
We ask this through Christ our Lord. **Amen.**

[Sing 'alleluia'.]

May we live in the light of Christ. **Amen.**

✞ All make the Sign of the Cross.

[Put out the candle.]

May 6, 2019

Tuesday Daily Prayer

[Light the Easter candle]

Introduction

Saints are people who are guided by the Spirit. One person like this was Mary Glowery. She was born in the western district of Victoria in 1887 and became a doctor. After hearing about the terrible death rate for babies in India, she decided to go there.

She joined a missionary group of sisters that served the medical and spiritual needs of poor people in India. Mary truly lived the gospel by her word and example. She died on May 5th in 1955.

Yesterday we read how Jesus appeared to Mary Magdalene on the morning he rose from the dead. In the evening of that same day he appeared to his disciples, breathed out his Spirit on them, and sent them out to be apostles of mercy and forgiveness.

✞ All make the Sign of the Cross.

Hymn

A Psalm for Early Eastertime

[Turn to page 72.]

Reading   *John 20:19-23*

Listen to the words of the holy gospel according to John:

On the evening of that same Sunday the disciples locked themselves in a room. Suddenly, Jesus appeared in the middle of the group. He greeted them and showed them his hands and his side. When the disciples saw the Lord, they became very happy.

After Jesus had greeted them again, he said, "I am sending you, just as the Father has sent me." Then he breathed on them and said, "Receive the Holy Spirit. If you forgive anyone's sins, they will be forgiven. But if you don't forgive their sins, they will not be forgiven."

The gospel of the Lord.

Reflection

What is Jesus' gift to the disciples? What does he send them to do? Do I find it easier to forgive others or to hold back my forgiveness?

Closing

Let us bring our hopes and needs to God, as we pray: **God of new life, hear our prayer.**

Let us pray with the words that Jesus taught us:

Our Father ...

Loving and glorious God,
we praise you with Easter joy
because Christ is our redeemer.
Through the eucharist we live the risen life
and share the mission of your Son.
Keep us faithful to Jesus,
who is always with us.
We ask this through Christ our Lord. **Amen.**

[Sing 'alleluia'.]

May we live in the light of Christ. **Amen.**

✞ All make the Sign of the Cross.

[Put out the candle.]

May 7, 2019

Wednesday Daily Prayer

[Light the Easter candle]

Introduction

At this time of the year we remember Blessed Edmund Rice. He was born in Ireland in 1762, inherited his uncle's business and became wealthy. His wife, Mary, died in an accident, leaving him to care for his disabled daughter.

At the age of 40, he sold his business and used the money to begin schools for the education of poor boys. He founded the congregation of the Christian Brothers. Many boys in Australia and New Zealand have been educated by them.

Today we read the story of Thomas the apostle. At first he refused to believe that Jesus had risen, but a week later he puts his faith in Jesus.

✞ All make the Sign of the Cross.

Hymn

A Psalm for Early Eastertime

[Turn to page 72.]

Reading   John 20:24-29

Listen to the words of the holy gospel according to John:

Although Thomas the Twin was one of the twelve disciples, he wasn't with the others when Jesus appeared to them. So they told him, "We have seen the Lord!"

But Thomas said, "First, I must see the nail scars in his hands and touch them with my finger. I must put my hand where the spear went into his side. I won't believe unless I do this!"

A week later the disciples were together again. This time, Thomas was with them. Jesus came in while the doors were still locked and stood in the middle of the group. He greeted his disciples and said to Thomas, "Put your finger here and look at my hands! Put your hand into my side. Stop doubting and have faith!"

Thomas replied, "You are my Lord and my God!" Jesus said, "Thomas, do you have faith because you have seen me? The people who have faith in me without seeing me are the ones who are really blessed!"

The gospel of the Lord.

Reflection

Why did Thomas refuse to believe at first? What made him change from doubt to faith? Why are those who haven't seen Jesus really blessed?

Closing

Let us bring our hopes and needs to God, as we pray: **God of new life, hear our prayer.**

Let us pray with the words that Jesus taught us:

Our Father …

Loving and glorious God,
we praise you with Easter joy
because Christ is our redeemer.
Through the eucharist we live the risen life
and share the mission of your Son.
Keep us faithful to Jesus,
who is always with us.
We ask this through Christ our Lord. **Amen.**

[Sing 'alleluia'.]

May we live in the light of Christ. **Amen.**

✞ All make the Sign of the Cross.

[Put out the candle.]

May 8, 2019

Thursday Daily Prayer

[Light the Easter candle]

Introduction

This coming Sunday is Mother's Day. Easter is a good time for Mother's Day because mothers are people who give life. They try to see that their children are fed, healed, comforted and protected. We give thanks for our mothers, stepmothers, grandmothers, godmothers, aunts and anyone who is like a mother to us.

Each of the four gospel writers tells the story of Jesus' resurrection in his own way. Some things are the same, others are different. Today we hear Mark's story. Like the others he tells us that the very first witnesses of the resurrection were some of Jesus' women followers.

✞ All make the Sign of the Cross.

Hymn

A Psalm for Early Eastertime

[Turn to page 72.]

Reading   Mark 16:2-7

Listen to the words of the holy gospel according to Mark:

Very early on Sunday morning, just as the sun was coming up, the women went to the tomb. On their way, they were asking one another, "Who will roll the stone away from the entrance for us?" But when they looked, they saw that the stone had already been rolled away. And it was a huge stone!
   The women went into the tomb, and on the right side they saw a young man in a white robe sitting there. They were alarmed.

The man said, "Don't be alarmed! You are looking for Jesus from Nazareth, who was nailed to a cross. God has raised him to life, and he is not here. You can see the place where they put his body. Now go and tell his disciples, and especially Peter, that he will go ahead of you to Galilee. You will see him there, just as he told you."

The gospel of the Lord.

Reflection

Do you think the young man in white may have been an angel (in many Bible stories angels are God's messengers)? What is his message to the women? Who are messengers of God for me today? Am I a messenger for others?

Closing

Let us bring our hopes and needs to God, as we pray: **God of new life, hear our prayer.**

Let us pray with the words that Jesus taught us:

Our Father …

Gracious God,
through the announcement of the holy women,
you bring the good news of your love
to people everywhere
Strengthen us to carry that good news
in our lives, in our hearts and in our words.
We ask this through Christ our Lord. **Amen.**

[Sing 'alleluia'.]

May we live in the light of Christ. **Amen.**

✞ All make the Sign of the Cross.

[Put out the candle.]

May 9, 2019

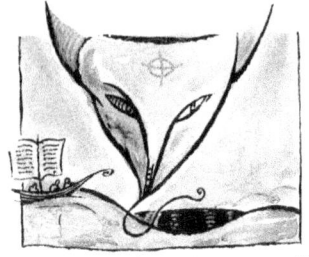

Friday Daily Prayer

[Light the Easter candle]

Introduction

On Sunday we read the Easter gospel in which Jesus speaks of himself as the shepherd of God's people. A good shepherd stays close to the sheep and pays attention to them. This way the shepherd can protect them from falling down rock hillsides or being attacked by wild animals.

The shepherd knows where the best pastures are and where there is clean water to drink. The sheep could not survive without the shepherd's care and so they learn to recognise the special sound of their own shepherd's call.

This is a time to rejoice that God has given us Jesus as our saviour and shepherd.

✝ All make the Sign of the Cross.

Hymn

A Psalm for Early Eastertime

[Turn to page 72.]

Reading   John 10:27-30

Listen to the words of the holy gospel according to John:

Jesus said to his disciples:
"My sheep know my voice, and I know them. They follow me, and I give them eternal life, so that they will never be lost. No one can snatch them out of my hand. My Father gave them to me, and he is greater than all others. No one can snatch them from his hands, and I am one with the Father."

The gospel of the Lord.

Reflection

What could possibly snatch us away from Jesus? How well does Jesus know me? How well do I know Jesus, our shepherd?

Closing

Let us bring our hopes and needs to God, as we pray: **Shepherding God, hear our prayer.**

Let us pray with the words that Jesus taught us:

Our Father ...

Loving and glorious God,
we praise you with Easter joy
because Christ is our redeemer.
Let him always be our good shepherd:
welcoming and leading us.
comforting and feeding us,
calling each by name.
We ask this through Christ our Lord. **Amen.**

[Sing 'alleluia'.]

May we live in the light of Christ. **Amen.**

✝ All make the Sign of the Cross.

[Put out the candle.]

May 10, 2019

Monday Daily Prayer

[Light the Easter candle]

Introduction

At the end of his gospel Mark adds another story of Jesus' resurrection. This one finishes with Jesus' command to his disciples to share the good news with everyone around the world.

One person who took the good news to a distant place was Fr Damien of Molokai (*MOL-uh-kye*). Born in Belgium in 1840, he spent many years on Molokai. This was an island where people were sent if they had the contagious (*con-TAY-jus*) disease called leprosy (*LEP-ruh-see*).

Damien touched and embraced those with the disease, ate with them, and cleaned and bandaged their wounds. He dug their graves and made their coffins. Some weeks before Father Damien died in 1889, he said that the Lord wanted him to spend Easter in heaven. He was made a saint in 2009.

✞ All make the Sign of the Cross.

Hymn

A Psalm for Early Eastertime

[Turn to page 72.]

Reading *Mark 16:9, 10–15*

Listen to the words of the holy gospel according to Mark:

Very early on the first day of the week, after Jesus had risen to life, he appeared to Mary Magdalene. She left and told his friends, who were crying and mourning. Even though they heard that Jesus was alive and that Mary had seen him, they would not believe it.

Later, Jesus appeared in another form to two disciples, as they were on their way out of the city. But when these disciples told what had happened, the others would not believe.

Afterwards, Jesus appeared to his eleven disciples as they were eating. He scolded them because they were too stubborn to believe the ones who had seen him after he had been raised to life. Then he told them: "Go and preach the good news to everyone in the world."

The gospel of the Lord.

Reflection

The faith of the disciples grew. It was not perfect all at once. Do I understand the word of God any better now than I did when I was younger? How has my faith grown this year?

Closing

Let us bring our hopes and needs to God, as we pray: **God of apostles, hear our prayer.**

Let us pray with the words that Jesus taught us:

Our Father ...

Lord God,
we thank you for sending apostles
to the whole world.
We welcome those who bring your good news.
We pray for them and listen to their teaching.
Call on us, one day, to become apostles, too.
We ask this through Christ our Lord. **Amen.**

[Sing 'alleluia'.]

May we live in the light of Christ. **Amen.**

✞ All make the Sign of the Cross.

[Put out the candle.]

May 13, 2019

Tuesday Daily Prayer

[Light the Easter candle]

Introduction

Today is the feast of Saint Matthias (*muth-EYE-us*). He was chosen as an apostle to take the place of Judas, who betrayed Jesus. We will read about his election today.

The meaning of the word "apostle" is "someone who is sent." All the apostles were sent to tell the good news that Jesus Christ is the risen Saviour.

✛ All make the Sign of the Cross.

Hymn

A Psalm for Early Eastertime

[Turn to page 72.]

Reading   Acts 1:15-16, 17, 21, 23-25, 26

Listen to the words of the Acts of the Apostles:

One day there were about one hundred and twenty of the Lord's followers meeting together, and Peter stood up to speak to them.

He said, "My friends. Judas was one of us and he worked with us, but he brought the mob to arrest Jesus. So we need someone else to help us tell others that Jesus has been raised from death."

Two men were suggested: One of them was Joseph Barsabbas (*bar-SAB-us*), known as Justus, and the other was Matthias (*muth-EYE-us*). Then they all prayed, "Lord, you know what everyone is like! Show us the one you have chosen to be an apostle and to serve in place of Judas." They drew names, and Matthias was chosen to join the group of eleven apostles.

The word of the Lord.

Reflection

Who are our church leaders? Do we ever pray for them? Who else teaches us about Jesus?

Closing

Let us bring our hopes and needs to God, as we pray: **God of apostles, hear our prayer.**

Let us pray with the words that Jesus taught us:

Our Father …

Lord God,
we thank you for sending apostles
to the whole world.
We welcome those who bring your good news.
We pray for them and listen to their teaching.
Call on us, one day, to become apostles, too.
We ask this through Christ our Lord. **Amen.**

[Sing 'alleluia'.]

May we live in the light of Christ. **Amen.**

✛ All make the Sign of the Cross.

[Put out the candle.]

May 14, 2019

Wednesday Daily Prayer

[Light the Easter candle]

Introduction

Today we remember Reverend John Flynn, born in 1880. While working in outback South Australia he realised that many people died because there was no medical help nearby. He had the idea of using planes.

Thanks to him, the Australian Royal Flying Doctor Service, a world first, was established on this day in 1928. Flynn's desire was to bring a 'mantle of safety' to Australia's outback. In his own way Flynn was a person of the Spirit, as we read today.

Today we read another story of Jesus appearing after his resurrection. It is about the women who discovered the empty tomb of Jesus and told the apostles what had happened. This news tested their faith. Peter was confused.

✝ All make the Sign of the Cross.

Hymn

A Psalm for Early Eastertime

[Turn to page 72.]

Reading — Luke 24:9-12

Listen to the words of the holy gospel according to Luke:

Mary Magdalene (*MAG-duh-lin*), Joanna, Mary, the mother of James, and some other women were the ones who had gone to the tomb. When they returned, they told the eleven apostles and the others what had happened. The apostles thought it was all nonsense, and they would not believe.

But Peter ran to the tomb, and when he stooped down and looked in, he saw only the burial clothes. Then he returned, wondering what had happened.

The gospel of the Lord.

Reflection

Why did no one believe the women? How would I feel if I had such good news and no one believed me? Why is it difficult to explain our faith to other people?

Closing

Let us bring our hopes and needs to God, as we pray: **God of Easter joy, hear our prayer.**

Let us pray with the words that Jesus taught us:

Our Father …

Gracious God,
through the announcement of the holy women,
you bring the good news of your love
to people everywhere.
Strengthen us to carry that good news
in our lives, in our hearts and in our words.
We ask this through Christ our Lord. **Amen.**

[Sing 'alleluia'.]

May we live in the light of Christ. **Amen.**

✝ All make the Sign of the Cross.

[Put out the candle.]

May 15, 2019

Thursday Daily Prayer

[Light the Easter candle]

Introduction

A few days ago it was International Day for Nurses. Today we remember a famous Australian nurse, Sister Elizabeth Kenny. She was born in 1880 and grew up in country New South Wales and Queensland. She became a bush nurse and was a pioneer in the treatment of polio. At first her methods were opposed but eventually were accepted and are still respected today. Sister Kenny died in 1952, two years before a polio vaccine was discovered.

Today we begin the long story of two disciples who were sad and confused. Jesus' death had ended their dreams, so they left Jerusalem and headed home. Even though they had heard the claim that Jesus had risen, they did not believe it. It seemed too good to be true.
We hear the first part of the story today and the rest next week.

✞ All make the Sign of the Cross.

Hymn

A Psalm for Early Eastertime

[Turn to page 72.]

Reading   Luke 24:13, 15–17, 19, 21, 22–23, 26–27

Listen to the words of the holy gospel according to Luke:

Two of Jesus' disciples were going to the village of Emmaus (ee-MAY-us). Jesus came near and started walking along beside them. But they did not know who he was. Jesus asked them, "What were you talking about as you walked along?"
They answered: "Those things that happened to Jesus from Nazareth. By what he did and said he showed that he was a powerful prophet. Then [he was] arrested and sentenced to die on a cross. We had hoped that he would be the one to set Israel free! But it has already been three days since all this happened.
"Some women in our group surprised us. They had gone to the tomb early in the morning, but did not find the body of Jesus. They came back, saying that they had seen a vision of angels who told them that he is alive."
Then Jesus asked the two disciples, "Didn't you know that the Messiah would have to suffer before he was given his glory?" Jesus then explained everything written about himself in the Scriptures.

The gospel of the Lord.

Reflection

Jesus walked along with his disciples. Why do you think they did not recognise him? Were they too sad? Did he look different? How does Jesus walk with his friends today?

Closing

Let us bring our hopes and needs to God, as we pray: **God of new life, hear our prayer.**

Let us pray with the words that Jesus taught us:

Our Father …

Loving and glorious God,
we praise you with Easter joy
because Christ is our redeemer.
Through the eucharist we live with risen life
and share the mission of your son.
Keep us faithful to Jesus
who is always with us.
We ask this through Christ our Lord. **Amen.**

[Sing 'alleluia'.]

May we live in the light of Christ. **Amen.**

✞ All make the Sign of the Cross.

[Put out the candle.]

May 16, 2019

Friday Daily Prayer

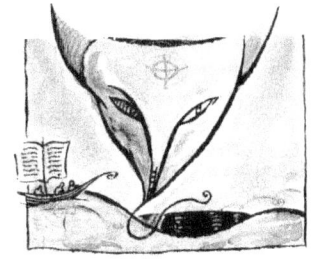

[Reminder: The Psalm for Late Easter is found on p. 92. Make a copy for each member of the class.]

[Light the Easter candle]

Introduction

Today we read from the gospel of John, which tells us of Jesus' command to love one another as he has loved us. This command is like a rule that is to be the foundation of life for all who follow Jesus. It is impossible to be a disciple of Jesus without the love that brings God among us. If we keep this command of love then we are bringers of life.

✞ All make the Sign of the Cross.

Hymn

A Psalm for Early Eastertime

[Turn to page 72.]

Reading   John 13:31, 33-35

Listen to the words of the holy gospel according to John:

After Judas had gone, Jesus said, "My children, I will be with you for a little while longer. Then you will look for me, but you won't find me. I tell you just as I told the people, 'You cannot go where I am going.'

"But I am giving you a new command. You must love one other, just as I have loved you. If you love one other, everyone will know that you are my disciples."

The gospel of the Lord.

Reflection

Have I made these words of Jesus a rule that I always keep? Would someone who saw us know by our love that we are disciples of Jesus?

Closing

Let us bring our hopes and needs to God, as we pray: **God of love, hear our prayer.**

Let us pray with the words that Jesus taught us:

Our Father ...

Loving and glorious God,
we praise you with Easter joy
because your Son Jesus
has shown his great love for us.
Increase our love for one another
so that all will know
that we are your faithful disciples.
We ask this through Christ our Lord. **Amen.**

[Sing 'alleluia'.]

May we live in the light of Christ. **Amen.**

✞ All make the Sign of the Cross.

[Put out the candle.]

May 17, 2019

THE PSALMS ARE SHOUTS

Can you remember a time when you just wanted to shout for joy? When you clapped your hands with excitement? When you felt like jumping or running or dancing? When you broke into song?

Have you ever been bursting to tell someone – maybe your mother or your father – how much you love them? Have you ever been surprised by how generous others can be to you?

Have you ever had your breath taken away by something beautiful? A rainbow after a storm? A glorious sunset? A thundering waterfall? The song of a bird? The sound of music? The scent of perfume?

Then you'll understand why so many of the psalms are shouts of praise and thanks. From the beginning God's people were thrilled at what they discovered about God and God's world. They wanted to shout out their joy. For them God was the most wonderful mystery that had been made known to them.

They came to see that God was the Creator of the whole universe. They learned that God had called them into a loving relationship. They believed that God was always with them, saving and protecting and blessing them. This inspired them to praise God for being such a great God, and to thank God for God's goodness to them. Here are a few examples:

"Tell the Lord how thankful you are, because he is kind and always merciful. Let Israel shout, "God is always merciful!" (*Psalm 118, Easter*)

"Shout praises to the Lord! With all that I am, I will shout God's praises." (*Psalm 146, June*)

"Sing a new song to the Lord! Everyone on this earth, sing praises to the Lord ... Tell the heavens and the earth to be glad and celebrate!" (*Psalm 96, September*)

Of course we don't always feel like shouting out in praise or bursting into song. That's where the psalms come in handy. We can let the words lead us out of ourselves. We can let the words teach us to be thankful deep in our hearts, even when we don't feel ready for it. God knows!

Late Eastertime

Monday, May 20,
to Friday, June 7

Late Eastertime 2019
Looking Ahead

About the Season

Easter's fifty days of joyful celebration continue for another three weeks. During this time we are reminded over and over how close the risen Jesus is to us.

Eastertime will conclude at the end of autumn. Our days are getting shorter and colder. In some parts of our country, trees may have lost their leaves or leaves still on trees might be colourful shades of green, gold, red and brown. In others, many native plants have bloomed into flower. We have seen an Eastertime filled with wonderful changes in our seasons and in nature, and also with God's message of resurrection and new life. There are many reasons for us to continue to sing 'alleluia!'

The coming of the Holy Spirit at Pentecost is celebrated on Sunday, June 9, ending the Easter Season. We celebrate Ascension on the Sunday before Pentecost day. The week between Ascension and Pentecost is the Week of Prayer for Christian Unity. During this week, we pray that all Christian churches will one day be united.

In the days before Pentecost, we are reminded of Jesus' promise to his disciples that he would always be with them. They were to wait for the coming of the Spirit and then do as the Spirit guided them. Jesus spoke to them of the Holy Spirit who would be God's everlasting presence. The Holy Spirit brings God's gifts of love, unity, wisdom and courage.

The Holy Spirit has been, and will continue to be with each of us and with our class and families during the year. In the power of that Spirit, we have been able to grow in our love of God and in our ability to see Christ in others. The Spirit of Jesus helps us to grow in respect for one another and to pray and work for people in need.

The fifty days of Easter conclude with the feast of Pentecost, June 9.

Readings

Our readings are taken mainly from the gospels of Luke and John. We begin with the story of Jesus travelling along the road to the town of Emmaus and meeting up with two disheartened followers. At first when Jesus joins them, they do not recognise him. But then Jesus opens up the words of the Scriptures to help them understand. Jesus blesses and breaks bread, and he gives it to his disciples to eat. It is only then that they recognise him—they know him because of these familiar actions. We also hear the story of Jesus having breakfast with his disciples after a great catch of fish. At first they do not recognise him, until he asks them to "come and eat". We read too the message that Jesus is the shepherd who cares for his sheep.

In the final week of Late Easter, we prepare for Pentecost and the gift of the Holy Spirit. Before Jesus returned to his Father, he told his followers not to be sad but to wait for the coming of the Holy Spirit. The Spirit would help them to grow in their understanding of all that Jesus had taught them. The Spirit would bring them unity, love and wisdom.

Our Friday readings will anticipate the Sunday readings. On the Sixth Sunday of Easter we will hear about Jesus' promise that the Holy Spirit will come and live with his followers. Then on Ascension Sunday we will hear Luke's account of the Ascension of Jesus. On Pentecost Sunday, Jesus breathes on his disciples with the words 'Receive the Holy Spirit'.

Feasts and Other Commemorations

- May 23, Mary Help of Christians. On this day, we turn to Australia's patron, Mary Help of Christians, and pray that she will protect our nation; we put ourselves into her care.
- May 30, The Visitation of Mary to her cousin Elizabeth.

The Week of Prayer for Christian Unity lasts from Ascension to Pentecost. We can join with the whole church in praying as a class for the unity of all Christian churches.

Other commemorations are Sorry Day which we will keep on May 27. National Reconciliation Week always occurs between May 27 and June 3. May 27 marks the anniversary of the 1967 referendum in which 91% of Australians voted to have Aboriginal people counted as citizens of Australia and to give the government power to make special laws for them. Until then, aboriginal people were not counted in the census. June 3 marks the anniversary of the Mabo case in 1992, which recognised the rights of Aboriginal and Torres Strait Islander peoples to their lands.

The Church observes a Week of Prayer for Reconciliation over these days.

On June 5 we celebrate World Environment Day and also Eid al-Fitr, the day that marks the end of the month long fast of Ramadan.

Preparation for Late Eastertime

The psalm for Late Easter is Psalm 23, the much loved 'Shepherd Psalm'. You will need to make copies for the class. Copy them on yellow paper to remind us of the Easter season.

It might be time to freshen up our Easter prayer space. Does it have signs of new life and resurrection? Does it need a new candle? Do we have a bowl of fresh water there for sprinkling and signing to help us remember the Easter sacrament of baptism?

A drop of perfume or scented oil can be added to the Easter water to remind us of chrism. Chrism is fragrant oil that is put on our heads at baptism and when we are confirmed. Chrism makes us a new Christ, because the word 'Christ' means 'anointed one.'

Suggested Hymns

See the hymn chart on pages viii-ix. In these weeks, you can continue singing the songs of Early Easter. Note that there are specific hymns for the Ascension and for the days leading up to Pentecost.

A Psalm for Late Easter

Psalm 23:1-6

LEADER
Christ is risen like the sun, alleluia!
ALL
**The light of Christ shines
over the whole world, alleluia!**

[Light a candle, and then say:]

LEADER
You, Lord, are my shepherd.
I will never be in need.
You let me rest in fields of green grass.

ALL
**You lead me to streams of peaceful water,
and you refresh my life.**

SIDE A
I may walk through valleys as dark as death,
but I won't be afraid.
You are with me,
and your shepherd's rod makes me feel safe.

SIDE B
You treat me to a feast, while my enemies watch.
You honour me as your guest,
and you fill my cup until it overflows.

SIDE A
Your kindness and love will always be with me
each day of my life,

SIDE B
and I will live forever in your house, Lord.

LEADER
The Lord is my shepherd, all that I need,
giving me rest in green and pleasant fields,
ALL
**reviving my life by finding fresh water,
guiding my ways with a shepherd's care.**

Glory be to the Father, and to the Son,
   and to the Holy Spirit:
as it was in the beginning, is now,
and ever shall be,
   world without end. Amen. Alleluia.

[Turn back to Daily Prayer for today.]

Monday Daily Prayer

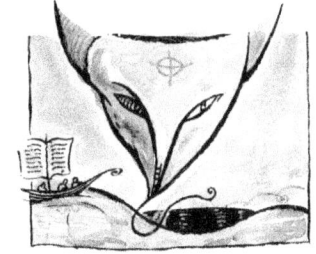

[Light the Easter candle.]

Introduction

Today we remember Father Ted Kennedy. He devoted himself to the aboriginal community in Redfern, an inner Sydney suburb. He understood their gifts and recognised their goodness. He opened his home to them and set up a medical service in the back part of the parish church.

Father Ted lived his belief that Christ was to be found in the lives of the poor. He was truly a person of the Holy Spirit. Many would see Father Ted as a future saint for Australia. He died in 2005.

Last week we began a wonderful story about two disciples who left Jerusalem in sadness when Jesus died on the cross. After his resurrection he met them on the road and explained the scriptures to them. Today we hear what happened next.

✞ All make the Sign of the Cross.

Hymn

A Psalm for Late Eastertime

[Turn to page 92.]

Reading   Luke 24:28-33

Listen to the words of the holy gospel according to Luke:

When the two disciples came near the village where they were going, Jesus seemed to be going further. They begged him, "Stay with us! It's already late, and the sun is going down." So Jesus went into the house to stay with them.

After Jesus sat down to eat, he took some bread. He blessed it and broke it. Then he gave it to them. At once they knew who he was, but he disappeared. They said to each other, "When he talked with us along the road and explained the Scriptures to us, didn't it warm our hearts?" So they got right up and returned to Jerusalem.

The gospel of the Lord.

Reflection

What helped the disciples to recognise Jesus? In what ways does Jesus continue to be present to his followers? How do we "break bread" with Jesus?

Closing

Let us bring our hopes and needs to God, as we pray: **God of new life, hear our prayer.**

Let us pray with the words that Jesus taught us:

Our Father …

Loving and glorious God,
we praise you with Easter joy
because Christ is our redeemer.
Through the eucharist we live with risen life
and share the mission of your son.
Keep us faithful to Jesus
who is always with us.
We ask this through Christ our Lord. **Amen.**

[Sing 'alleluia'.]

May we live in the light of Christ. **Amen.**

✞ All make the Sign of the Cross.

[Put out the candle.]

May 20, 2019

Tuesday Daily Prayer

[Light the Easter candle.]

Introduction

Today we remember two modern-day martyrs of Australia.

Irene McCormack, a Sister of St Joseph, was born in a rural area of Western Australia. After many years teaching in Catholic schools in Australia, Irene volunteered to work with the poor of Peru. On the night of 21 May, 1991, Irene and four men from the village were murdered by terrorists.

Graham Staines was a Christian missionary from Queensland who worked with lepers in Orissa, India. In 1999, Graham and his two sons were burnt alive by an anti-Christian gang. After his death, Graham's daughter stated: "I praise God that he has found my father worthy to die for Christ."

Today we continue the story of the disciples who meet Jesus on the road to Emmaus. They rush back to the other apostles and disciples to tell them what had happened.

☦ All make the Sign of the Cross.

Hymn

A Psalm for Late Eastertime

[Turn to page 92.]

Reading
Luke 24:33, 35–39

Listen to the words of the holy gospel according to Luke:

The two disciples found the eleven apostles and the others gathered together. Then the disciples from Emmaus (*ee-MAY-us*) told what happened on the road and how they knew he was the Lord when he broke the bread.

While Jesus' disciples were talking about what had happened, Jesus appeared and greeted them. They were frightened and terrified.

But Jesus said, "Why are you so frightened? Why do you doubt? Look at my hands and my feet and see who I am! Touch me and find out for yourselves. Ghosts don't have flesh and bones as you see I have."

The gospel of the Lord.

Reflection

Can you think of ways in which the Emmaus story is like Mass? At the end of Mass, are we like the two disciples who were bursting with good news to share with others? What story do we have to tell?

Closing

Let us bring our hopes and needs to God, as we pray: **God of new life, hear our prayer.**

Let us pray with the words that Jesus taught us:

Our Father …

Loving and glorious God,
we praise you with Easter joy
because Christ is our redeemer.
Through the eucharist we live with risen life
and share the mission of your son.
Keep us faithful to Jesus
who is always with us.
We ask this through Christ our Lord. **Amen.**

[Sing 'alleluia'.]

May we live in the light of Christ. **Amen.**

☦ All make the Sign of the Cross.

[Put out the candle.]

May 21, 2019

Wednesday Daily Prayer

[Reminder: Tomorrow we will celebrate the feast of Mary Help of Christians. You may wish to prepare for this with a statue or image of Mary, flowers and a candle or lamp.]

[Light the Easter candle.]

Introduction

In our reading this week we have heard that Jesus opens the meaning of the Scriptures to his followers, he strengthens their faith, and he hands on to them his own mission. The mission to be messengers, which his first disciples received, is also given to us. When we hear the gospel words of Jesus today, they are being spoken to us.

✞ All make the Sign of the Cross.

Hymn

A Psalm for Late Eastertime

[Turn to page 92.]

Reading   Luke 24:44–49

Listen to the words of the holy gospel according to Luke:

Jesus said to the disciples, "While I was still with you, I told you that everything written about me in the [Scriptures] had to happen."

Then he helped them understand the Scriptures. He told them: "The Scriptures say that the Messiah must suffer, then three days later he will rise from death. They also say that all people of every nation must be told in my name to turn to God, in order to be forgiven. So beginning in Jerusalem, you must tell everything that has happened. I will send you the one my Father has promised, but you must stay in the city until you are given power from heaven."

The gospel of the Lord.

Reflection

For Christians, the Scriptures mean the whole Bible, both Old Testament and New Testament. Why is it so important to understand the meaning of the Scriptures? What is the message of the Bible? What does it tell us about Jesus?

Closing

Let us bring our hopes and needs to God, as we pray: **God of new life, hear our prayer.**

Let us pray with the words that Jesus taught us:

Our Father …

Loving and glorious God,
we praise you with Easter joy
because Christ is our redeemer.
Through the eucharist we live with risen life
and share the mission of your son.
Keep us faithful to Jesus
who is always with us.
We ask this through Christ our Lord. **Amen.**

[Sing 'alleluia'.]

May we live in the light of Christ. **Amen.**

✞ All make the Sign of the Cross.

[Put out the candle.]

May 22, 2019

Thursday Daily Prayer

~ Feast of Mary Help of Christians

At this time we celebrate the Feast of Mary Help of Christians. A statue or other image of Mary can be placed in the prayer space. Bring some flowers to place before the image. Use a special candle or a lamp that can be used on this day and on other feasts of Mary.

Introduction

In 1884, the bishops of Australia decided to make Mary Help of Christians the patron of Australia. We turn to Mary today for the protection that our nation needs, and put ourselves into her care, just as she put herself into the care of God.

[Place the lighted candle and the flowers before the image of Mary.]

☩ All make the Sign of the Cross.

Hymn

A Psalm for Late Eastertime

[Turn to page 92.]

Reading   Acts 1:12-14

Listen to the words of the Acts of the Apostles:

The Mount of Olives was about half a mile from Jerusalem. The apostles who had gone there were Peter, John, James, Andrew, Philip, Thomas, Bartholomew (*bar-THOL-uh-mew*), Matthew, James the son of Alphaeus (*AL-fee-uss*), Simon, known as the Eager One, and Judas the son of James.

After the apostles returned to the city they went upstairs to the room where they had been staying.

The apostles often met together and prayed with a single purpose in mind. The women and Mary the mother of Jesus would meet with them, and so would the brothers.

The word of the Lord.

Reflection

Why would Mary's presence be important for the disciples after the death and resurrection of Jesus? On this feast day, we remember Mary's presence in our church. What are some of the needs of Australia for which we might ask Mary's help?

Closing

Let us bring our hopes and needs to God, as we pray: **God of help, hear our prayer.**

Let us pray with the words that Jesus taught us:

Our Father …

We turn to you for protection,
Mary, the help of all Christians.
Hear our prayers and help us in our need.
Save us from every danger,
and, through your son, Jesus,
may you bring the blessing of peace and unity
to all the peoples of Australia.
We make this prayer through Christ,
who lives and reigns for ever and ever. **Amen.**

[Sing 'alleluia'.]

☩ All make the Sign of the Cross.

[Sing a closing song.]

May 23, 2019

Friday Daily Prayer

[Light the Easter candle]

Introduction

The gospel of Sunday's Mass raises a question for us. Have you ever wanted to see God, just to know for sure that God has not forgotten about you? Jesus knew that his followers would sometimes be lonely and discouraged. So he promised to be with them. He promised them his Spirit, and he promised them his peace. Today's reading strengthens us for the times when God may seem far away.

☩ All make the Sign of the Cross.

Hymn

A Psalm for Late Eastertime

[Turn to page 92.]

Reading   John 14:23-24, 25-27, 29

Listen to the words of the holy gospel according to John:

Jesus said, "If anyone loves me, they will obey me. Then my Father will love them, and we will come to them and live in them. But anyone who doesn't love me, won't obey me.

"I have told you these things while I am still with you. But the Holy Spirit will come and help you, because the Father will send the Spirit to take my place. The Spirit will teach you everything and will remind you of what I said while I was with you.

"I give you peace, the kind of peace that only I can give. It isn't like the peace that this world can give. So don't be worried or afraid.

"I am telling you this before I leave, so that when it does happen, you will have faith in me."

The gospel of the Lord.

Reflection

Jesus says that he and the Father will make a home with those who keep his word. Can I imagine God living with me? How can I become more prepared for God to make a home in me?

Closing

Let us all say:
Christ, our light and our salvation!
Christ, our light and our salvation!

You are the sun that shines on everyone, the day that knows no ending:
Christ, our light and our salvation!

You are the promised hope of the universe and the saviour of the world:
Christ, our light and our salvation!

Let us also remember our other hopes and needs as we pray: **God of peace, hear our prayer.**

Let us pray with the words that Jesus taught us:

Our Father …

[Sing 'alleluia'.]

May we live in the light of Christ. **Amen.**

☩ All make the Sign of the Cross.

[Put out the candle.]

May 24, 2019

Monday Daily Prayer

[Light the Easter candle]

Introduction

Yesterday was National Sorry Day. On this day all Australians are invited to be sorry for all that Aboriginal and Torres Strait Islander peoples have suffered as a result of white settlement.

National Reconciliation Week runs from May 27 to June 3. On May 27 in 1967, almost all Australians voted "yes" for a national change in support of Aboriginal and Torres Strait Islander peoples.

On June 3 in 1992, the High Court of Australia recognised the special relationship that Aboriginal and Torres Strait Islander peoples have always had with the land. This was called the "Mabo case."

Today we begin reading another story of the risen Jesus appearing to the apostles.

✞ All make the Sign of the Cross.

Hymn

A Psalm for Late Eastertime

[Turn to page 92.]

Reading   *John 21:3-6, 9, 12*

Listen to the words of the holy gospel according to John:

Simon Peter said, "I'm going fishing!" The others said, "We'll go with you." They went out in their boat. But they didn't catch a thing that night.

Early the next morning Jesus stood on the shore, but the disciples did not realise who he was. Jesus shouted, "Friends, have you caught anything?" "No!" they answered. So he told them, "Let your net down on the right side of your boat, and you will catch some fish."

They did, and the net was so full of fish that they could not drag it up into the boat.

When the disciples got out of the boat, they saw some bread and a charcoal fire with fish on it. Jesus said, "Come and eat!" but none of the disciples dared ask who he was. They knew he was the Lord.

The gospel of the Lord.

Reflection

How did the disciples recognise that it was Jesus? Is the great catch of fish a sign of the church's mission to "catch people for God"? Why does Jesus invite the disciples to eat with him?

Closing

Let us bring our hopes and needs to God, as we pray: **Ever-present God, hear our prayer.**

Let us pray with the words that Jesus taught us:

Our Father ...

Ever-present God,
we praise you with Easter joy
because Christ is our redeemer.
Through the eucharist we live the risen life
and share the mission of your Son.
Keep us faithful to Jesus,
who is always with us.
We ask this through Christ our Lord. **Amen.**

[Sing 'alleluia'.]

May we live in the light of Christ. **Amen.**

✞ All make the Sign of the Cross.

[Put out the candle.]

May 27, 2019

Tuesday Daily Prayer

[Light the Easter candle]

Introduction

Many stories tell of Jesus appearing to the disciples after the resurrection. Each visit strengthened their faith that Jesus had truly risen, and that he was truly the Messiah. Jesus is still present to his disciples, sharing meals and opening hearts to the meaning of the Scriptures.

✟ All make the Sign of the Cross.

Hymn

A Psalm for Late Eastertime

[Turn to page 92.]

Reading   *John 21:9-14*

Listen to the words of the holy gospel according to John:

When the disciples got out of the boat, they saw some bread and a charcoal fire with fish on it. Jesus told his disciples, "Bring some of the fish you just caught." Simon Peter got back into the boat and dragged the net to shore. In it were one hundred and fifty-three large fish, but still the net did not rip
  Jesus said, "Come and eat!" But none of the disciples dared ask who he was. They knew he was the Lord. Jesus took the bread in his hands and gave some of it to his disciples. He did the same with the fish. This was the third time that Jesus appeared to his disciples after he was raised from death.

The gospel of the Lord.

Reflection

Can you remember another story of Jesus feeding people with bread and fish? Did this help the disciples recognise Jesus? How does Jesus feed his people today? Why is this a good story to read during Easter?

Closing

Let us bring our hopes and needs to God, as we pray: **Ever-present God, hear our prayer.**

Let us pray with the words that Jesus taught us:

Our Father ...

Ever-present God,
we praise you with Easter joy
because Christ is our redeemer.
Through the eucharist we live the risen life
and share the mission of your Son.
Keep us faithful to Jesus,
who is always with us.
We ask this through Christ our Lord. **Amen.**

[Sing 'alleluia'.]

May we live in the light of Christ. **Amen.**

✟ All make the Sign of the Cross.

[Put out the candle.]

May 28, 2019

Wednesday Daily Prayer

[Light the Easter candle]

Introduction

Caroline Chisholm (CHIZ-*um*) was a woman on a mission. She was born in England in 1808. At the time she came to Australia with her husband, many women travelled alone from England to find employment. Their living conditions were shocking.

Caroline spent her life finding them homes and work. She also worked hard to improve conditions on board the ships bringing the women to Australia. When she died in 1877, the words on her grave called her 'the emigrant's friend'.

When Jesus was arrested, the apostle Simon Peter denied him three times, then was very sorry. After Jesus had risen from the dead he gave Peter the chance to make up for his failure. Each time Peter replied Jesus told him he had an important mission.

✞ All make the Sign of the Cross.

Hymn

A Psalm for Late Eastertime

[Turn to page 92.]

Reading   John 21:15-16.17

Listen to the words of the holy gospel according to John:

When Jesus and his disciples had finished eating, he asked, "Simon son of John, do you love me more than the others do?"
Simon Peter answered, "Yes, Lord, you know I do!"
"Then feed my lambs," Jesus said.

Jesus asked a second time, "Simon son of John, do you love me?"
Peter answered, "Yes, Lord, you know I love you!"
"Then take care of my sheep," Jesus told him.

Jesus asked a third time, "Simon son of John, do you love me?"
Peter was hurt because Jesus had asked him three times if he loved him. So he told Jesus, "Lord, you know everything. You know I love you."
Jesus replied, "Feed my sheep.

The gospel of the Lord.

Reflection

Jesus forgives Peter and appoints him to shepherd his sheep. What does Jesus ask Peter to do? Do you know any "pastors"? Are you able to admit your mistakes and make a fresh start?

Closing

Let us bring our hopes and needs to God, as we pray: **God of new life, hear our prayer.**

Let us pray with the words that Jesus taught us:

Our Father …

Loving and glorious God,
we praise you with Easter joy
because Christ is our redeemer.
He promises us his Spirit
so that our hearts may burn with his love.
Help us to follow the way of Jesus
and to live with love for one another.
We ask this through Christ our Lord. **Amen.**

[Sing 'alleluia'.]

May we live in the light of Christ. **Amen.**

✞ All make the Sign of the Cross.

[Put out the candle.]

May 29, 2019

Thursday Daily Prayer

[Light the Easter candle]

Introduction

Tomorrow is the Feast of the Visitation. Mary learned that her cousin Elizabeth was going to have a baby. So Mary visited her. Today we celebrate that visit. Elizabeth's child was John the Baptist. Mary's child was Jesus. That is why Elizabeth told Mary she was so blessed.

✞ All make the Sign of the Cross.

Hymn

A Psalm for Late Eastertime

[Turn to page 92.]

Reading   *Luke 1:39–42, 45–48*

Listen to the words of the holy gospel according to Luke:

Mary hurried to a town in the hill country of Judea. She went into Zechariah's (*zek-uh-RYE-uhz*) home, where she greeted Elizabeth. When Elizabeth heard Mary's greeting, her baby moved within her.
 The Holy Spirit came upon Elizabeth. Then in a loud voice she said to Mary: "God has blessed you more than any other woman! He has also blessed the child you will have. The Lord has blessed you because you believe that he will keep his promise."
 Mary said:
 "With all my heart I praise the Lord,
 and I am glad because of God my Saviour.
 God cares for me, his humble servant.
 From now on, all people will say
 God has blessed me."

The gospel of the Lord.

Reflection

Why does Elizabeth call Mary blessed? What promise did God keep? Mary brought Jesus to Elizabeth and her baby. How do I bring Jesus to the people who know me?

Closing

Let us bring our hopes and needs to God, as we pray: **God of promise, hear our prayer.**

Let us pray with the words that Jesus taught us:

Our Father …

Mary, our mother,
you sheltered Jesus in your own body.
You raised him with a mother's care
and followed him in faith.
Teach us all to celebrate God's saving love.

Let us all say:
**Hail, Mary, full of grace,
the Lord is with you!
Blessed are you among women,
and blessed is the fruit of your womb, Jesus.
Holy Mary, Mother of God,
pray for us sinners
now and at the hour of our death. Amen.**

[Sing 'alleluia'.]

✞ All make the Sign of the Cross.

[Put out the candle.]

May 30, 2019

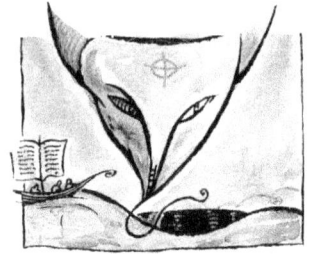

Friday Daily Prayer

[Light the Easter candle]

Introduction

This Sunday is Ascension Day, a day of great joy! While we do not see Jesus with our eyes, we know that he is still with us. Or perhaps we see Jesus whenever we look at another person. Jesus is closer to us than we are to each other.

In the Southern Hemisphere the coming week is observed as a Week of Prayer for Christian Unity. Christians take this time to pray in a special way for the many different Christian churches to be re-united.

✞ All make the Sign of the Cross.

Hymn

A Psalm for Late Eastertime

[Turn to page 92.]

Reading   Acts 1:3-4, 5, 8-11

Listen to the words of the Acts of the Apostles:

For forty days after Jesus had suffered and died, he proved in many ways that he had been raised from death. He appeared to his apostles and spoke to them about God's kingdom.
   While he was still with them, he said: "John baptised with water, but in a few days you will be baptised with the Holy Spirit.
   "The Holy Spirit will come upon you and give you power. Then you will tell everyone about me in the world." After Jesus had said this and while they were watching, he was taken up into a cloud. They could not see him, but as he went up, they kept looking up into the sky.
   Suddenly two men dressed in white clothes were standing there beside them. They said, "Why are you standing here and looking up into the sky? Jesus has been taken to heaven. But he will come back in the same way that you have seen him go."

The word of the Lord.

Reflection

In one way Jesus has left the world, but in another way he is here with us more than ever. How is Jesus here with us now? What can we tell everyone about Jesus?

Closing

Let us bring our hopes and needs to God, as we pray: **Ever-present God, hear our prayer.**

Let us pray with the words that Jesus taught us:

Our Father …

Lord God,
you give us great joy
as we celebrate
   the feast of the ascension of your Son, Jesus
Make us witnesses to his gospel,
and may we always seek his presence
   here among us.
We ask this through Christ our Lord. **Amen.**

[Sing 'alleluia'.]

May we live in the light of Christ. **Amen.**

✞ All make the Sign of the Cross.

[Put out the candle.]

May 31, 2019

Monday Daily Prayer

[Light the Easter candle]

Introduction

This week we prepare for Pentecost and the gift of the Holy Spirit. Before Jesus ascended into heaven, he told his followers not to be sad but to wait for the coming of the Holy Spirit. The Spirit would help them to grow in their understanding of all that Jesus had taught them. The Spirit would bring them unity and love and wisdom.

In today's reading Saint Paul tells the Christians of Ephesus (*EFF-uh-sus*) that only the Spirit of God can help them to live in peace. The Spirit of God helps them to live each day and to face difficult times.

Prayer for Christian Unity takes place through this week.

✝ All make the Sign of the Cross.

Hymn

A Psalm for Late Eastertime

[Turn to page 92.]

Reading *Ephesians 4:1–5*

Listen to the words of the apostle Paul:

I beg you to live in a way that is worthy of the people God has chosen to be his own. Always be humble and gentle. Patiently put up with each other and love each other. Try your best to let God's Spirit keep your hearts united. Do this by living at peace. All of you are part of the same body. There is only one Spirit of God, just as you were given one hope when you were chosen to be God's people. We have only one Lord, one faith, and one baptism.

The word of the Lord.

Reflection

How should we live as God's people? Am I patient and kind with others at school and at home? What should I do if there are arguments?

Closing

Please respond to each petition:
'Come, Holy Spirit.'

That the Spirit of peace may bring unity among our families and friends,
let us pray to the Lord: **Come, Holy Spirit.**

That the Spirit of understanding
may do away with hatred,
let us pray to the Lord: **Come, Holy Spirit.**

That the Spirit of knowledge
may teach us to live as Christians,
let us pray to the Lord: **Come, Holy Spirit.**

Let us also remember our other hopes and needs as we pray: **Gentle God, hear our prayer.**

Let us pray with the words that Jesus taught us:

Our Father …

[Sing 'alleluia'.]

May we live in the light of Christ. **Amen.**

✝ All make the Sign of the Cross.

[Put out the candle.]

June 3, 2019

Tuesday Daily Prayer

[Light the Easter candle]

Introduction

It's easy to list some of the difficult challenges that the human family has to face: climate change and global warming, millions of refugees, wars and terrorism. Our own families can have struggles, and so can each of us. Where can we find help? Paul tells us that God is with us and for us. He has given us his Spirit to strengthen and inspire us. The Spirit helps us pray.

☥ All make the Sign of the Cross.

Hymn

A Psalm for Late Eastertime

[Turn to page 92.]

Reading   *Romans 8:26-28, 31*

Listen to the words of the apostle Paul:

In certain ways we are weak, but the Spirit is here to help us. For example, when we don't know what to pray for, the Spirit prays for us in ways that cannot be put into words.
　All of our thoughts are known to God. He can understand what is in the mind of the Spirit, as the Spirit prays for God's people. We know that God is always at work for the good of everyone who loves him.
　What can we say about all this? If God is on our side, can anyone be against us?

The word of the Lord.

Reflection

What have I learned about prayer during Lent and Easter? Have I found some favourite ways to pray? Has prayer taught me that God always works for everyone's good?

Closing

Please respond to each petition:
'Come, Holy Spirit.'

That the Spirit of prayer
may open our hearts to God,
let us pray to the Lord: **Come, Holy Spirit.**

That the Spirit of compassion
may open our hearts to our neighbours,
let us pray to the Lord: **Come, Holy Spirit.**

That the Spirit of joy
may shape our living and our growing,
let us pray to the Lord: **Come, Holy Spirit.**

Let us also remember our other hopes and needs as we pray: **Companion God, hear our prayer.**

Let us pray with the words that Jesus taught us:

Our Father …

[Sing 'alleluia'.]

May we live in the light of Christ. **Amen.**

☥ All make the Sign of the Cross.

[Put out the candle.]

June 4, 2019

Wednesday Daily Prayer

[Light the Easter candle]

Introduction

Today is World Environment Day. This was established by the United Nations in 1972 to make us more aware of our need to respect and protect our environment.

In 2015 Pope Francis wrote a letter called *Laudato Si'* to the whole human family. He pointed out that our way of life was causing great harm to the planet. He called us to change our lifestyle to care for one another and for the world in which we live. It's our common home.

Last evening followers of the Islamic faith marked the end of the month long fast of Ramadan. They began to celebrate the holiday of Eid al Fitr (*EED-ull-FITTer*).

Today we read from Paul's letter to the church at Ephesus (*EFF-uh-sus*). Paul prays that the Spirit will help us to understand the blessings God gives.

✝ All make the Sign of the Cross.

Hymn

A Psalm for Late Eastertime

[Turn to page 92.]

Reading   *Ephesians 1:17-20*

Listen to the words of the apostle Paul:

Brothers and sisters: I ask the glorious Father and God of our Lord Jesus Christ to give you his Spirit. The Spirit will make you wise and let you understand what it means to know God. My prayer is that light will flood your hearts and that you will understand the hope that was given to you when God chose you. Then you will discover the glorious blessings that will be yours together with all of God's people.

I want you to know about the great and mighty power that God has for us followers. It is the same wonderful power he used when he raised Christ from death and let him sit at his right hand in heaven.

The word of the Lord.

Reflection

What special gift does Paul want the Spirit to give us? What blessings has God given to this class? What blessings has God given me?

Closing

Please respond to each petition:
'Come, Holy Spirit.'

That the Spirit of wisdom
may guide the leaders of our church,
let us pray to the Lord: **Come, Holy Spirit.**

That the Spirit of awe
may teach us to care for our planet,
let us pray to the Lord: **Come, Holy Spirit.**

That the Spirit of peace may bring unity among our families and friends,
let us pray to the Lord: **Come, Holy Spirit.**

Let us also remember our other hopes and needs as we pray: **Wise God, hear our prayer.**

Let us pray with the words that Jesus taught us:

Our Father ...

[Sing 'alleluia'.]

May we live in the light of Christ. **Amen.**

✝ All make the Sign of the Cross.

[Put out the candle.]

June 5, 2019

Thursday Daily Prayer

[Light the Easter candle]

Introduction

On this day in 1925, a man named Matt Talbot died in Dublin, Ireland. When Matt was a young man, he became addicted to alcohol. By the time he was 25 he had no job, money or home. He finally prayed for God's help and became sober. He never drank again and led a life of prayer and penance.

Many people are praying for Matt Talbot to be named a saint. He is a model for others who struggle with addictions.

Our last reading before Pentecost speaks of the many wonderful gifts the Holy Spirit brings. Paul writes to the Christian community in Corinth about the variety of these gifts. Each gift is special, but they are all the work of the one Spirit. They are meant to go together to support the shared life of the community.

☦ All make the Sign of the Cross.

Hymn

A Psalm for Late Eastertime

[Turn to page 92.]

Reading   1 Corinthians 12:7–11

Listen to the words of the apostle Paul:

The Spirit has given each of us a special way of serving others. Some of us can speak with wisdom, while others can speak with knowledge, but these gifts come from the same Spirit. To others the Spirit has given great faith or the power to heal the sick or the power to work mighty miracles. Some of us are prophets, and some of us recognise when God's Spirit is present. Others can speak different kinds of languages, and still others can tell what these languages mean. But it is the Spirit who does all this and decides which gifts to give to each of us.

The word of the Lord.

Reflection

Do I have a special way of serving others? What kinds of gifts does the Spirit give to people our age? How do our gifts help in building up the church and the world around us?

Closing

Please respond to each petition:
'Come, Holy Spirit.'

That the Spirit of understanding
may do away with hatred,
let us pray to the Lord: **Come, Holy Spirit.**

That the Spirit of courage
may strengthen us to be faithful to Jesus,
let us pray to the Lord: **Come, Holy Spirit.**

That the Spirit of awe may bring people joy,
let us pray to the Lord: **Come, Holy Spirit.**

Let us also remember our other hopes and needs as we pray: **God our teacher, hear our prayer.**

Let us pray with the words that Jesus taught us:

Our Father …

[Sing 'alleluia'.]

May we live in the light of Christ. **Amen.**

☦ All make the Sign of the Cross.

[Put out the candle.]

June 6, 2019

Friday Daily Prayer

[Reminder: Easter ends with the Feast of Pentecost. The Psalm for June is on page 112. Make a copy for each member of the class.]

[Light the Easter candle]

Introduction

This Sunday is the Feast of Pentecost, a great day in our Christian year. It is the fiftieth day of Easter. On this day we rejoice that Jesus keeps his promises. He promised that he would send the Holy Spirit to unify and strengthen his followers, and he did just that. Today's reading tells us how.

✞ All make the Sign of the Cross.

Hymn

A Psalm for Late Eastertime

[Turn to page 92.]

Reading   Acts 2:1-4, 6-7, 11

Listen to the words of the Acts of the Apostles:

On the day of Pentecost all the Lord's followers were together in one place. Suddenly there was a noise from heaven like the sound of a mighty wind! It filled the house where they were meeting. Then they saw what looked like fiery tongues moving in all directions, and a tongue came and settled on each person there. The Holy Spirit took control of everyone, and they began speaking whatever languages the Spirit let them speak.

When they heard this noise, a crowd gathered. But they were surprised, because they were hearing everything in their own languages. They were excited and amazed, and said, "Don't all these who are speaking come from Galilee (GAL-uh-lee)? Yet we all hear them using our own languages to tell the wonderful things God has done."

The word of the Lord.

Reflection

Why are fire and wind good symbols of the Holy Spirit? At Pentecost, people from many countries were gathered. Why were they surprised when they heard the disciples speaking in their own language? What were the disciples telling them?

Closing

Please respond to each petition:
'Come, Holy Spirit.'

That the Spirit of knowledge
may open the scriptures to us,
let us pray to the Lord: **Come, Holy Spirit.**

That the Spirit of courage
will give strength to those who are suffering,
let us pray to the Lord: **Come, Holy Spirit.**

That the Spirit of awe
may bring people to joy and delight,
let us pray to the Lord: **Come, Holy Spirit.**

Let us also remember our other hopes and needs as we pray: **Mighty God, hear our prayer.**

Let us pray with the words that Jesus taught us:

Our Father …

[Sing 'alleluia'.]

May we live in the light of Christ. **Amen.**

✞ All make the Sign of the Cross.

[Put out the candle.]

June 7, 2019

PSALMS ARE CRIES

It may surprise you to learn that many of the psalms are full of complaint. You may not have thought of complaining as a form of prayer. Yet there's a lot of it in the psalms. How come? How can it be prayer?

The place to start is with your own life. Are you always bubbling with joy? Do you always feel happy? Do you always feel safe? If so, you would be a very unusual person. At one time or another all of us are anxious or afraid or angry or disappointed or jealous or hurt or alone. These are all the common things we feel as human beings. They are painful. They disturb our peace. We wish they would go away.

When we are upset, we can turn to those who love us, like our parents or friends. We can beg them for help. Or we can accuse them of not doing enough for us. Or we can blame them for all our problems.

Another way we try to deal with our pain is by saying nothing. We keep it inside ourselves. We hide it and pretend everything is OK. But it's not. God's first people never made that mistake. They told God exactly what they thought and felt. They didn't hold back. They cried out to God. They poured out their troubles over and over. And a strange thing used to happen. After all their complaining, they often came to see that God was still there for them. So their cries of complaint eventually turned into words of trust. They were able to put new faith in God's goodness for them.

Here are some examples:

"When I call for help, I am safe from my enemies ... From the depths I cried out, my plea reached the heavens. God heard me." (*Psalm 18, Lent*)

"From a sea of troubles, I call out to you Lord. Won't you please listen as I beg for mercy? ... With all my heart, I am waiting, Lord, for you! I trust your promises." (*Psalm 130, Lent*)

"When I was really hurting I prayed to the Lord. The Lord answered my prayer and took my worries away." (*Psalm 118, Easter*)

"God gives justice to the poor and food to the hungry. The Lord sets prisoners free and heals blind eyes ... He defends the rights of orphans and widows." (*Psalm 146, June*).

June

Tuesday June 11,
to Friday, June 28

Ordinary Time ~ June 2019
Looking Ahead

Note: because of overlapping school holidays throughout Australia, there is a gap in Daily Prayer from Monday, July 1 – Friday, July 12.

About the Month

Wherever we live there will soon be many signs of winter. The sun is low in the sky and everywhere days are shorter and nights longer. Winter clothes come out of wardrobes. Netball, football, soccer and rugby are signs that this is the winter season.

The month of June is named after Juno. In Roman myths, Juno was the goddess of hearth and home. The hearth is the fireplace, which was once the gathering spot for cooking, conversation and storytelling. As we move into winter, we know that there will be cold days and nights ahead. These are times when we like to gather around warm fires.

While, for some, winter means cold and often wet days; for others it might be cool mornings and evenings and warm days. In parts of Australia, it is the dry season and grass turns brown. The more southern parts experience cold days and nights and rain. In these places grass is green. In parts close to mountains, snow may even fall. In these cooler parts of the country many trees now stand like skeletons pointing towards the sky. Desert parts of Australia experience, for a time, cold nights and desert winds during the day.

The Lent-Easter cycle is complete and the fifty days of Easter finished on Pentecost Sunday. Early June this year signals the return to Ordinary Time. Ordinary Time does not mean unimportant or boring time, but rather time that is counted in order of weeks.

In the church's year, there are two parts to Ordinary Time. The first weeks occur between the end of the Christmas season and the beginning of Lent. Now we come to the second part of Ordinary Time which, this year, begins with the 10th week. Ordinary Time will continue until the 34th week. And then Advent will begin.

Readings

During June and July we will often hear readings from the Old Testament. They will come from the first and second books of Kings (really one book in two parts). The first book tells the story of King David's son Solomon and the kings that followed him. Some were faithful to God and some were not. We also hear about one person who tried to keep them faithful, Elijah the prophet. These are very old stories.

Our readings for Fridays will anticipate the gospels of the feasts of the Holy Trinity, the Body and Blood of Jesus, and the Nativity of John the Baptist, and then the 12th Sunday of Ordinary Time.

Feasts and Other Commemorations

Important feasts occur during the month of June.

- On Sunday, June 16, the church celebrates the feast of the Holy Trinity. One of our oldest traditions has been to call God by the name of the Father, Son and Holy Spirit. These are the three persons of the Holy Trinity, and yet we know that there is only one God. Even though this is difficult to understand with our minds, we try to take hold of it in our hearts.
- The following Sunday is the feast of the Body and Blood of the Lord. This is a day of gratitude for the gift of eucharist and of being reminded what it means to live as a member of the Body of Christ.

- The Birth of John the Baptist, the cousin of Jesus, is celebrated on June 24.
  Mary's cousin Elizabeth and her husband Zechariah were blessed with a son late in life. It was a surprise when they called him John.
- The feast of the Sacred Heart falls on Friday, June 28. This feast celebrates the great love that Jesus has for us. It is an opportunity to show our love for those who suffer because of lack of food, clothing or shelter.

Feasts in early July

Two weeks of July are omitted this year as many schools are on holidays for some or all of this time. If you are still at school during the week of July 1 to July 5 we suggest that you pray a simple daily prayer on the feast-day of St Thomas.

1. Begin with the Sign of the Cross
2. Read the passage about the saint
3. Pray the Psalm for July
4. Read the scripture passage indicated below.
5. Reflect in silence after the reading
6. Pray intercessions in the usual way
7. Use the Closing Prayer for July.

TUESDAY, JULY 3
ST THOMAS THE APOSTLE

Reading: *John 20:24-29*

Thomas was probably born in Galilee but the gospels don't record how Jesus invited him to be a disciple. He was known as 'the Twin'. When Jesus planned to go to Jerusalem even though it was dangerous, Thomas immediately said to the other apostles, "Come on, let us also go so we can die with him: (John 11:16). Tradition has called him 'Doubting Thomas'. After today's gospel we know why.

Preparation for June

The Psalm for June is Psalm 146 (page 112). In this psalm, we praise God for all that he has created, for his goodness to the poor and for his helping hand to all. Once again, each member of the class will need a copy. Since green is the colour for Ordinary Time, copy them on green paper. Keep these pages in your special prayer folder.

Have we anything in our prayer space which shows that it is Ordinary Time? We could use a green cloth, green candles and green ribbons as markers in this book for our daily prayer.

Some parishes and schools celebrate a special Mass on the Feast of the Sacred Heart and invite people to bring gifts of food and clothing for people who are in need. If this does not happen, then maybe we could make this gift-giving part of Daily Prayer. Remember that food must be non-perishable, and clothing needs to be in good condition. Helping people with these kinds of gifts represents the way we should care all year long for the poor, the hungry and the homeless people of the world. The gifts we bring can be given to the local Saint Vincent de Paul Society for distribution. Discuss possibilities with your teacher ahead of time.

Suggested Hymns

See the hymn chart on pages viii-ix for hymns suitable for the following feasts: Holy Trinity, the Body and Blood of Christ and the Sacred Heart.

As we return to Ordinary Time, remember that general hymns of praise are suitable: 'This day God gives me', 'Morning has broken', 'Sing praises to the Lord', 'All the earth', 'Strong and Constant' and 'Clap your hands', all you nations' are always good hymns to begin prayer.

A Psalm for June

Psalm 95:1-2, 4-7

LEADER
Sing joyful songs to the Lord!
Praise the mighty rock where we are safe.
ALL
**Come to worship God
with thankful hearts and songs of praise.**

SIDE A
God holds the deepest part of the earth
  in his hands,
and the mountain peaks belong to him.

SIDE B
**The ocean is the Lord's
because he made it,
and with his own hands
he formed the dry land.**

SIDE A
Bow down and worship the Lord our Creator!
The Lord is our God,
and we are his people.

SIDE B
**We are the sheep he takes care of
in his own pasture.**

LEADER
Sing joyful songs to the Lord!
Praise the mighty rock where we are safe.
ALL
**Come to worship God
with thankful hearts and songs of praise.**

Glory be to the Father, and to the Son,
and to the Holy Spirit.
**As it was in the beginning, is now,
and ever shall be,
world without end. Amen. Alleluia.**

[Turn back to Daily Prayer for today.]

Tuesday Daily Prayer

Introduction

During June and July we will often hear readings from the Old Testament. They will come from the first and second books of Kings (really one book in two parts). The first book tells the story of King David's son Solomon and the kings that followed him. Some were faithful to God and some were not. We will also hear about one person who tried to keep them faithful, Elijah (*ee-LIE-juh*) the prophet. These are very old stories.

Today we remember Marcellin Champagnat (*sham-PAN-yah*). He joined the Marist Fathers in 19th century France. With two other priests, he began to teach the faith to children from poor families. This gave birth to the Marist Brothers. They still teach young people here in Australia and overseas today.

✝ All make the Sign of the Cross.

Hymn

A Psalm for June

[Turn to page 112.]

Reading   *1 Kings* 2:1-4

Listen to the words of the first book of Kings:

Not long before David died, he told Solomon: My son, I will soon die, as everyone must. But I want you to be strong and brave. Do what the Lord your God commands and follow his teachings. Obey everything written in the Law of Moses. Then you will be a success, no matter what you do or where you go. You and your descendants must always faithfully obey the Lord. If you do, he will keep the solemn promise he made to me that someone from our family will always be king of Israel.

The word of the Lord.

Reflection

What is David's advice to his son Solomon? Why is following God's ways the most important thing in life? How do we know what God asks of us?

Closing

Let us bring our hopes and needs to God, as we pray: **God, our provider, hear our prayer.**

Let us pray with the words that Jesus taught us:

Our Father …

Saving God,
in ancient times you led your people Israel
by the guidance of prophets and kings.
Give your church today true pastors
to teach and nourish us
like Christ our good shepherd.
We ask this through the same Christ our Lord.
Amen.

[Sing 'alleluia'.]

✝ All make the Sign of the Cross.

June 11, 2019

Wednesday Daily Prayer

Introduction

The School of the Air opened in Alice Springs in June 1951. It was the inspiration of a teacher from South Australia, Miss Adelaide Miethke (*MEETH-key*). When she saw how the Flying Doctor Service used radio to bring medical care to people in remote parts of the country, she realised it could also bring school to children in the outback. They could participate in lessons conducted by trained teachers as well as communicate with other students.

The School of the Air still plays a vital role in the education of children in distant places. It covers a broadcast area of over one billion square kilometres.

King David's son Solomon became famous because he asked God for wisdom rather than power and wealth.

✢ All make the Sign of the Cross.

Hymn

A Psalm for June

[Turn to page 112.]

Reading   1 Kings 3:5.6.7.9

Listen to the words of the first book of Kings:

One night while Solomon was in Gibeon, the Lord God appeared to him in a dream and said, "Solomon, ask for anything you want, and I will give it to you."
Solomon answered:
"Lord God, I'm your servant, and you've made me king in my father's place. But I'm very young and know so little about being a leader. And now I must rule your chosen people, even though there are too many of them to count. Please make me wise and teach me the difference between right and wrong. Then I will know how to rule your people. If you don't, there is no way I could rule this great nation of yours."

The word of the Lord.

Reflection

What did Solomon ask God for? What other things might he have wanted? If God promised to give you whatever you asked for, what would be the most important thing on your list?

Closing

Let us bring our hopes and needs to God, as we pray: **God, our provider, hear our prayer.**

Let us pray with the words that Jesus taught us:

Our Father …

Saving God,
in ancient times you led your people Israel
by the guidance of prophets and kings.
Give your church today true pastors
to teach and nourish us
like Christ our good shepherd.
We ask this through the same Christ our Lord.
Amen.

[Sing 'alleluia'.]

✢ All make the Sign of the Cross.

June 12, 2019

Thursday Daily Prayer

Introduction

Today's story of King Solomon tells how he decided to build a temple for the people to worship God. His father David had this dream but was unable to make it happen. The Temple of Solomon was a sign of God's presence among his people and of his special love for them.

✞ All make the Sign of the Cross.

Hymn

A Psalm for June

[Turn to page 112.]

Reading   1 Kings 5:1-5

Listen to the words of the first book of Kings:

King Hiram of Tyre had always been friends with Solomon's father David. When Hiram learned that Solomon was king, he sent some of his officials to meet with Solomon.
Solomon sent a message back to Hiram:
Remember how my father David wanted to build a temple where the Lord his God could be worshiped? But enemies kept attacking my father's kingdom, and he never had the chance. Now, thanks to the Lord God, there is peace in my kingdom and no trouble or threat of war anywhere.
  The Lord God promised my father that when his son became king, he would build a temple for worshiping the Lord. So I've decided to do that.

The word of the Lord.

Reflection

Why did David and Solomon want to build a temple? What is a temple for? What is a church building for?

Closing

Let us bring our hopes and needs to God, as we pray: **God, our provider, hear our prayer.**

Let us pray with the words that Jesus taught us:

Our Father …

Saving God,
in ancient times you led your people Israel
by the guidance of prophets and kings.
Give your church today true pastors
to teach and nourish us
like Christ our good shepherd.
We ask this through the same Christ our Lord.
Amen.

[Sing 'alleluia'.]

✞ All make the Sign of the Cross.

June 13, 2019

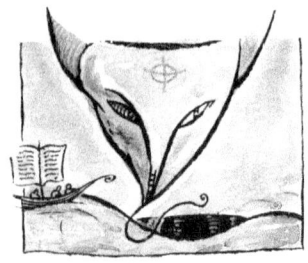

Friday Daily Prayer

Introduction

On Sunday, the church celebrates the Holy Trinity. One of our oldest traditions has been to call God by the names of Father, Son and Holy Spirit. These are the three persons of the Holy Trinity. And yet we know that there is only one God.

God's life is a mystery, but it is a mystery of infinite love shared within the "family" of God and with all that is. It is hard to understand with our minds, but we can deepen the understanding of our hearts.

☩ All make the Sign of the Cross.

Hymn

A Psalm for June

[Turn to page 112.]

Reading   Matthew 28:16-20

Listen to the words of the holy gospel according to Matthew:

Jesus' eleven disciples went to a mountain in Galilee, where Jesus had told them to meet him. They saw him and worshipped him, but some of them doubted.

Jesus came to them and said, "I have been given all authority in heaven and on earth! Go to the people of all nations and make them my disciples. Baptise them in the name of the Father, the Son, and the Holy Spirit, and teach them to do everything I have told you.

"I will be with you always, even until the end of the world."

The gospel of the Lord.

Reflection

Jesus tells his disciples to go to all the nations and make disciples. Do these words apply to me too? In what way? How is Jesus with us always?

Closing

Let us bring our hopes and needs to God, as we pray: **God of mystery, hear our prayer.**

Let us pray with the words that Jesus taught us:

Our Father …

Our response is: 'We praise you.'

Holy Trinity, one God: **We praise you.**
God our Father, endless in mercy:
    We praise you.
Son of God, Saviour of the world:
    We praise you.
Holy Spirit, strength of God's people:
    We praise you.

O holy, undivided Trinity,
one God in three Persons.
We praise and bless you
for sharing your life with us
now and for ever. **Amen.**

[Sing 'alleluia'.]

☩ All make the Sign of the Cross.

Monday Daily Prayer

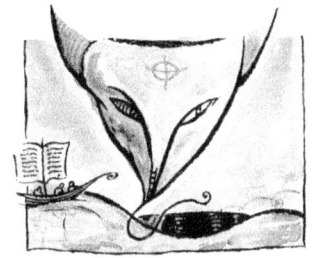

Introduction

After Solomon finished building the temple, he went inside it with the people and made a long prayer to God. He asks God for many blessings on the temple. Today we hear a short part of that prayer.

✝ All make the Sign of the Cross.

Hymn

A Psalm for June

[Turn to page 112.]

Reading   1 Kings 8:22.27-30

Listen to the words of the first book of Kings:

Solomon stood facing the altar with everyone standing behind him. Then he lifted his arms toward heaven and prayed:
Lord God of Israel, no other god in heaven or on earth is like you!
There's not enough room in all of heaven for you, Lord God. How could you possibly live on earth in this temple I have built? But I ask you to answer my prayer. This is the temple where you have chosen to be worshiped. Please watch over it day and night and listen when I turn toward it and pray. I am your servant, and the people of Israel belong to you. So whenever any of us look toward this temple and pray, answer from your home in heaven and forgive our sins.

The word of the Lord.

Reflection

God's home is in heaven, but Solomon asks for the temple to be a place on earth where the people can turn to God. He asks for it to be a place of mercy and forgiveness. Where can we find forgiveness when we turn away from God and don't show love to one another?

Closing

Let us bring our hopes and needs to God, as we pray: **God, our provider, hear our prayer.**

Let us pray with the words that Jesus taught us:

Our Father ...

Saving God,
in ancient times you led your people Israel
by the guidance of prophets and kings.
Give your church today true pastors
to teach and nourish us
like Christ our good shepherd.
We ask this through the same Christ our Lord.
Amen.

[Sing 'alleluia'.]

✝ All make the Sign of the Cross.

June 17, 2019

Tuesday Daily Prayer

Introduction

In the ancient world wisdom was considered a great gift. Solomon became very famous for his wisdom and other rulers admired him for it. One of those was the Queen of Sheba (*SHEE-buh*), as we hear in today's reading. No-one knows for sure who she was but in the story she is fabulously wealthy. She came to see Solomon for herself and was very impressed. Even today we talk about the "wisdom of Solomon."

✜ All make the Sign of the Cross.

Hymn

A Psalm for June

[Turn to page 112.]

Reading   1 Kings 10:1-3.6-7.9

Listen to the words of the first book of Kings:

The Queen of Sheba (*SHEE-buh*) heard how famous Solomon was, so she went to Jerusalem to test him with difficult questions. She took along several of her officials, and she loaded her camels with gifts of spices, jewels, and gold. When she arrived, she and Solomon talked about everything she could think of. He answered every question, no matter how difficult it was.
The Queen said:
Solomon, in my own country I had heard about your wisdom and all you've done. But I didn't believe it until I saw it with my own eyes! And there's so much I didn't hear about. You are wiser and richer than I was told.
I praise the Lord your God. He is pleased with you and has made you king of Israel. The Lord loves Israel, so he has given them a king who will rule fairly and honestly.

The word of the Lord.

Reflection

The Queen of Sheba went to great trouble to search out Solomon and his wisdom. Then she gave him gifts. Can you think of a gospel story where wise men went in search of a king? What did they find? What gifts did they give him?

Closing

Let us bring our hopes and needs to God, as we pray: **God, our provider, hear our prayer.**

Let us pray with the words that Jesus taught us:

Our Father …

Saving God,
in ancient times you led your people Israel
by the guidance of prophets and kings.
Give your church today true pastors
to teach and nourish us
like Christ our good shepherd.
We ask this through the same Christ our Lord.
Amen.

[Sing 'alleluia'.]

✜ All make the Sign of the Cross.

June 18, 2019

Wednesday Daily Prayer

Introduction

Today we remember Mother Suzanne Aubert, (*soo-ZAN oh-BEAR*). She was born on this day in France in 1835 and went to New Zealand as a missionary. She worked among the Maori people. She founded the Sisters of Compassion whose members still work with sick and needy people today. The Church in New Zealand is hoping that she will be officially declared a saint.

In the reading for today we meet the prophet Elijah (*ee-LIE-juh*). His mission was to keep the people and the king faithful to God. The power of God was with him to do wonderful things.

✞ All make the Sign of the Cross.

Hymn

A Psalm for June

[Turn to page 112.]

Reading   *1 Kings 17:1.10-11.12.13-14.16*

Listen to the words of the first book of Kings:

Elijah (*ee-LIE-juh*) was a prophet from Tishbe in Gilead.

When Elijah came near the town gate of Zarephath (*ZAR-uh-fath*), he saw a widow gathering sticks for a fire. "Would you please bring me a cup of water?" he asked. As she left to get it, he asked, "Would you also please bring me a piece of bread?"

The widow answered, "In the name of the living Lord your God, I swear that I don't have any bread. All I have is a handful of flour and a little olive oil."

Elijah said, "Everything will be fine. Do what you said. Go home and fix something for you and your son. But first, please make a small piece of bread and bring it to me. The Lord God of Israel has promised that your jar of flour won't run out and your bottle of oil won't dry up before he sends rain for the crops."

The Lord kept the promise that his prophet Elijah had made, and she did not run out of flour or oil.

The word of the Lord.

Reflection

The widow has almost nothing to give but she puts her trust in God and Elijah and is given much in return. Are there any stories like this in the gospels? What did Jesus mean when he told the crowds not to worry about anything (Matthew 6:25-33)?

Closing

Let us bring our hopes and needs to God, as we pray: **God, our provider, hear our prayer.**

Let us pray with the words that Jesus taught us:

Our Father …

Saving God,
in ancient times you led your people Israel
by the guidance of prophets and kings.
Give your church today true pastors
to teach and nourish us
like Christ our good shepherd.
We ask this through the same Christ our Lord.
Amen.

[Sing 'alleluia'.]

✞ All make the Sign of the Cross.

June 19, 2019

Thursday Daily Prayer

Introduction

Today is World Refugee Day. We remember the millions of displaced people, refugees and asylum seekers around the world. We see their great courage and perseverance when they have lost everything. Often facing injustice, hardship and hostility, they show us how to stay strong and hopeful even when everything seems to go wrong. They can be a great blessing for us.

Yesterday we read how Elijah (*ee-LIE-juh*) used the power of God to provide food for the poor widow and her son. Today he brings the boy back to life.

✢ All make the Sign of the Cross.

Hymn

A Psalm for June

[Turn to page 112.]

Reading   1 Kings 17:17.19.20-24

Listen to the words of the first book of Kings:

Several days later, the son of the woman who owned the house got sick, and he kept getting worse, until finally he died.
   "Bring me your son," Elijah (*ee-LIE-juh*) said. Then he took the boy from her arms and carried him upstairs to the room where he was staying. Elijah laid the boy on his bed and prayed, "Lord God, why did you do such a terrible thing to this woman? She's letting me stay here, and now you've let her son die." Elijah stretched himself out over the boy three times, while praying, "Lord God, bring this boy back to life!"
   The Lord answered Elijah's prayer, and the boy started breathing again. He gave the boy to his mother and said, "Look, your son is alive."
   "You are God's prophet!" the woman replied. "Now I know that you really do speak for the Lord."

The word of the Lord.

Reflection

It is not Elijah who brings the boy back to life but God. This story will remind you of Jesus' powerful deeds. Can you think of any stories of Jesus bringing someone back to life? What do they teach us?

Closing

Let us bring our hopes and needs to God, as we pray: **God, our provider, hear our prayer.**

Let us pray with the words that Jesus taught us:

Our Father …

Saving God,
in ancient times you led your people Israel
by the guidance of prophets and kings.
Give your church today true pastors
to teach and nourish us
like Christ our good shepherd.
We ask this through the same Christ our Lord.
Amen.

[Sing 'alleluia'.]

✢ All make the Sign of the Cross.

Friday Daily Prayer

Introduction

On Sunday we celebrate the feast of the Body and Blood of Christ. This is a day of gratitude for the gift of the Eucharist.

Each time we gather at Mass, we listen to God's word. We pray for the world and for the church, and we give thanks to God with bread and wine. Then, united with God and with one another, we share the bread and wine. They have become the Body and Blood of Christ. Christians have promised to do this every Sunday in memory of Jesus, just as he asked.

☧ All make the Sign of the Cross.

Hymn

A Psalm for June

[Turn to page 112.]

Reading   *Luke 9:12-17*

Listen to the words of the holy gospel according to Luke:

Late in the afternoon the twelve apostles came to Jesus and said, "Send the crowd to the villages and farms around here. They need to find a place to stay and something to eat. There is nothing in this place. It is like a desert!"

Jesus answered, "You give them something to eat." But they replied, "We have only five small loaves of bread and two fish. If we are going to feed all these people we will have to go and buy food." There were about five thousand in the crowd.

Jesus said to his disciples, "Have the people sit in groups of fifty." They did this, and all the people sat down. Jesus took the five loaves and the two fish. He looked up toward heaven and blessed the food. Then he broke the bread and fish and handed them to his disciples to give to the people.

Everyone ate all they wanted. What was left over filled twelve baskets.

The gospel of the Lord.

Reflection

This story of Jesus feeding the crowd with a few fish and some bread is in all the gospels. At Mass we are fed with Jesus himself in the form of bread and wine. Why did Jesus tell us to keep remembering him in this way? What hunger of ours is God wanting to satisfy?

Closing

Let us bring our hopes and needs to God, as we pray: **Jesus, bread from heaven, hear our prayer.**

Let us pray with the words that Jesus taught us:

Our Father …

Loving God,
through the bread and wine of the Eucharist
you give us a share in the life, death,
and resurrection of your son, Jesus.
Guide us by his Holy Spirit
and lead us to the heavenly banquet table.
We ask this through Christ our Lord. **Amen.**

[Sing 'alleluia'.]

☧ All make the Sign of the Cross.

June 21, 2019

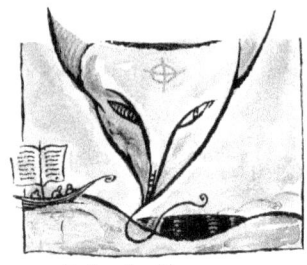

Monday Daily Prayer

Introduction

Today we remember the birth of Saint John the Baptist, the prophet sent by God to prepare the way for Jesus. We celebrate this feast six months from Christmas Eve, because Luke's gospel tells us that John was born six months before Jesus his cousin.

John the Baptist pointed out Jesus to his disciples, and he said of him, "He must increase, I must decrease."

✝ All make the Sign of the Cross.

Hymn

A Psalm for June

[Turn to page 112.]

Reading *Luke 1:57-64*

Listen to the words of the holy gospel according to Luke:

When Elizabeth's son was born, her neighbours and relatives heard how kind the Lord had been to her, and they too were glad.

Eight days later they did for the child what the Law of Moses commands. They were going to name him Zechariah (*zek-uh-RIE-uh*), after his father. But Elizabeth said, "No! His name is John."

The people argued, "No one in your family has ever been named John." So they motioned to Zechariah to find out what he wanted to name his son.

Zechariah asked for a writing tablet. Then he wrote, "His name is John." Everyone was amazed. Right away Zechariah started speaking and praising God.

The gospel of the Lord.

Reflection

After he learned that Elizabeth would give birth to a son, Zechariah lost the power of speech. Have I ever been left speechless by the wonders of God? How do I use my voice in God's service? Do I pray with enthusiasm when I praise God with others?

Closing

Let us bring our hopes and needs to God, as we pray: **God of wonder, hear our prayer.**

Let us pray with the words that Jesus taught us:

Our Father …

God of the prophets
you raised up John the Baptist
to prepare the way
for the coming of your Son, Jesus.
You made him a fiery prophet to your people.
Give us the strength
to be prophets in our lives.
We ask this through Christ our Lord. **Amen.**

[Sing 'alleluia'.]

✝ All make the Sign of the Cross.

June 24, 2019

Tuesday Daily Prayer

Introduction

Today we remember an Australian Franciscan brother, Kevin Lawler. He was born in Scotland and, as a small boy, came to Australia with his family as a migrant. They settled in Victoria. In 1982, Kevin responded to a call for volunteers for the Franciscan African Mission. He died as a victim of violence for the sake of the gospel in Nairobi, Kenya, on this day in 1986.

Last week we heard a story of Elijah (*ee-LIE-juh*) providing food for a widow and her son. Today it is Elijah himself who needs to be fed by God.

☦ All make the Sign of the Cross.

Hymn

A Psalm for June

[Turn to page 112.]

Reading   *1 Kings 19:1-2.3.4-6.8-9*

Listen to the words of the first book of Kings:

Ahab told his wife Jezebel what Elijah (*ee LIE-juh*) had done. She sent a message to Elijah: "You killed my prophets. Now I'm going to kill you!"

  Elijah was afraid when he got her message, and he ran to the town of Beersheba, then walked another whole day into the desert. Finally, he came to a large bush and sat down in its shade. He begged the Lord, "I've had enough. Just let me die! I'm no better off than my ancestors." Then he lay down in the shade and fell asleep.

  Suddenly an angel woke him up and said, "Get up and eat." Elijah looked around, and by his head was a jar of water and some baked bread.

The food and water made him strong enough to walk forty more days. At last, he reached Mount Sinai, the mountain of God, and he spent the night there in a cave.

The word of the Lord.

Reflection

God gave Elijah the food and water he needed to survive the desert, just as he gave the Israelites manna on their way from Egypt to the Promised Land. How does God feed us for our journey through life? Is the teaching of Jesus a kind of food for our minds and hearts?

Closing

Let us bring our hopes and needs to God, as we pray: **God, our provider, hear our prayer.**

Let us pray with the words that Jesus taught us:

Our Father …

Saving God,
in ancient times you led your people Israel
by the guidance of prophets and kings.
Give your church today true pastors
to teach and nourish us
like Christ our good shepherd.
We ask this through the same Christ our Lord.
Amen.

[Sing 'alleluia'.]

☦ All make the Sign of the Cross.

June 25, 2019

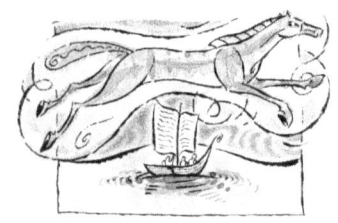

Wednesday Daily Prayer

Introduction

Our last story from the first book of the Kings is about a mysterious meeting between God and the prophet Elijah. It takes place on God's holy mountain in the desert. It suggests that God reveals himself to us in quietness, not in noisy and impressive events.

✟ All make the Sign of the Cross.

Hymn

A Psalm for June

[Turn to page 112.]

Reading   1 Kings 19:9.11-13

Listen to the words of the first book of Kings:

While Elijah was on Mount Sinai, the Lord asked, "Elijah, why are you here?"

He answered, "Lord God All-Powerful, I've always done my best to obey you. But your people have broken their solemn promise to you."

"Go out and stand on the mountain," the Lord replied. "I want you to see me when I pass by."

All at once, a strong wind shook the mountain and shattered the rocks. But the Lord was not in the wind. Next, there was an earthquake, but the Lord was not in the earthquake. Then there was a fire, but the Lord was not in the fire.

Finally, there was a gentle breeze, when Elijah heard it, he covered his face with his coat. He went out and stood at the entrance to the cave.

The word of the Lord.

Reflection

What can we do to hear God speaking to us? How can we listen carefully? Do we need to find a quiet place and quiet time? What do you think God might want to say to us?

Closing

Let us bring our hopes and needs to God, as we pray: **God, our provider, hear our prayer.**

Let us pray with the words that Jesus taught us:

Our Father ...

Saving God,
in ancient times you led your people Israel
by the guidance of prophets and kings.
Give your church today true pastors
to teach and nourish us
like Christ our good shepherd.
We ask this through the same Christ our Lord.
Amen.

[Sing 'alleluia'.]

✟ All make the Sign of the Cross.

June 26, 2019

Thursday Daily Prayer

[Reminder: Tomorrow is the feast of the Sacred Heart. In many places people bring gifts for those in need on this day.]

Introduction

Tomorrow is the feast of the Sacred Heart of Jesus but we will remember it today. The heart of Christ is a symbol of Jesus' love for us.

Jesus' generous love for us was sometimes shown in paintings and statues with his heart crowned with thorns, bringing to mind his suffering. It reminds us that love and suffering often go together.

This feast is an opportunity to remember in a special way those who suffer because of lack of food, clothing or shelter. We often have special Masses on this day and bring gifts of food and clothing to be shared among these people.

☦ All make the Sign of the Cross.

Hymn

A Psalm for June

[Turn to page 112.]

Reading   Luke 15:3–7

Listen to the words of the holy gospel according to Luke:

Jesus told this story:

"If any of you has a hundred sheep, and one of them gets lost, what will you do? Won't you leave the ninety-nine in the field and go look for the lost sheep until you find it? And when you find it, you will be so glad that you will put it on your shoulder and carry it home. Then you will call in your friends and neighbours and say, 'Let's celebrate! I've found my lost sheep.'"

Jesus said, "In the same way there is more happiness in heaven because of one sinner who turns to God than over ninety-nine good people who don't need to."

The gospel of the Lord.

Reflection

Why is this gospel chosen for the feast of the Sacred Heart? What other titles or images of Jesus do I know? Are there pictures, ideas or titles of God that help me remember that God loves me as no one else can?

Closing

Let us bring our hopes and needs to God, as we pray: **Shepherd God, hear our prayer.**

Let us pray with the words that Jesus taught us:

Our Father …

Generous God,
you are always loving and merciful.
Give us loving hearts
so that we will never be separated
from the love of your Son, Jesus.
May we always remember
those who do not have food, clothing or shelter.
We ask this through Christ our Lord. **Amen.**

[Sing 'alleluia'.]

☦ All make the Sign of the Cross.

June 27, 2019

Friday Daily Prayer

[Reminder: The Psalm for July is on page 130. Make a copy for each member of the class.]

Introduction

Usually on a Friday we read part of the gospel from Sunday Mass. Sometimes we turn to one of the other readings. Today we hear from a letter which Saint Paul wrote to the church in Galatia (*gal-AY-shuh*).

The words 'freedom' and 'service' occur in this reading. We often think that freedom is doing anything we want to do. But Paul speaks about freeing ourselves from selfishness and from anything that destroys love of other people. This kind of freedom means that we will go out of our way to respect and love each other.

✞ All make the Sign of the Cross.

Hymn

A Psalm for June

[Turn to page 112.]

Reading   *Galatians 5:1, 13-15*

Listen to the words from the apostle Paul:

Christ has set us free! You were chosen to be free. So don't use your freedom as an excuse to do anything you want. Use it as an opportunity to serve each other with love. All that the Law says can be summed up in the command to love others as much as you love yourself. But if you keep attacking each other like wild animals, you had better watch out or you will destroy yourselves.

The word of the Lord.

Reflection

When did you do what you wanted even though it hurt somebody else? When did you do something loving for another person even though this meant that you had to give up something yourself?

Closing

Let us bring our hopes and needs to God, as we pray: **God of love, hear our prayer.**

Let us pray with the words that Jesus taught us:

Our Father …

Loving God,
free us from sadness and worry.
Free us from jealousy and greed.
Free us to follow you with all our hearts.
We ask this through Christ our Lord. **Amen.**

[Sing 'alleluia'.]

✞ All make the Sign of the Cross.

June 28, 2019

July

Monday, July 15,
to Wednesday, July 31

Ordinary Time ~ July 2019
Looking Ahead

About the Month

July, the seventh month of the year is named for the ancient Roman emperor Julius Caesar.

In most parts of Australia and in New Zealand, July is the middle month of winter. Middles are often more difficult than beginnings and endings. The months of winter can often seem a time of 'hanging in there'. It is good that there is always a school term break during July. In the northern parts of Australia, July is the dry season, and temperatures during the day are quite warm.

We will experience July differently according to whatever part of the country we live in. Often, July is the time for winter colds and flu. It is also the time for planting bulbs so that they will be ready to flower when spring comes. It would be nice to plant some bulbs in pots for the classroom. They would be ready to be part of our prayer space during the months of Spring.

We begin our July prayer in the fifteenth week of Ordinary Time. Sunday is the heart of Ordinary Time, and there is usually a total of thirty-four Sundays.

Readings

Last month we heard a number of readings from the first book of the kings in the Old Testament. This month we will read from the second book of the Kings and similar books. We begin with the stories of Elisha, the prophet who succeeded Elijah. Next we hear of a reforming king, followed by the disaster of Jerusalem being captured by enemies and the people going into exile. Finally there is the good news of their return home and a fresh start.

Our readings for Fridays will anticipate the gospels of the Sixteenth and Seventeenth Sundays of Ordinary Time.

Feasts

- The feast of St Mary Magdalene is celebrated on July 22. In the early church, Mary Magdalene was called 'apostle to the apostles'. She was the first to witness that Jesus had risen from the dead and she was the one who brought this good news to the apostles. Recently, Pope Francis wrote that Mary Magdalene's feast-day is a call for all Christians to reflect more deeply on the dignity of women … and the greatness of God's mercy."

- The feast of St James the apostle is on July 25. James, a fisherman, and his brother John were invited by Jesus to come with him and learn to fish for human beings. James was one of the favoured apostles. He was a witness to many of Jesus' miracles, and was present at the Transfiguration and at the Agony in the Garden.

- The feast of Joachim and Anne is on July 26, honouring them as the parents of Mary and the grandparents of Jesus. Nothing is mentioned of them in the gospels.

Preparation for July

The Psalm for July is Psalm 146 and is on page 130. This is a psalm of praise and thanksgiving in which we thank God for creation. God keeps his word and is always there to help. Make copies of the psalm for each member of the class.

Suggested Hymns

See hymn chart on pages viii-ix. Don't forget that hymns such as 'This day God gives me', 'Morning has broken' or a hymn of praise are always suitable for prayer in the morning. Try to expand your repertoire of hymns suitable for Ordinary Time.

A Psalm for July

Psalm 146:1-2, 5-8, 9

Leader
Let us offer God praise and thanksgiving.

Leader
Shout praises to the Lord!
With all that I am, I will shout God's praises.
All
**I will sing and praise the Lord God
for as long as I live.**

Side A
The Lord God of Jacob blesses everyone
who trusts him and depends on him.

Side B
God made heaven and earth;
he created the sea and everything else.

Side A
God always keeps his word.
He gives justice to the poor
and food to the hungry.

Side B
The Lord sets prisoners free
and heals blind eyes.

Side A
He gives a helping hand
to everyone who falls.

Side B
He defends the rights of orphans and widows.

Leader
Shout praises to the Lord!
With all that I am, I will shout God's praises.
All
**I will sing and praise the Lord God
for as long as I live.**

Glory be to the Father, and to the Son,
and to the Holy Spirit.
As it was in the beginning, is now,
and ever shall be,
world without end. Amen. Alleluia.

(Turn back to Daily Prayer for today.)

Monday Daily Prayer

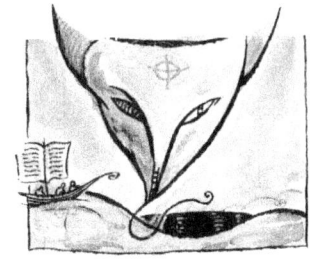

[Reminder: The Psalm for July is found on p. 130. Make a copy for each member of the class.]

Introduction

Last month we had a number of readings from the first book of the Kings in the Old Testament. This month we hear from the second book of the Kings and similar books. We begin with stories of Elisha (*ell-EESH-uh*), the prophet who succeeded Elijah (*ee-LIE-juh*).

Next we hear of a reforming king, followed by the disaster of Jerusalem being captured by enemies and the people going into exile. Finally there is the good news of their return home and a fresh start.

Today's story is about how Elisha was given Elijah's power.

✝ All make the Sign of the Cross.

Hymn

A Psalm for July

[Turn to page 130.]

Reading   2 Kings 2:9.11.13-15

Listen to the words of the second book of the Kings:

After they had reached the other side, Elijah (*ee-LIE-juh*) said, "Elisha (*ell-EESH-uh*), the Lord will soon take me away. What can I do for you before that happens?"
Elisha answered, "Please give me twice as much of your power as you give the other prophets, so I can be the one who takes your place as their leader."
Elijah and Elisha were walking along and talking, when suddenly there appeared between them a flaming chariot pulled by fiery horses. Right away, a strong wind took Elijah up into heaven.
Elijah's coat had fallen off, so Elisha picked it up and walked back to the Jordan River. He struck the water with the coat and wondered, "Will the Lord perform miracles for me as he did for Elijah?" As soon as Elisha did this, a dry path opened up through the water, and he walked across.
When the prophets from Jericho (JE-rick-o) saw what happened, they said to each other, "Elisha now has Elijah's power."

The word of the Lord.

Reflection

What do you think happened to Elijah at the end of his life? It's very mysterious, isn't it? What does Elisha do that reminds you of Moses?

Closing

Let us bring our hopes and needs to God, as we pray: **God of holiness, hear our prayer.**

Let us pray with the words that Jesus taught us:

Our Father …

Loving God, have mercy on all your people.
Help us to listen when you call us.
Give us courage to do what you ask.
Keep us close to your heart.
We ask this through Christ our Lord. **Amen.**

[Sing 'alleluia'.]

✝ All make the Sign of the Cross.

July 15, 2019

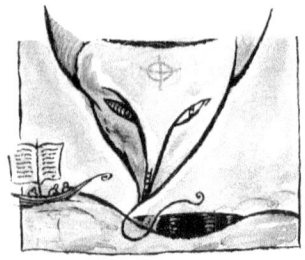

Tuesday Daily Prayer

Introduction

In the ancient world of the Bible, olive oil was used for many different everyday purposes such as cooking, healing and lighting. This made it a valuable asset. Today we read about how Elisha used God's power to provide a poor widow with oil to sell. She could pay her debts and live on with her sons.

✞ All make the Sign of the Cross.

Hymn

A Psalm for July

[Turn to page 130.]

Reading   2 *Kings* 4:1-4.7

Listen to the words of the second book of the Kings:

One day the widow of one of the Lord's prophets said to Elisha (*ell-EESH-uh*), "You know that before my husband died, he was a follower of yours and a worshiper of the Lord. But he owed a man some money, and now that man is on his way to take my two sons as his slaves."

"Maybe there's something I can do to help," Elisha said. "What do you have in your house?"
"Sir, I have nothing but a small bottle of olive oil."

Elisha told her, "Ask your neighbours for their empty jars. And after you've borrowed as many as you can, go home and shut the door behind you and your sons. Then begin filling the jars with oil and set each one aside as you fill it.

Sell the oil and use part of the money to pay what you owe the man. You and your sons can live on what is left."

The word of the Lord.

Reflection

In many societies in the past (and even in some today), a woman whose husband had died was powerless and poor. Why was that so? How does Elisha come to this widow's rescue? Is this a sign of God's care for the weak?

Closing

Let us bring our hopes and needs to God, as we pray: **God of holiness, hear our prayer.**

Let us pray with the words that Jesus taught us:

Our Father ...

Loving God, have mercy on all your people.
Help us to listen when you call us.
Give us courage to do what you ask.
Keep us close to your heart.
We ask this through Christ our Lord. **Amen.**

[Sing 'alleluia'.]

✞ All make the Sign of the Cross.

July 16, 2019

Wednesday Daily Prayer

Introduction

Today we read another story of how God's power was with the prophet Elisha. It teaches us something important. Elisha does not use this power to show off or make himself famous. He uses it for the good of others. He uses it to show God's loving care for his people.

✞ All make the Sign of the Cross.

Hymn

A Psalm for July

[Turn to page 130.]

Reading 2 Kings 4:42-44

Listen to the words of the second book of the Kings:

A man from the town of Baal-Shalishah (*BARL shar-li-SHAR*) brought Elisha (*ell-EESH-uh*) some freshly cut grain and twenty loaves of bread made from the first barley that was harvested. Elisha said, "Give it to the people so they can eat."
  "There's not enough here for a hundred people," his servant said.
  "Just give it to them," Elisha replied. "The Lord has promised there will be more than enough."
So the servant served the bread and grain to the people. They ate and still had some left over, just as the Lord had promised.

The word of the Lord.

Reflection

Like Elisha, Jesus fed crowds of people with a few loaves and had much left over. They show how God's love can take what seems little and make it more than enough for everyone. How can we let God make our little love grow into something great?

Closing

Let us bring our hopes and needs to God, as we pray: **God of holiness, hear our prayer.**

Let us pray with the words that Jesus taught us:

Our Father …

Loving God, have mercy on all your people.
Help us to listen when you call us.
Give us courage to do what you ask.
Keep us close to your heart.
We ask this through Christ our Lord. **Amen.**

[Sing 'alleluia'.]

✞ All make the Sign of the Cross.

July 17, 2019

Thursday Daily Prayer

Introduction

Today we read the last of the stories about Elisha the prophet. This time he cures a foreigner of leprosy. As a result the man comes to believe in the one true God. Jesus cured lepers and welcomed outsiders. But when the religious authorities started to turn against him, he reminded them of this story and how it was a foreigner who found faith in the God of Israel.

☩ All make the Sign of the Cross.

Hymn

A Psalm for July

[Turn to page 130.]

Reading   2 *Kings* 5:1.9-10.14.15

Listen to the words of the second book of the Kings:

Naaman (*NAH-man*) was the commander of the Syrian army. The Lord had helped him and his troops defeat their enemies, so the king of Syria respected Naaman very much. Naaman was a brave soldier, but he had leprosy.
  Naaman left [his country] with his horses and chariots and stopped at the door of Elisha's house. Elisha sent someone outside to say to him, "Go wash seven times in the Jordan River. Then you'll be completely cured."
  Naaman walked down to the Jordan; he waded out into the water and stooped down in it seven times, just as Elisha had told him. Right away, he was cured, and his skin became as smooth as a child's.
  Naaman and his officials went back to Elisha. Naaman stood in front of him and announced, "Now I know that the God of Israel is the only God in the whole world."

The word of the Lord.

Reflection

Once again, what Elisha did reminds us of Jesus. Jesus reached out to people like lepers who were kept apart and ignored. Do we welcome those who are different from us? Do we reach out to those who are made fun of or treated badly?

Closing

Let us bring our hopes and needs to God, as we pray: **God of holiness, hear our prayer.**

Let us pray with the words that Jesus taught us:

Our Father ...

Loving God, have mercy on all your people.
Help us to listen when you call us.
Give us courage to do what you ask.
Keep us close to your heart.
We ask this through Christ our Lord. **Amen.**

[Sing 'alleluia'.]

☩ All make the Sign of the Cross.

July 18, 2019

Friday Daily Prayer

Introduction

Today's reading tells a story from Sunday's gospel that is easy to understand. It is about two sisters who do not agree on how to divide their work. Martha, the unhappy sister, wisely brings her problem to Jesus. He helps her to understand things better.

✞ All make the Sign of the Cross.

Hymn

A Psalm for July

[Turn to page 130.]

Reading *Luke 10:38-42*

Listen to the words of the holy gospel according to Luke:

The Lord and his disciples were travelling along and came to a village. When they got there, a woman named Martha welcomed him into her home. She had a sister named Mary, who sat down in front of the Lord and was listening to what he said. Martha was worried about all that had to be done. Finally, she went to Jesus and said, "Lord, doesn't it bother you that my sister has left me to do all the work by myself? Tell her to come and help me!"
  The Lord answered, "Martha, Martha! You are worried and upset about so many things, but only one thing is necessary. Mary has chosen what is best, and it will not be taken away from her."

The gospel of the Lord.

Reflection

Does Jesus seem unfair to Martha? Why was Mary's choice a better one? Do I ever become so busy with my work or my play that I forget the presence of Jesus in my life, or ignore other people around me?

Closing

Let us all say:
All the ends of the earth
have seen the power of God.
**All the ends of the earth
have seen the power of God.**

Let us bring our hopes and needs to God, as we pray: **Gracious God, hear our prayer.**

Let us pray with the words that Jesus taught us:

Our Father ...

Gracious God,
in the home of Martha and Mary your Son found
a generous welcome,
hearts open to the gospel,
and hands ready to serve.
Bless us with Martha's generous spirit
and Mary's faithful attention to your word.
We make this prayer through Christ our Lord.
Amen.

[Sing 'alleluia'.]

✞ All make the Sign of the Cross.

July 19, 2019

Monday Daily Prayer

Introduction

Today we remember Saint Mary Magdalene (*MAG-duh-lun*). Mary Magdalene was very dear to Jesus. She went with him on his preaching journeys. She followed him to Calvary and stayed with him until he died. She was also one of the women who went to the tomb to anoint his body.

As we hear in today's reading, Mary was the first to see the risen Lord. Because Mary Magdalene brought the good news of Christ's resurrection to the Twelve, she is called 'apostle to the apostles.'

✠ All make the Sign of the Cross.

Hymn

A Psalm for July

[Turn to page 130.]

Reading   *John 20:11.14b–18*

Listen to the words of the holy gospel according to John:

Mary Magdalene (*MAG-duh-lun*) stood crying outside the tomb. She was still weeping, when she stooped down and saw two angels inside.

She turned around and saw Jesus standing there. But she did not know who he was. Jesus asked her, "Why are you crying? Who are you looking for?"

She thought he was the gardener and said, "Sir, if you have taken his body away, please tell me, so I can go and get him." Then Jesus said to her, "Mary!" She turned and said to him, "Teacher."

Jesus told her, "Don't hold on to me! I have not yet gone to the Father. But tell my disciples I am going to the one who is my Father and my God, as well as your Father and your God." Mary Magdalene then went and told the disciples she had seen the Lord. She also told them what he had said to her.

The gospel of the Lord.

Reflection

How did Jesus make Mary aware of his presence? How does he make me aware of his presence? How can I be a messenger of the good news like Mary Magdalene? Who are some holy women who have taught me about Jesus?

Closing

Let us bring our hopes and needs to God, as we pray: **Gentle God, hear our prayer.**

Let us pray with the words that Jesus taught us:

Our Father …

Loving God,
through the joyful words of Mary Magdalene
you bring the good news of your love
to all the peoples of the earth.
Strengthen us to carry that good news
in our lives, in our hearts and in our words.
We ask this through Christ our Lord. **Amen.**

[Sing 'alleluia'.]

✠ All make the Sign of the Cross.

July 22, 2019

Tuesday Daily Prayer

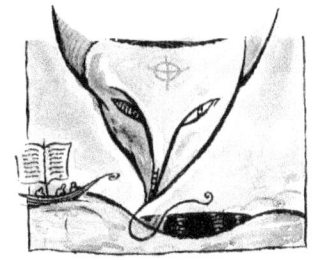

Introduction

Many of the kings of Israel were unfaithful to God and led the people astray. Today we read about one of the good kings, Josiah (*joe-SIGH-uh*). When the scroll with God's Law was found again in the temple, he asked everyone to turn back to God and to obey his commands.

✞ All make the Sign of the Cross.

Hymn

A Psalm for July

[Turn to page 130.]

Reading   2 *Kings* 22:3.8.9.10; 23:1.2.3

Listen to the words of the second book of the Kings:

After Josiah (*joe-SIGH-uh*) had been king for eighteen years, he told Shaphan (*SHAR-fan*), one of his highest officials:
"Go to the Lord's temple."
　While Shaphan was at the temple, Hilkiah (*hill-KIGH-uh*) handed him a book and said, "Look what I found here in the temple – The Book of God's Law."
　Shaphan read it, then went back to Josiah and reported, "The priest Hilkiah gave me this book." Then Shaphan read it out loud.
King Josiah called together the older leaders of Judah and Jerusalem. When everybody was there, he read aloud The Book of God's Law that had been found in the temple.
　After Josiah had finished reading, he stood by one of the columns. He asked the people to promise in the Lord's name to faithfully obey the Lord and to follow his commands. The people agreed to do everything written in the book.

The word of the Lord.

Reflection

For God's people, the Law was a blessing. It taught them how to live well. Jesus summed it all up in one commandment: to love God and our neighbour. How did Jesus show his love for God and others? How can we grow in love?

Closing

Let us bring our hopes and needs to God, as we pray: **God of holiness, hear our prayer.**

Let us pray with the words that Jesus taught us:

Our Father …

Loving God, have mercy on all your people.
Help us to listen when you call us.
Give us courage to do what you ask.
Keep us close to your heart.
We ask this through Christ our Lord. **Amen.**

[Sing 'alleluia'.]

✞ All make the Sign of the Cross.

July 23, 2019

Wednesday Daily Prayer

Introduction

Today we remember Saint Charbel (*SHAR-bell*) of the Lebanese Maronite church. He was born in 1828 in Lebanon. At a young age went to live in a monastery, then became a hermit. He was truly a man of prayer. In 1977 he was named a saint. There are Maronite parishes in Australia and New Zealand.

The story we read today is very sad. It tells of a disaster that happened to God's people about six hundred years before Jesus Christ. A foreign power invades their country, destroys the holy city of Jerusalem, and takes the people into exile in Babylon (*BAB-uh-lon*). Everything seemed lost.

✢ All make the Sign of the Cross.

Hymn

A Psalm for July

[Turn to page 130.]

Reading   2 Kings 25:1.9-11

Listen to the words of the second book of the Kings:

In Zedekiah's (*zed-uh-KIGH-uh's*) ninth year as king, on the tenth day of the tenth month, King Nebuchadnezzar (*neb-yoo-kuhd-NED-zar*) of Babylonia (*bab-i-LOAN-i-uh*) led his entire army to attack Jerusalem.
   In Nebuchadnezzar's nineteenth year as king, Nebuzaradan (*neb-yoo-ZAR-uh-dan*), who was his official in charge of the guards, arrived in Jerusalem. Nebuzaradan burned down the Lord's temple, the king's palace, and every important building in the city, as well as all the houses. Then he ordered the Babylonian soldiers to break down the walls around Jerusalem. He led away as prisoners the people left in the city, including those who had become loyal to Nebuchadnezzar. Only some of the poorest people were left behind to work the vineyards and the fields.

The word of the Lord.

Reflection

This terrible event in the history of Israel is known as the Exile. It seemed like the end. But those who survived kept their faith in God. How can we keep believing and trusting when things seem to go wrong for us? What can help us hope for a fresh start?

Closing

Let us bring our hopes and needs to God, as we pray: **God of holiness, hear our prayer.**

Let us pray with the words that Jesus taught us:

Our Father …

Loving God, have mercy on all your people.
Help us to listen when you call us.
Give us courage to do what you ask.
Keep us close to your heart.
We ask this through Christ our Lord. **Amen.**

[Sing 'alleluia'.]

✢ All make the Sign of the Cross.

July 24, 2019

Thursday Daily Prayer

Introduction

Today is the feast of Saint James the apostle. James and his brother John were the sons of Zebedee (*ZEBB-uh-dee*). They were working as fishermen when Jesus called them to be his disciples. They must have been energetic and excitable people, as Jesus nicknamed them 'sons of thunder.'

James was one of the three closest apostles to Jesus. He was present when Jesus raised the daughter of Jairus (*JEYE-rus*) from the dead and was with Jesus in the Garden of Olives. And he may have been the first of the apostles to die for preaching about Jesus.

✠ All make the Sign of the Cross.

Hymn

A Psalm for July

[Turn to page 130.]

Reading   *Matthew 20:20–21.26-28*

Listen to the words of the holy gospel according to Matthew:

The mother of James and John came to Jesus with her two sons. She knelt down and started begging him to do something for her. Jesus asked her what she wanted, and she said, "When you come into your kingdom, please let one of my sons sit at your right side and the other at your left."

Jesus answered, "If you want to be great, you must be the servant of all the others. And if you want to be first, you must be the slave of the rest. The Son of Man did not come to be a slave master, but a slave who will give his life to rescue many people."

The gospel of the Lord.

Reflection

Do I want the top place wherever I go? What advice does Jesus give about wanting to be great? What kind of a leader was he?

Closing

Let us bring our hopes and needs to God, as we pray: **God of apostles, hear our prayer.**

Let us pray with the words that Jesus taught us:

Our Father ...

Lord God, we thank you for sending apostles to the whole world.
We welcome those who bring your good news.
We pray for them and listen to their teaching.
Call on us, one day, to become apostles too.
We ask this through Christ our Lord. **Amen.**

[Sing 'alleluia'.]

✠ All make the Sign of the Cross.

Friday Daily Prayer

Introduction

In today's reading from the Sunday gospel Jesus teaches us how to pray and to give praise and honour to God. He also teaches us the spirit of forgiveness. Each time we say the Lord's Prayer, we ask God to forgive us, and we promise to forgive others.

✠ All make the Sign of the Cross.

Hymn

A Psalm for July

[Turn to page 130.]

Reading   Luke 11:1-4

Listen to the words of the holy gospel according to Luke:

When Jesus had finished praying, one of his disciples said to him, "Lord, teach us to pray, just as John taught his followers to pray."
   So, Jesus told them, "Pray in this way:
   'Father, help us to honour your name.
   Come and set up your kingdom.
   Give us each day the food we need.
   Forgive our sins,
   as we forgive everyone who has done wrong to us.
   And keep us from being tempted.' "

The gospel of the Lord.

Reflection

This reading is a version of the 'Our Father,' the prayer we call the 'Lord's Prayer.' Can you put each of the five petitions in your own words? What is their importance in our lives?

Closing

Let us bring our hopes and needs to God, as we pray: **Gracious God, hear our prayer.**

Let us pray with the words that Jesus taught us:

Our Father …

Loving God,
you are quick to forgive
all who ask forgiveness.
Show us our mistakes.
Open our hearts to have sorrow for sin.
Help us to ask pardon from those we hurt.
We ask this through Christ our Lord. **Amen.**

[Sing 'alleluia'.]

✠ All make the Sign of the Cross.

July 26, 2019

Monday Daily Prayer

Introduction

On this day we remember Francis Vernon Douglas. Francis was born in New Zealand in 1910. He became a Columban priest and went to the Philippines as a missionary. He worked with the people in a poor parish called Pililla (*puh-LILL-uh*). In 1943, Francis disappeared after being accused of spying. He is remembered for his great courage.

Last week we heard the story of the disaster for the Jewish people called the Exile. Today there is good news. The leader of a new empire, Cyrus (*SIGH-rus*) king of Persia, sends the exiles back to Jerusalem to rebuild the temple and the city. This allows them to begin their life together again as God's chosen people in the Promised Land.

✞ All make the Sign of the Cross.

Hymn

A Psalm for July

[Turn to page 130.]

Reading   *Ezra 1:1-4*

Listen to the words of the book of Ezra:

Years ago the Lord sent Jeremiah (*jeh-ruh-MIGH-uh*) with a message about a promise for the people of Israel. Then in the first year that Cyrus (*SIGH-rus*) was king of Persia, the Lord kept his promise by having Cyrus send this official message to all parts of his kingdom:
"I am King Cyrus of Persia.
   The Lord God of heaven, who is also the God of Israel, has made me the ruler of all nations on earth. And he has chosen me to build a temple for him in Jerusalem, which is in Judah. The Lord God will watch over and encourage any of his people who want to go back to Jerusalem and help build the temple. Everyone else must provide what is needed. They must give money, supplies, and animals, as well as gifts for rebuilding God's temple."

The word of the Lord.

Reflection

Millions of people in the world today are in exile from their homeland. Most of them would love to return home, but would have to start all over again. Can you see that they might feel both happy and worried at the same time? Are there things that you look forward to but are also a little afraid of?

Closing

Let us bring our hopes and needs to God, as we pray: **God of holiness, hear our prayer.**

Let us pray with the words that Jesus taught us:

Our Father ...

Loving God, have mercy on all your people.
Help us to listen when you call us.
Give us courage to do what you ask.
Keep us close to your heart.
We ask this through Christ our Lord. **Amen.**

[Sing 'alleluia'.]

✞ All make the Sign of the Cross.

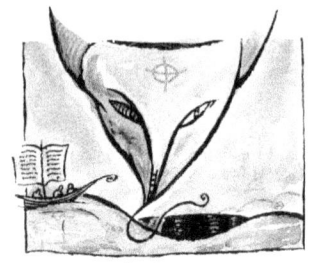

Tuesday Daily Prayer

Introduction

When the exiles returned home to Jerusalem from exile in Babylon, they had to build the city again. Their great goal was to rebuild the temple. It was a long and difficult task, but with much encouragement they succeeded. It was a great achievement and something to celebrate well.

✞ All make the Sign of the Cross.

Hymn

A Psalm for July

[Turn to page 130.]

Reading   Ezra 6:14.16.18

Listen to the words of the book of Ezra:

With great success the Jewish leaders continued working on the temple, while Haggai (HAGG-eye) and Zechariah (zeck-uh-RIGH-uh) encouraged them by their preaching. And so, the temple was completed at the command of the God of Israel and by the orders of kings Cyrus (SIGH-rus), Darius (duh-RIGH-us), and Artaxerxes (ah-tuh-GSERK-sees) of Persia.

The people of Israel, the priests, the Levites, and everyone else who had returned from exile were happy and celebrated as they dedicated God's temple.
  Then the priests and Levites were assigned their duties in God's temple in Jerusalem, according to the instructions Moses had written.

The word of the Lord.

Reflection

Why was it so important for the people to rebuild the temple? What did the temple mean to them? What is the importance of a parish church?

Closing

Let us bring our hopes and needs to God, as we pray: **God of holiness, hear our prayer.**

Let us pray with the words that Jesus taught us:

Our Father …

Loving God, have mercy on all your people.
Help us to listen when you call us.
Give us courage to do what you ask.
Keep us close to your heart.
We ask this through Christ our Lord. **Amen.**

[Sing 'alleluia'.]

✞ All make the Sign of the Cross.

Wednesday Daily Prayer

(Reminder: The Psalm for August is on page 148. Make a copy for each member of the class.)

Introduction

After the people came home from exile, they rebuilt the temple and their way of life. They were able to celebrate their feast days again. We read about one of these today. It's called the Festival of Shelters. It reminded them of their journey through the desert and of the Law that God gave them through Moses. Jewish people still celebrate this feast today. They call it Sukkot or the Feast of Tabernacles.

✝ All make the Sign of the Cross.

Hymn

A Psalm for July

[Turn to page 130.]

Reading   *Nehemiah 8:13-14.17-18*

Listen to the words of the book of Nehemiah (*nee-huh-MIGH-uh*):

On the second day of the seventh month, the leaders of all the family groups came together with the priests and the Levites, so Ezra could teach them the Law that the Lord had given to Moses. They learned from the Law that the people of Israel were to live in shelters when they celebrated the festival in the seventh month of the year.
    Everyone who had returned from Babylonia (*bab-i-LOAN-i-uh*) built shelters. They lived in them and joyfully celebrated the Festival of Shelters for the first time since the days of Joshua son of Nun. On each of the first seven days of the festival, Ezra read to the people from God's Law. Then on the eighth day, everyone gathered for worship, just as the Law had said they must.

The word of the Lord.

Reflection

This feast reminded Jews of being pilgrims guided by God's Law. What do Christians do to remember they are on a journey of faith? What guides them on their way?

Closing

Let us bring our hopes and needs to God, as we pray: **God of holiness, hear our prayer.**

Let us pray with the words that Jesus taught us:

Our Father ...

Loving God, have mercy on all your people.
Help us to listen when you call us.
Give us courage to do what you ask.
Keep us close to your heart.
We ask this through Christ our Lord. **Amen.**

[Sing 'alleluia'.]

✝ All make the Sign of the Cross.

July 31, 2019

The Psalms Are Cosmic Chants

Have you ever watched nature shows on television? Aren't they amazing? We can see the extraordinary lives of birds, animals, fish, insects and plants in a way that no human beings have ever seen them before. The photography is mind-blowing. It shows unbelievable beauty as well as the brutal struggle that some creatures have to survive. How they find ways of adapting to their environment is incredible.

God's first people, the Israelites, did not have telescopes, microscopes, time-lapse cameras or underwater videocams to show them the wonders of nature. But they did have sharp eyes and keen ears and they used them well. They watched the stars, tuned in to the seasons, and kept a close eye on the weather. They observed the ways of animals, tame and wild. They learned how to grow crops and fruit. They knew their way around the plains and valleys and rocky ranges of their homeland.

And all that they saw led them to praise God, the Creator of all things. They came to believe that everything came from God's hands and stayed in God's hands. It was all so wonderful that they couldn't stop praising God. The psalms they prayed are cosmic chants:

"Our Lord, by your wisdom you made so many things; the whole earth is covered with your living creatures." (*Psalm 104, August*)

"You take care of the earth and send rain to help the soil grow all kinds of crops." (*Psalm 65, July*).

They even went further. They even imagined the whole of creation joining in their song of praise:

"Bless God, sun and moon ... Bless God, stars of heaven ... Bless God, light and darkness. Give praise and glory." (*Daniel, October*).

The psalms help us keep our sense of wonder at the world in which we live. Once upon a time all we wanted to do was to conquer nature and use it up. Now more than ever we need to learn how to live in harmony with it. The psalms remind us that we are not masters of the universe. Only God is Master. We are stewards of God's wonderful world.

August

Thursday, August 1,
to Friday, August 30

Ordinary Time ~ August 2019
Looking Ahead

About the Month

Moving into August means that we are beginning to move out of winter. We begin to observe some changes. We will see new signs of life beginning to stir in the earth. As the sap rises in the trees, some early leaves and buds may begin to grow. We will really begin to notice the longer days.

Two Roman rulers from ancient times have months of the year named after them. One is July, named after Julius Caesar, and the other is August, named after his grandnephew Emperor Augustus Caesar. It was after Augustus Caesar defeated Antony and Cleopatra that he became emperor of Rome and so he was honoured by naming a month after him. Originally, August had only 30 days but, so that it would not seen as inferior to July which honoured Julius Caesar, it was lengthened to 31 days.

August 1 is known as the birthday of thoroughbred horses. They are bred to be born on this day so that when the time comes for the foal to be broken in, it is the right time of the year for them to race!

As we begin August, we are in the seventeenth week of Ordinary Time. Sunday is the heart of Ordinary Time. We count Sunday by Sunday until, in November, we reach the 34th Sunday, which is the Feast of Christ the King.

Readings

During August our readings will come from two long and important letters that the apostle Paul wrote to the Christians in Corinth. Corinth was a large port city in southern Greece. It was a centre of power for the Roman Empire and a wealthy trading post. People from many parts of the world and with many different beliefs lived there. Paul preached the gospel and founded the church there. The community was very blessed but also troubled. Paul wrote to them to teach and advise them.

Our readings for Fridays will anticipate the gospels for the following Sunday. They will be the Sunday readings from the Eighteenth to the Twenty-Second Sundays in Ordinary Time. This keeps us connected with Christian assemblies who will hear the same reading on the actual Sunday.

Feasts and Other Commemorations

- The feast of the Transfiguration on August 6. It is a celebration of the life and glory of God that shone out in Jesus like a brilliant light. God's message was to listen to Jesus. But on this day we also remember the many thousands who died in the atomic bombing of Hiroshima, Japan, in 1945.
- On August 8 we remember Saint Mary MacKillop, who is Australia's first saint. Known as Mary of the Cross, she began the Australian religious order named the Sisters of Saint Joseph. She is remembered for her concern that children in isolated places of Australia be educated and also for her unselfish care for the poor.

- On August 15 we celebrate the feast of the Assumption of Mary. The feast of the Assumption celebrates Mary's sharing in the new life won by her son's victory over death.
- August 9 is the International Day of the World's Indigenous People (observed here on August 12). It is a day to become more aware of the problems faced by the original or first peoples of countries. We also remember, people who have fought and continue to fight for indigenous rights.
- Sunday September 1 is Father's Day. We will remember and pray for fathers and all those who are father to us on Thursday August 29.

Preparation for August

The Psalm for August is Psalm 104 and is on page 148. In this psalm, we join with the psalmist in praising God for the wonders of God's creation. Make a copy for each member of the class.

As we pray the psalm let us remember that we are praying to God with God's own words.

Make sure that you give attention to your prayer space so that it looks fresh and cared for. The liturgical colour for Ordinary Time is green, a colour of life and hope.

Suggested Hymns

For the feast of the Transfiguration see Feasts of the Lord in the hymn chart. For the feast of the Assumption select a hymn for a feast of Mary. See the hymn chart on pages viii-ix for other selections.

A Psalm for August

Psalm 104:1, 5, 13-15, 24, 30

LEADER
I praise you, Lord God, with all my heart.
ALL
With all my heart I sing praise.

SIDE A
You built foundations for the earth,
and it will never be shaken.
From your home above you send rain on the hills and water the earth.

SIDE B
**You let the earth produce grass for cattle,
plants for our food,
wine to cheer us up,
olive oil for our skin, and grain for our health.**

SIDE A
Our Lord, by your wisdom you made so many things;
the whole earth is covered with your living creatures.

SIDE B
**You created all of them by your Spirit,
and you give new life to the earth.**

LEADER
I praise you, Lord God, with all my heart.
ALL
With all my heart I sing praise.

Glory be to the Father, and to the Son,
and to the Holy Spirit:
as it was in the beginning, is now,
and ever shall be,
world without end. Amen. Alleluia.

[Turn back to Daily Prayer for today.]

Thursday Daily Prayer

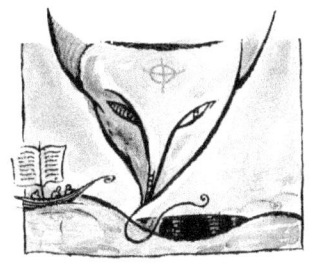

[Reminder: The Psalm is on page 148. Make a copy for each member of the class.]

Introduction

During August our readings will come from two long and important letters that the apostle Paul wrote to the Christians in Corinth. Corinth was a large port city in southern Greece. It was a centre of power for the Roman Empire and a wealthy trading post.

People from many parts of the world and with many different beliefs lived there. Paul preached the gospel and founded the church there. The community was very blessed but also troubled. Paul wrote to them to teach and advise them.

✛ All make the Sign of the Cross.

Hymn

A Psalm for August

[Turn to page 148.]

Reading   1 Corinthians 1:1-6

Listen to the words of the apostle Paul.

From Paul, chosen by God to be an apostle of Christ Jesus, and from Sosthenes (*SOSS-the-nees*), who is also a follower.

To God's church in Corinth. Christ Jesus chose you to be his very own people, and you worship in his name, as we and all others do who call him Lord.

My prayer is that God our Father and the Lord Jesus Christ will be kind to you and will bless you with peace!

I never stop thanking my God for being kind enough to give you Christ Jesus, who helps you speak and understand so well. Now you are certain that everything we told you about our Lord Christ Jesus is true.

The word of the Lord.

Reflection

Many of Paul's letters begin beautifully with a greeting and a prayer of thanks. How does he greet the Corinthians? What does he thank God for? What do you thank God for?

Closing

Let us bring our hopes and needs to God, as we pray: **God of all grace, hear our prayer.**

Let us pray with the words that Jesus taught us:

Our Father ...

God, always loving,
you call us to be ready to follow Jesus your son,
and to be generous in his service.
Teach us to be fearless and faithful even in hard times.
We ask this through Christ our Lord. **Amen**.

[Sing 'alleluia'.]

✛ All make the Sign of the Cross.

August 1, 2019

Friday Daily Prayer

Introduction

The rich man in today's parable from the Sunday gospel is very selfish. Listen to how many times he keeps on saying, 'I', 'I', 'I'! All he can think about is himself and his own possessions. He never shares what he has or thinks about how God gives the gifts of rain and good soil to help his crops grow. He even forgets that his own life is a gift from God. He gets a great shock when God reminds him of this and tells him that it is time for him to die.

✞ All make the Sign of the Cross.

Hymn

A Psalm for August

[Turn to page 148.]

Reading　　　　Luke 12:15-21

Listen to the words of the holy gospel according to Luke:

Jesus said to the crowd, "Don't be greedy! Owning a lot of things won't make your life safe." So Jesus told them this story: A rich man's farm produced a big crop, and he said to himself, "What can I do? I don't have a place large enough to store everything." Later, he said, "I know what I'll do. I'll tear down my barns and build bigger ones, where I can store all my grain and other goods. Then I'll say to myself, 'You have stored up enough good things to last for years to come. Live it up! Eat, drink, and enjoy yourself.'"

But God said to him, "You fool! Tonight you will die. Then who will get what you have stored up?"

"This is what happens to people who store up everything for themselves, but are poor in the sight of God."

The gospel of the Lord.

Reflection

What could this story tell us about money, clothes, the latest mobile phones, computer games and iPads? Why are possessions the source of so much trouble between people? How do I handle my money and possessions?

Closing

Let us bring our hopes and needs to God, as we pray: **God of the poor, hear our prayer.**

Let us pray with the words that Jesus taught us:

Our Father …

Merciful God,
we have been cared for and protected.
We have eaten and been filled.
Show us, your children,
how to share what we have been given.
We ask this through Christ our Lord. **Amen.**

[Sing 'alleluia'.]

✞ All make the Sign of the Cross.

August 2, 2019

Monday Daily Prayer

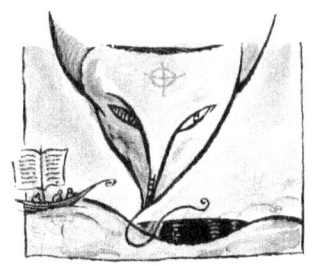

Introduction

In today's reading Paul tells the Christians at Corinth that the cross of Christ is good news. This message sounded very strange to some of Paul's listeners. For his fellow Jews it was too difficult to understand and accept. For people who weren't Jewish – they're called Gentiles (*JEN-tiles*) – Paul's message about the cross seemed mad. But it made sense to Paul.

✢ All make the Sign of the Cross.

Hymn

A Psalm for August

[Turn to page 148.]

Reading   *1 Corinthians 1:17.18.23-25*

Listen to the words of the apostle Paul.

Christ sent me to tell the good news without using big words that would make the cross of Christ lose its power.
   The message about the cross doesn't make any sense to lost people. But for those of us who are being saved, it is God's power at work. We preach that Christ was nailed to a cross. Most Jews have problems with this, and most Gentiles think it is foolish. Our message is God's power and wisdom for the Jews and the Greeks that he has chosen. Even when God is foolish, he is wiser than everyone else, and even when God is weak, he is stronger than everyone else.

The word of the Lord.

Reflection

Paul teaches that God did something strange and foolish – he became a weak human being who died on the cross. How is this good news for us? How does it show that love is the most powerful thing of all?

Closing

Let us bring our hopes and needs to God, as we pray: **God of all grace, hear our prayer.**

Let us pray with the words that Jesus taught us:

Our Father …

God, always loving,
you call us to be ready to follow Jesus your son,
and to be generous in his service.
Teach us to be fearless and faithful even in hard times.
We ask this through Christ our Lord. **Amen.**

[Sing 'alleluia'.]

✢ All make the Sign of the Cross.

August 5, 2019

Tuesday Daily Prayer

Introduction

Today is the feast of the Transfiguration of the Lord. It is also the anniversary of the dropping of the first atomic bomb on Hiroshima (hih-ROSH-ih-ma), Japan, in 1945.

The Transfiguration is a celebration of the life and glory of God, which shone out in Jesus like a brilliant light. Hiroshima is a day of sad memories of the death of seventy thousand people caused by war and the destructive white blast of the bomb.

If we obey the Father's mountain message from the cloud and listen to Jesus, we will choose the way of life and peace, not violence and death.

✞ All make the Sign of the Cross.

Hymn

A Psalm for August

[Turn to page 148.]

Reading   Luke 9:28-31, 33, 34-36

Listen to the words of the holy gospel according to Luke:

Jesus took Peter, John and James with him and went up on a mountain to pray. While he was praying, his face changed, and his clothes became shining white. Suddenly Moses and Elijah (ee-LYE-juh) were speaking with him. They appeared in heavenly glory and talked about all that Jesus' death in Jerusalem would mean.

Peter said to Jesus, "Master, it is good for us to be here! Let us make three shelters, one for you, one for Moses, and one for Elijah." While Peter was still speaking, a shadow from a cloud passed over them, and they were frightened as the cloud covered them. From the cloud a voice spoke, "This is my chosen son. Listen to what he says!"

After the voice had spoken, Peter, John, and James saw only Jesus.

The gospel of the Lord.

Reflection

What does the voice tell us about Jesus? Do I obey the command to listen? How can our remembrance of Hiroshima (hih-ROSH-ih-ma) today, urge us to work for peace and for an end to violence?

Closing

Let us bring our hopes and needs to God, as we pray: **God of light and love, hear our prayer.**

Let us pray with the words that Jesus taught us:

Our Father ...

God of glory,
it is good for us to be here.
Reveal your Son to us now
in the message of the prophets
and the witness of the apostles.
Help us listen to his voice
and welcome him in faith.
We ask this through Christ our Lord. **Amen.**

[Sing 'alleluia'.]

✞ All make the Sign of the Cross.

August 6, 2019

Wednesday Daily Prayer

Introduction

One of the problems in the church at Corinth was that people were choosing their own favourite leader. This broke the community up into rival groups. Some wanted to follow Paul, others Apollos, and others Peter. Paul makes it clear that this is wrong. These preachers are not in competition. They are all God's servants.

✢ All make the Sign of the Cross.

Hymn

A Psalm for August

[Turn to page 148.]

Reading   1 Corinthians 3:4-9

Listen to the words of the apostle Paul.

Some of you say that you follow me, and others claim to follow Apollos. Isn't that how ordinary people behave? Apollos and I are merely servants who helped you to have faith. It was the Lord who made it all happen. I planted the seeds, Apollos watered them, but God made them sprout and grow. What matters isn't those who planted or watered, but God who made the plants grow. The one who plants is just as important as the one who waters. And each one will be paid for what they do. Apollos and I work together for God, and you are God's garden and God's building.

The word of the Lord.

Reflection

Like Jesus, Paul is not trying to make a big name for himself. He is God's servant. Do I realise that all my talents are God's gift to me? Do I appreciate other people's gifts? Do I remember to thank God?

Closing

Let us bring our hopes and needs to God, as we pray: **God of all grace, hear our prayer.**

Let us pray with the words that Jesus taught us:

Our Father …

God, always loving,
you call us to be ready to follow Jesus your son,
and to be generous in his service.
Teach us to be fearless and faithful even in hard times.
We ask this through Christ our Lord. **Amen.**

[Sing 'alleluia'.]

✢ All make the Sign of the Cross.

Thursday Daily Prayer

Introduction

Today is the feast day of Saint Mary MacKillop, who is Australia's first saint. Born in Melbourne in 1842, Mary grew up in Penola, a small town in South Australia. In 1866, Mary began a religious order named the Sisters of Saint Joseph. She and her sisters opened schools in isolated places and served the poor in many other ways. Their unselfish work won the respect of many people.

It was usual for bishops to decide how women religious should live, but Mother Mary received permission from the pope for her sisters to govern themselves. Because of this, some bishops tried to interfere in her work and she was unjustly accused of being a poor leader. This caused Mother Mary great suffering, but instead of becoming bitter, she tried to accept it as willingly as Jesus had accepted his cross. Mary MacKillop died in Sydney on August 8 in 1909.

✝ All make the Sign of the Cross.

Hymn

A Psalm for August

[Turn to page 148.]

Reading *Colossians 3:12-14*

Listen to the words of the apostle Paul:

God loves you and has chosen you as his own special people. So be gentle, kind, humble, meek, and patient. Put up with each other, and forgive anyone who does you wrong, just as Christ has forgiven you. Love is more important than anything else. It is what ties everything completely together.

The word of the Lord.

Reflection

What do you know about Mary MacKillop? In what ways did she put Paul's advice about love into practice? Were there any people that she forgave for treating her badly? Why is she a model leader for Australia?

Closing

Let us bring our hopes and needs to God, as we pray: **God of strength, hear our prayer.**

Let us pray with the words that Jesus taught us:

Our Father ...

Loving God,
you show us in Mary MacKillop
a woman of faith
who accepted the cross of suffering.
Through her example,
may we grow in the selfless love
and deep respect she showed for all.
We ask this through Christ our Lord. **Amen.**

[Sing 'alleluia'.]

✝ All make the Sign of the Cross.

August 8, 2019

Friday Daily Prayer

Introduction

The gospel for this Sunday speaks about servants who are faithful and wise, and servants who are lazy when the master is away. A responsible follower of Jesus is always ready to listen to him and to do his will day in and day out.

✞ All make the Sign of the Cross.

Hymn

A Psalm for August

[Turn to page 148.]

Reading   Luke 12:41-48

Listen to the words of the holy gospel according to Luke:

Jesus said to Peter, "Who are the faithful and wise servants? Who are the ones the master will put in charge of giving the other servants their food supplies at the proper time? Servants are fortunate if the master comes and finds them doing their job. A servant who is always faithful will surely be put in charge of everything the master owns.

"But suppose one of the servants thinks that the master won't return until late. Suppose that servant starts beating all the other servants and eats and drinks and gets drunk. If that happens, the master will come on a day and at a time when the servant least expects him. That servant will then be punished and thrown out with the servants who can't be trusted.

"If servants are not ready or willing to do what their master wants them to do, they will be beaten hard. But servants who don't know what their master wants them to do won't be beaten so hard for doing wrong. If God has been generous with you, he will expect you to serve him well. But if he has been more than generous, he will expect you to serve him even better."

The gospel of the Lord.

Reflection

Who do you think is the "master" in this parable? Who are the "servants"? What responsibilities do you think Jesus gives to those who are "put in charge" of the master's household? Do I ever misuse gifts or a responsibility I have been given?

Closing

Let us bring our hopes and needs to God, as we pray: **Generous God, hear our prayer.**

Let us pray with the words that Jesus taught us:

Our Father …

God, always loving,
you call us to be ready to follow Jesus your son,
and to be generous in his service.
Teach us to be fearless and faithful even in hard times.
We ask this through Christ our Lord. **Amen.**

[Sing 'alleluia'.]

✞ All make the Sign of the Cross.

August 9, 2019

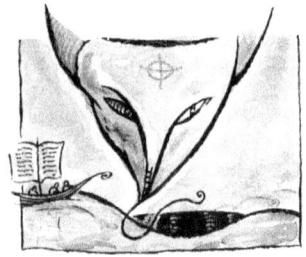

Monday Daily Prayer

Introduction

Friday was the International Day of the World's Indigenous (*in-DIDGE-en-us*) People. This is a day to become more aware of the original or first peoples of countries and the problems they face. We also remember, people who have fought for indigenous rights.

Whina Cooper was one of the great Maori leaders of the 20th Century. She fought for the rights of the original people of New Zealand. 'Mum' Shirl was a Wiradjuri (*wuh-RAJ-uri*) woman. She lived most of her life in Sydney where she fought strongly for aboriginal rights. She visited gaols and was like a 'mum' to prisoners. She died in 1998.

In today's reading Paul writes about his mission as an apostle.

✢ All make the Sign of the Cross.

Hymn

A Psalm for August

[Turn to page 148.]

Reading   *1 Corinthians 9:1.22-25*

Listen to the words of the apostle Paul.

I am free. I am an apostle. I have seen the Lord Jesus and have led you to have faith in him. When I am with people whose faith is weak, I live as they do to win them. I do everything I can to win everyone I possibly can. I do all this for the good news, because I want to share in its blessings.

You know that many runners enter a race, and only one of them wins the prize. So run to win! Athletes work hard to win a crown that cannot last, but we do it for a crown that will last forever.

The word of the Lord.

Reflection

Paul doesn't just tell people what to believe or how to behave. He tries to reach out to them and work with them as they are. Can you put yourself in someone else's shoes and understand the way they feel? Is this an important lesson to learn?

Closing

Let us bring our hopes and needs to God, as we pray: **God of all grace, hear our prayer.**

Let us pray with the words that Jesus taught us:

Our Father …

God, always loving,
you call us to be ready to follow Jesus your son,
and to be generous in his service.
Teach us to be fearless and faithful even in hard times.
We ask this through Christ our Lord. **Amen.**

[Sing 'alleluia'.]

✢ All make the Sign of the Cross.

August 12, 2019

Tuesday Daily Prayer

Introduction

Today we remember Florence Nightingale, known around the world for her dedication to nursing. While she was still quite young she made visits to the sick in local villages, though nursing was not considered suitable for well-educated women.

During the Crimean (*cry-MEE-un*) War, Florence worked in military hospitals and nursed the wounded. At first the doctors did not want nurses there, but she soon gained their respect. Her great achievement was to make nursing a respected profession for women.

Today's reading tells the story of the Last Supper at which Jesus gave us the mystery of the eucharist. This is what we do at every Mass.

✞ All make the Sign of the Cross.

Hymn

A Psalm for August

[Turn to page 148.]

Reading   *1 Corinthians 11:23-26*

Listen to the words of the apostle Paul.

I have already told you what the Lord Jesus did on the night he was betrayed. And it came from the Lord himself.

He took some bread in his hands. Then after he had given thanks, he broke it and said, "This is my body, which is given for you. Eat this and remember me."

After the meal, Jesus took a cup of wine in his hands and said, "This is my blood, and with it God makes his new agreement with you. Drink this and remember me."
The Lord meant that when you eat this bread and drink from this cup, you tell about his death until he comes.

The word of the Lord.

Reflection

As Jesus commanded, the church remembers him by blessing bread and wine and sharing them in communion. What does bread mean to us? What about wine? What is the "new agreement" that God makes by means of this holy meal?

Closing

Let us bring our hopes and needs to God, as we pray: **God of all grace, hear our prayer.**

Let us pray with the words that Jesus taught us:

Our Father ...

God, always loving,
you call us to be ready to follow Jesus your son,
and to be generous in his service.
Teach us to be fearless and faithful even in hard times.
We ask this through Christ our Lord. **Amen.**

[Sing 'alleluia'.]

✞ All make the Sign of the Cross.

August 13, 2019

Wednesday Daily Prayer

Introduction

Today we remember a modern saint, Maximilian Kolbe (*max-i-MILL-yun KOL-bee*), a Polish priest who is honoured for his bravery and generosity.

During the Second World War, Father Kolbe risked his life by giving shelter to thousands of Polish people. Early in 1941 he was arrested and sent to a cruel prison camp. He often gave away his small ration of food to other prisoners. When ten men were chosen for execution, Father Kolbe took the place of one who had a wife and children. He was declared a saint in 1982.

In today's reading Paul writes that all our different gifts come the same Spirit of God.

✝ All make the Sign of the Cross.

Hymn

A Psalm for August

[Turn to page 148.]

Reading   *1 Corinthians 12:7-11*

Listen to the words of the apostle Paul.

The Spirit has given each of us a special way of serving others. Some of us can speak with wisdom, while others can speak with knowledge, but these gifts come from the same Spirit. To others the Spirit has given great faith or the power to heal the sick or the power to work mighty miracles. Some of us are prophets, and some of us recognize when God's Spirit is present. Others can speak different kinds of languages, and still others can tell what these languages mean. But it is the Spirit who does all this and decides which gifts to give to each of us.

The word of the Lord.

Reflection

Different people have different gifts. What are your best gifts? Are you able to be glad for other people's gifts? How can everyone's gifts work together for good?

Closing

Let us bring our hopes and needs to God, as we pray: **God of all grace, hear our prayer.**

Let us pray with the words that Jesus taught us:

Our Father ...

God, always loving,
you call us to be ready to follow Jesus your son,
and to be generous in his service.
Teach us to be fearless and faithful even in hard times.

We ask this through Christ our Lord. **Amen.**

[Sing 'alleluia'.]

✝ All make the Sign of the Cross.

August 14, 2019

Thursday Daily Prayer

Introduction

Today we celebrate the feast called the Assumption of Mary into heaven. It celebrates Mary's total sharing in the new life won by her son's death and resurrection. It is the national feast for New Zealand.

In today's reading we hear Mary's song of praise for the wonderful things God has done for her in making her the mother of Jesus. In life, she was the first among her son's disciples. In death she joyfully meets her own son in heaven.

✞ All make the Sign of the Cross.

Hymn

A Psalm for August

[Turn to page 148.]

Reading *Luke 1:46-49*

Listen to the words of the holy gospel according to Luke:

Mary said:
With all my heart I praise the Lord,
and I am glad because of God my Saviour.
He cares for me, his humble servant.
From now on,
all people will say God has blessed me.
God All-Powerful has done great things for me
and his name is holy.

The gospel of the Lord.

Reflection

Mary's life and death were a wonderful example of praise and thanksgiving to God. What is one thing for which I can praise and thank God? Is there anything about Mary's life, which could help me to be a better follower of Jesus? What images of Mary do we have in our classroom and in our homes? What do they tell us about Mary?

Closing

Let us bring our hopes and needs to God, as we pray: **God of holiness, hear our prayer.**

Let us pray with the words that Jesus taught us:

Our Father ...

Mary our mother,
you sheltered Jesus in your own body,
raised him with a mother's care,
and followed him in faith.
With you, we celebrate God's saving love.

Let us all say:
**Hail Mary, full of grace,
the Lord is with you!
Blessed are you among women,
and blessed is the fruit
of your womb, Jesus.
Holy Mary, Mother of God,
prayer for us sinners,
now and at the hour of our death. Amen.**

[Sing 'alleluia'.]

✞ All make the Sign of the Cross.

August 15, 2019

Friday Daily Prayer

Introduction

Sometimes the things that Jesus says in the gospels can be difficult to understand or to put into practice. Today's short reading is one of these. It's a puzzle when Jesus says he did not come to bring peace. Just as he had to make the hard choice to risk his life, so his followers too will have to make tough decisions. To put Jesus first may put them in conflict with others, even members of their own families.

✠ All make the Sign of the Cross.

Hymn

A Psalm for August

[Turn to page 148.]

Reading   *Luke 12:22.59-51*

Jesus said to his disciples:
I came to set fire to the earth, and I wish it were already on fire! I am going to be put to a hard test. And I will have to suffer a lot of pain until it is over. Do you think that I came to bring peace to earth? No indeed! I came to make people choose sides.

The gospel of the Lord.

Reflection

It isn't always easy to stick to what we know is right and true. Have you ever had to make a hard choice that others did not agree with? What gave you the courage?

Closing

Let us bring our hopes and needs to God, as we pray: **God and Father of Jesus, hear our prayer.**

Let us pray with the words that Jesus taught us:

Our Father …

God, always loving,
you call us your children
and remain with us even in times of difficulty.
Help us to be always faithful,
and strengthen us in times of trouble.
We ask this through Christ our Lord. **Amen.**

[Sing 'alleluia'.]

✠ All make the Sign of the Cross.

August 16, 2019

Monday Daily Prayer

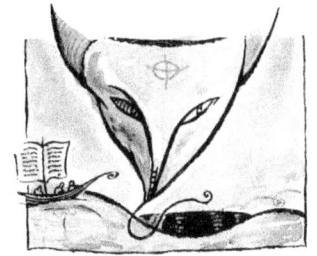

Introduction

Today we remember Brother Roger Schütz. He called together a community of brothers in the French village of Taizé (*TAY-zay*) during the Second World War. His great desire was for reconciliation and love between Christians. Millions of young people from around the world have made their way to Taizé to share in the life and prayer of the community. Tragically Brother Roger was killed while at prayer with a large crowd in the community's church.

Today's reading is a very famous hymn in praise of love.

✢ All make the Sign of the Cross.

Hymn

A Psalm for August

[Turn to page 148.]

Reading   *1 Corinthians 13:1-8*

Listen to the words of the apostle Paul.

What if I could speak all languages of humans and of angels?
   If I did not love others, I would be nothing more than a noisy gong or a clanging cymbal. What if I could prophesy and understand all secrets and all knowledge?
And what if I had faith that moved mountains? I would be nothing, unless I loved others.
What if I gave away all that I owned
   and let myself be burned alive?
I would gain nothing, unless I loved others.
Love is kind and patient, never jealous, boastful, proud, or rude.
Love isn't selfish or quick tempered.
It doesn't keep a record of wrongs that others do.
Love rejoices in the truth, but not in evil.
Love is always supportive, loyal, hopeful, and trusting.
Love never fails!

The word of the Lord.

Reflection

Have you heard this reading before? It is very popular. Paul teaches us that nothing is more important than love. How does Paul describe love? Are there any other words you would use to say what love is?

Closing

Let us bring our hopes and needs to God, as we pray: **God of all grace, hear our prayer.**

Let us pray with the words that Jesus taught us:

Our Father ...

God, always loving,
you call us to be ready to follow Jesus your son,
and to be generous in his service.
Teach us to be fearless and faithful even in hard times.
We ask this through Christ our Lord. **Amen.**

[Sing 'alleluia'.]

✢ All make the Sign of the Cross.

Tuesday Daily Prayer

Introduction

In his letters Paul sometimes includes a short hymn or poem or saying that sums up the good news. Today's reading is one of these. The key belief that Christians have is that Jesus Christ died for us and rose to life again. His death and resurrection have brought us into friendship with God.

✞ All make the Sign of the Cross.

Hymn

A Psalm for August

[Turn to page 148.]

Reading   1 Corinthians 15:1.2.3.4-7

Listen to the words of the apostle Paul.

My friends, I want you to remember the message that I preached and that you believed and trusted. You will be saved by this message, if you hold firmly to it.
Christ died for our sins, as the Scriptures say.
He was buried,
and three days later he was raised to life,
 as the Scriptures say.
Christ appeared to Peter, then to the twelve.
After this, he appeared to more than five hundred other followers.
Most of them are still alive, but some have died.
He also appeared to James,
 and then to all of the apostles.

The word of the Lord.

Reflection

The word "gospel" means good news. What is this good news? What are the most important things that Christians believe?

Closing

Let us bring our hopes and needs to God, as we pray: **God of all grace, hear our prayer.**

Let us pray with the words that Jesus taught us:

Our Father ...

God, always loving,
you call us to be ready to follow Jesus your son,
and to be generous in his service.
Teach us to be fearless and faithful even in hard times.
We ask this through Christ our Lord. **Amen.**

[Sing 'alleluia'.]

✞ All make the Sign of the Cross.

August 20, 2019

Wednesday Daily Prayer

Introduction

On this day we remember three Australian War Nurses who served in World War II. They are Vivian Bullwinkel from South Australia, Betty Jeffrey from Tasmania, and Wilma Young from Victoria. They were taken as prisoners of war in Sumatra, and during that time, under terrible conditions, they nursed the ill and the dying.

Often they were without food, clothing, shelter, bedding and adequate medical supplies. These three women survived the war and continued to work in different parts of Australia. They are remembered for their courage, endurance and bravery.

Today we begin reading from Paul's second letter to the Christians at Corinth. Like the first, it begins with a greeting and a prayer. Later on Paul deals with some difficult problems in the community, but this does not stop him from starting the letter with these beautiful words of faith.

☩ All make the Sign of the Cross.

Hymn

A Psalm for August

[Turn to page 148.]

Reading   2 Corinthians 1:1-4

Listen to the words of the apostle Paul.

From Paul, chosen by God to be an apostle of Jesus Christ, and from Timothy, who is also a follower.

To God's church in Corinth and to all of God's people in Achaia (*uh-KAI-uh*).

I pray that God our Father and the Lord Jesus Christ will be kind to you and will bless you with peace!

Praise God, the Father of our Lord Jesus Christ! The Father is a merciful God, who always gives us comfort. He comforts us when we are in trouble, so that we can share that same comfort with others in trouble.

The word of the Lord.

Reflection

What is Paul's prayer for the Christians at Corinth? What does he teach them about God and about Jesus? How can we share God's comfort with others?

Closing

Let us bring our hopes and needs to God, as we pray: **God of all grace, hear our prayer.**

Let us pray with the words that Jesus taught us:

Our Father …

God, always loving,
you call us to be ready to follow Jesus your son,
and to be generous in his service.
Teach us to be fearless and faithful even in hard times.
We ask this through Christ our Lord. **Amen.**

[Sing 'alleluia'.]

☩ All make the Sign of the Cross.

August 21, 2019

Thursday Daily Prayer

Introduction

Today we remember Blessed Frederic Ozanam (OZ-uh-nam). A family man and scholar, Ozanam was the principal founder of the Saint Vincent de Paul Society whose aim is to serve the poor. Throughout his life, his simple hope was to "become better – to do a little good." Today there are thousands of Saint Vincent de Paul societies in 131 countries. Ozanam died at the age of 40 in 1853 and was declared 'Blessed' by Pope John Paul II in 1997.

In today's reading Paul sums up Jesus Christ in one word. That word is "Yes!" Jesus is God's "Yes" to us, and at the same time is our "Yes" (or "**Amen**") to God. All of God's promises to us have come true in Jesus. And all our gratitude has been given to God by Jesus.

✞ All make the Sign of the Cross.

Hymn

A Psalm for August

[Turn to page 148.]

Reading   2 Corinthians 1:18-19a.20-22

Listen to the words of the apostle Paul.

God can be trusted, and so can I, when I say that our answer to you has always been "Yes" and never "No." This is because Jesus Christ the Son of God is always "Yes" and never "No." Christ says "Yes" to all of God's promises. That's why we have Christ to say "**Amen**" for us to the glory of God. And so God makes it possible for you and us to stand firmly together with Christ. God is also the one who chose us and put his Spirit in our hearts to show that we belong only to him.

The word of the Lord.

Reflection

Paul knows that when God and Jesus say "Yes!" they mean it. When we give our word, do we always mean it? Are we sometimes really saying "Yes, but …" or "Yes and No"?

Closing

Let us bring our hopes and needs to God, as we pray: **God of all grace, hear our prayer.**

Let us pray with the words that Jesus taught us:

Our Father …

God, always loving,
you call us to be ready to follow Jesus your son,
and to be generous in his service.
Teach us to be fearless and faithful even in hard times.
We ask this through Christ our Lord. **Amen**.

[Sing 'alleluia'.]

✞ All make the Sign of the Cross.

Friday Daily Prayer

Introduction

Today we have another short reading from Sunday's gospel that makes us think hard. Jesus tells the people that they shouldn't just take things easy and expect to be saved. They have to make a real choice. If they want to follow Jesus, they have to be prepared to commit themselves fully.

☦ All make the Sign of the Cross.

Hymn

A Psalm for August

[Turn to page 148.]

Reading *Luke 13:22-24*

Listen to the words of the holy gospel according to Luke:

As Jesus was on his way to Jerusalem, he taught the people in the towns and villages. Someone asked him, "Lord, are only a few people going to be saved?"
Jesus answered:
    Do all you can to go in by the narrow door! A lot of people will try to get in, but will not be able to.

The gospel of the Lord.

Reflection

Because Jesus has made his own choice to stay true to God, he asks others to do the same. What difficulties did Jesus face in his mission? What difficulties do Christians face today?

Closing

Let us bring our hopes and needs to God, as we pray: **God and Father of Jesus, hear our prayer.**

Let us pray with the words that Jesus taught us:

Our Father …

God, always loving,
you call us your children
and are faithful to us even in times of difficulty.
Teach us to listen to you,
and to know that you are constant in your love.
We ask this through Christ our Lord. **Amen.**

[Sing 'alleluia'.]

☦ All make the Sign of the Cross.

August 23, 2019

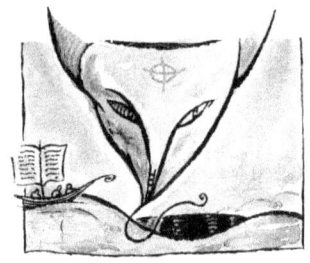

Monday Daily Prayer

Introduction

Today we remember Dom Helder Camara (ka-MAR-uh). In 1952 he was ordained a bishop for one of the poorest parts of Brazil. He was known for his concern for the poor and his fight for justice. He preached non-violence as the only lasting way to improve the lot of the poor, and he lived the simple life that he preached. Dom Helder Camara died on August 27th in 1999.

In today's reading Paul gives us the fine image of a treasure (God's power) stored in clay jars (our bodies).

✞ All make the Sign of the Cross.

Hymn

A Psalm for August

[Turn to page 148.]

Reading   2 Corinthians 4:1.7-11

Listen to the words of the apostle Paul.

God has been kind enough to trust us with this work. That's why we never give up.
We are like clay jars in which this treasure is stored. The real power comes from God and not from us. We often suffer, but we are never crushed. Even when we don't know what to do, we never give up. In times of trouble, God is with us, and when we are knocked down, we get up again. We face death every day because of Jesus. Our bodies show what his death was like, so that his life can also be seen in us.

The word of the Lord.

Reflection

Paul struggled and suffered a lot while spreading the gospel. His strength came from God's spirit in him. What gives you strength to be good and honest and loving? Do you ask for God's help in times of trouble?

Closing

Let us bring our hopes and needs to God, as we pray: **God of all grace, hear our prayer.**

Let us pray with the words that Jesus taught us:

Our Father ...

God, always loving,
you call us to be ready to follow Jesus your son,
and to be generous in his service.
Teach us to be fearless and faithful even in hard times.
We ask this through Christ our Lord. **Amen.**

[Sing 'alleluia'.]

✞ All make the Sign of the Cross.

August 26, 2019

Tuesday Daily Prayer

Introduction

Today we remember a mother and son who were both saints. Monica was a strong Christian woman of North Africa. When her son Augustine turned away from Christianity she never stopped praying for him to come back. Augustine studied many other beliefs but was never satisfied until he heard God's word calling him back to Christ.

His mother's prayer was answered and he returned home to Africa. There he became a great bishop, preacher and writer. His most famous book, called Confessions, is the story of God's love pursuing him. In it he also wrote of his great love for his mother. She died in 387, he in 430.

Our reading from Paul tells us that God has made everything new in Christ.

✞ All make the Sign of the Cross.

Hymn

A Psalm for August

[Turn to page 148.]

Reading   2 Corinthians 5:16-19

Listen to the words of the apostle Paul.

We are careful not to judge people by what they seem to be, though we once judged Christ in that way. Anyone who belongs to Christ is a new person. The past is forgotten, and everything is new. God has done it all! He sent Christ to make peace between himself and us, and he has given us the work of making peace between himself and others.

What we mean is that God was in Christ, offering peace and forgiveness to the people of this world. And he has given us the work of sharing his message about peace.

The word of the Lord.

Reflection

Paul teaches us that God does not blame us for our past mistakes. He sets us free and makes us new. Is this how we treat others? Do we make peace with them and give them a fresh chance?

Closing

Let us bring our hopes and needs to God, as we pray: **God of all grace, hear our prayer.**

Let us pray with the words that Jesus taught us:

Our Father ...

God, always loving,
you call us to be ready to follow Jesus your son,
and to be generous in his service.
Teach us to be fearless and faithful even in hard times.
We ask this through Christ our Lord. **Amen.**

[Sing 'alleluia'.]

✞ All make the Sign of the Cross.

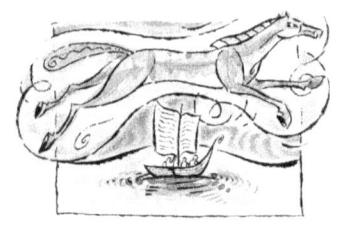

Wednesday Daily Prayer

Introduction

Today's reading is about an appeal Paul is making for the Christian community in Jerusalem. It was poor and in need of support. He asks the community in Corinth to give generously to a collection he is taking up for their fellow believers.

✞ All make the Sign of the Cross.

Hymn

A Psalm for August

[Turn to page 148.]

Reading   2 Corinthians 9:1.7-8.11

Listen to the words of the apostle Paul.

I don't need to write you about the money you plan to give for God's people.
Each of you must make up your own mind about how much to give. But don't feel sorry that you must give and don't feel that you are forced to give. God loves people who love to give. God can bless you with everything you need, and you will always have more than enough to do all kinds of good things for others. You will be blessed in every way, and you will be able to keep on being generous. Then many people will thank God when we deliver your gift.

The word of the Lord.

Reflection

Are you happy to give to others who are in need? What other valuable things can we give besides money? How does generous giving bring a blessing?

Closing

Let us bring our hopes and needs to God, as we pray: **God of all grace, hear our prayer.**

Let us pray with the words that Jesus taught us:

Our Father …

God, always loving,
you call us to be ready to follow Jesus your son,
and to be generous in his service.
Teach us to be fearless and faithful even in hard times.
We ask this through Christ our Lord. **Amen.**

[Sing 'alleluia'.]

✞ All make the Sign of the Cross.

August 28, 2019

Thursday Daily Prayer

Introduction

In the reading for today Paul writes about the dangers and hardships he has had to face while travelling to preach the good news. It's a long list of difficult trials. But Paul says he is happy to suffer these things if it means he can make Christ known.

✢ All make the Sign of the Cross.

Hymn

A Psalm for August

[Turn to page 148.]

Reading   2 Corinthians 11:16.26-27; 12:10

Listen to the words of the apostle Paul.

I don't want any of you to think that I am a fool. But if you do, then let me be a fool and brag a little.
   During my many travels, I have been in danger from rivers, robbers, my own people, and foreigners. My life has been in danger in cities, in deserts, at sea, and with people who only pretended to be the Lord's followers.
   I have worked and struggled and spent many sleepless nights. I have gone hungry and thirsty and often had nothing to eat. I have been cold from not having enough clothes to keep me warm.
   Yes, I am glad to be weak or insulted or mistreated or to have troubles and sufferings, if it is for Christ. Because when I am weak, I am strong.

The word of the Lord.

Reflection

When we really believe something is worth doing, it's amazing how hard we will work to achieve it and how much we will give up. Can you think of something you have worked hard for? What did Paul believe was worth all his pain and struggle?

Closing

Let us bring our hopes and needs to God, as we pray: **God of all grace, hear our prayer.**

Let us pray with the words that Jesus taught us:

Our Father …

God, always loving,
you call us to be ready to follow Jesus your son,
and to be generous in his service.
Teach us to be fearless and faithful even in hard times.
We ask this through Christ our Lord. **Amen.**

[Sing 'alleluia'.]

✢ All make the Sign of the Cross.

Friday Daily Prayer

[Reminder: The Psalm for September is on page 174. Make a copy for each member of the class.]

Introduction

This coming Sunday is Father's Day. It's a special day to give thanks for our fathers, stepfathers, grandfathers, godfathers, uncles, and anyone who is like a father to us.

In today's reading from the Sunday gospel we hear that, one day, Jesus was invited to dinner by an important person, and everyone was carefully watching him. He pointed out that we shouldn't show favour to people just so that they will return the favour to us.

✞ All make the Sign of the Cross.

Hymn

A Psalm for August

[Turn to page 148.]

Reading   Luke 14:1, 12-14

Listen to the words of the holy gospel according to Luke:

One Sabbath Jesus was having dinner in the home of an important Pharisee, and everyone was carefully watching Jesus.
   Jesus said to the man who had invited him: "When you give a dinner or a banquet, don't invite your friends and family and relatives and rich neighbours. If you do, they will invite you in return, and you will be paid back.
   When you give a feast, invite the poor, the crippled, the lame, and the blind. They cannot pay you back. But God will bless you and reward you.

The gospel of the Lord.

Reflection

Do I sometimes do good things without expecting return favours? How can I share friendship with people who are not in my family or group of friends? Who is welcome at the banquet in God's kingdom?

Closing

Let us bring our hopes and needs to God, as we pray: **God of the poor, hear our prayer.**

Let us pray with the words that Jesus taught us:

Our Father …

God of the hungry and the humble,
your son, Jesus always welcomed the poor
   and the lowly.
Make us attentive to the sufferings of your Son
   in other people.
Make our hearts generous
in showing kindness to all.
We ask this through Christ our Lord. **Amen.**

[Sing 'alleluia'.]

✞ All make the Sign of the Cross.

August 30, 2019

September

Monday, September 2,
to Friday, September 27

Ordinary Time ~ September 2019
Looking Ahead

About the Month

In Australia, the first day of September is known as Wattle Day. Some of the early wattles and blossoms have been flowering or will begin to flower, and their scent is in the air. Some early flowers and desert wildflowers may begin to pop up, and trees that have lost their leaves may even be budding. We begin to hear the chirping of birds that have been elsewhere during winter. With the sun higher in the sky, we notice the lengthening hours of daylight. If we live in warmer parts of the country, temperatures are beginning to rise.

Let us remember to thank God for all that is happening around us in nature and in the skies.

The weeks of Ordinary Time are mounting up, or are we counting them down? As we begin September, we will move into the twenty-second week of Ordinary Time.

Readings

During this month we are going to be reading from some books of the Old Testament called the 'Wisdom Books'. In the ancient world, wisdom had many different forms. It could mean very down-to-earth practical advice about daily living. It could also mean understanding how God worked in the world. Sometimes, wisdom is spoken of as a person, a woman who is close to God and teaches us God's ways.

Our readings for Fridays will anticipate the gospels of the Twenty-third to the Twenty-sixth Sundays of Ordinary Time.

Feasts and Other Commemorations

- In 2015 Pope Francis declared September 1 as the World Day of Prayer for Creation, as the Orthodox Church has done since 1989. This annual day of prayer, which we will keep on September 2, reminds us that God has entrusted creation to our care.
- On September 14, Christians celebrate the feast of the Triumph of the Cross. We will keep this feast on Thursday September 12. When we trace on ourselves the Sign of the Cross, we are reminded that we are followers of Jesus who suffered death on a cross and rose to new life.
- On September 23, we will celebrate the feast of the apostle Matthew who worked as a tax collector until he met Jesus.

This year all schools in Australia are on holidays during the week of Monday, 30 September, to Friday, 4 October. They will miss the feast days that occur this week: St Jerome (30 September), St Thérèse of the Child Jesus (1 October), the Guardian Angels (2 October) and St Francis of Assisi (4 October).

Most will also miss two Jewish festivals. Jewish people around the world begin the New Year celebration of Rosh Hashanah on the evening of September 29. In each Jewish meeting place, a shofar, which is a ram's horn, is blown. The shofar calls Jews to remember the past year and to make plans to practise their faith better during the coming year.

At sundown on October 7, the Jewish observance of Yom Kippur begins. This feast is called the Day of Atonement, a "Great Day of Forgiveness". It is the most holy day on the Jewish calendar. The need to ask God for forgiveness is so important that Jewish people do not work or travel on this day. It is a day, just like the Sabbath. They pray and fast. They apologise to people they have hurt.

Preparation for September

The Psalm for September, Psalm 96, is on page 174. It is a psalm that praises God who fills the earth with vibrant life. Make copies for each member of the class.

Spring is a season of freshness and new life. As we begin the spring months, make sure that your prayer space is bright and fresh. Perhaps you can add a brighter green and use spring flowers as they come into bloom.

Suggested Hymns

See the hymn chart on pages viii-ix for hymns for Ordinary Time and for the feast of the Holy Cross.

A Psalm for September

Psalm 96:1-3, 4, 8, 11-13

LEADER
Sing a new song to the Lord!
Everyone on this earth, sing praises to the Lord.
ALL
Let all people sing and praise God's name.

SIDE A
Day after day announce, "The Lord has saved us!"
Tell every nation on earth, "The Lord is wonderful and does marvellous things!

SIDE B
The Lord is great and deserves our greatest praise!
He is the only God worthy of our worship.
Give honour and praise to the Lord."

SIDE A
Tell everyone of every nation,
"Praise the glorious power of the Lord.
God is wonderful! Praise him."

SIDE B
Tell the heavens and the earth to be glad and celebrate!
Command the ocean to roar with all of its creatures and the fields to rejoice with all of their crops.
Then every tree in the forest
will sing joyful songs to the Lord.

LEADER
Sing a new song to the Lord!
Everyone on this earth, sing praises to the Lord.
ALL
Let all people sing and praise God's name.

Glory be to the Father, and to the Son,
and to the Holy Spirit:
As it was in the beginning, is now,
and ever shall be,
world without end. **Amen.** Alleluia.

[Turn back to Daily Prayer for today.]

Monday Daily Prayer

Introduction

In 2015 Pope Francis wrote a letter to the world about caring for the earth, our common home. It was called *Laudato Si'*. Later that year he declared September 1 to be a *World Day of Prayer for the Care of Creation*. It's a reminder to spend every day caring for the world we live in and all its wonderful creatures.

During this month we are going to be reading from some books of the Old Testament called the "Wisdom Books." In the ancient world, wisdom had many different forms. It could mean very down-to-earth practical advice about daily living. It could also mean understanding how God worked in the world. Sometimes, as in today's reading, wisdom is spoken of as a person, a woman who is close to God and teaches us God's ways.

✢ All make the Sign of the Cross.

Hymn

A Psalm for September

[Turn to page 174.]

Reading   *Wisdom 6:12-16*

Listen to the words of the book of Wisdom.

Wisdom shines brightly and never fades.
She is easily recognised by those who love her.
Wisdom wants to be known by those who desire her.
If you get up early to look for Wisdom,
   you find her at your door.
Just thinking about Wisdom leads to full understanding,
and caring about Wisdom
will soon set you free from all other cares.
Wisdom searches eagerly for those who are seeking,
and she lets them find her in all of their thoughts.

The word of the Lord.

Reflection

What does this tell us about wisdom? Can you think of someone who is wise in this way? Do you want to become wise?

Closing

Let us bring our hopes and needs to God, as we pray: **God of wisdom, hear our prayer.**

Let us pray with the words that Jesus taught us

Our Father ...

God of grace and wisdom,
you continually raise up good people
who show with their lives
that they follow a holy and loving God.
Let our lives be true to all that our faith teaches,
so that we will grow more and more
in your son's likeness.
  We ask this through Christ our Lord. **Amen.**

[Sing 'alleluia'.]

✢ All make the Sign of the Cross.

September 2, 2019

Tuesday Daily Prayer

Introduction

The world that is all around us is full of wonder and mystery. There is so much still to explore and discover. Only God and God's spirit of Wisdom knows all its secrets. Today's reading gives us a glimpse into the hidden workings of God's creation.

✞ All make the Sign of the Cross.

Hymn

A Psalm for September

[Turn to page 174.]

Reading   Wisdom 7:17-22

Listen to the words of the book of Wisdom.

From God came my knowledge about the universe and how its parts work;
about the way a calendar is determined;
about the movement of the sun and the changing seasons;
about the way the years come and go on schedule;
about the groups of stars and the way animals behave,
   both tame and wild;
about the motion of the wind and the thoughts of humans;
about all kinds of plants and the value of roots.
I learned hidden mysteries and things known to all,
because I was taught by Wisdom,
   who made everything.

The word of the Lord.

Reflection

Isn't the world is an amazing and awesome place? Do you understand how it all works? What would you like to know more about?

Closing

Let us bring our hopes and needs to God, as we pray: **God of wisdom, hear our prayer.**

Let us pray with the words that Jesus taught us:

Our Father …

God of grace and wisdom,
you continually raise up good people
who show with their lives
that they follow a holy and loving God.
Let our lives be true to all that our faith teaches,
so that we will grow more and more
in your son's likeness.
We ask this through Christ our Lord. **Amen.**

[Sing 'alleluia'.]

✞ All make the Sign of the Cross.

September 3, 2019

Wednesday Daily Prayer

Introduction

Today's reading comes from the book of Sirach (*SEAR-rack*). This is a wisdom book that is included in the Catholic Bible but not in some other Christian Bibles or in the official writings of the Jewish people. It is called Sirach after the name of the writer's grandfather. Today he gives wise advice about how to live well by caring for others, especially those who are in need.

☦ All make the Sign of the Cross.

Hymn

A Psalm for September

[Turn to page 174.]

Reading   Sirach 4:7-10

Listen to the words of the book of Sirach.

Be friendly to everyone in the community
 and show proper respect to the town leaders.
When the poor greet you,
 be polite and greet them in return.
Rescue everyone
 who suffers from injustice;
Have the courage to make the right decisions;
provide for orphans and widows,
 as if they were your own children or wife.
Then you will be a true child of God Most High,
 and he will love you more than your own mother does.

The word of the Lord.

Reflection

This advice comes from the other side of the world a long time ago. Is it still good advice for us here? What do you think is the most important thing?

Closing

Let us bring our hopes and needs to God, as we pray: **God of wisdom, hear our prayer.**

Let us pray with the words that Jesus taught us:

Our Father …

God of grace and wisdom,
you continually raise up good people
who show with their lives
that they follow a holy and loving God.
Let our lives be true to all that our faith teaches,
so that we will grow more and more
in your son's likeness.
We ask this through Christ our Lord. **Amen.**

[Sing 'alleluia'.]

☦ All make the Sign of the Cross.

September 4, 2019

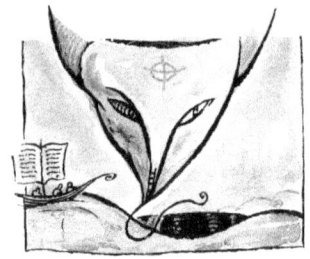

Thursday Daily Prayer

Introduction

On this day in 1997 Mother Teresa died in India. She was a holy woman who lived out her solemn promise to give 'wholehearted and free service to the poorest of the poor'. Because of this she is now known as St Teresa of Calcutta. The thousands of men and women who join in her work are called the Missionaries of Charity. They serve the sick and the dying who have no one else to care for them, bringing God's love to forgotten corners of crowded cities.

Our second reading from the book of Sirach (*SEAR-rack*) comes from the very last chapter. The writer looks back on his life. From the time he was young he chose to let wisdom guide him. He urges us to do the same.

☦ All make the Sign of the Cross.

Hymn

A Psalm for September

[Turn to page 174.]

Reading   Sirach 51:13-14.18-19.29-30

Listen to the words of the book of Sirach.

When I was young and before I had travelled,
I prayed in the temple courtyard
   and openly asked for Wisdom.
And I will look for her every day of my life.
I chose to live by Wisdom and always do right,
   and I have never had a reason to be ashamed.
Whenever I had to struggle to follow her completely,
I would lift my hands in prayer
and tell God I was sorry
 I knew so little of Wisdom.
Celebrate the mercy of God!
Don't be ashamed to tell others how great he is.
Work when it is time to work,
   and God will reward you when the time is right.

The word of the Lord.

Reflection

It seems that living wisely wasn't always easy for Sirach. There were times of struggle. What makes it difficult to live wisely? Where can we go to find wisdom for life?

Closing

Let us bring our hopes and needs to God, as we pray: **God of wisdom, hear our prayer.**

Let us pray with the words that Jesus taught us:

Our Father ...

God of grace and wisdom,
you continually raise up good people
who show with their lives
that they follow a holy and loving God.
Let our lives be true to all that our faith teaches,
so that we will grow more and more
in your son's likeness.
 We ask this through Christ our Lord. **Amen.**

[Sing 'alleluia'.]

☦ All make the Sign of the Cross.

September 5, 2019

Friday Daily Prayer

Introduction

Today's reading from the gospel for Sunday may seem to ask too much of us. Jesus tells us that we should love him above everyone and everything else. Love of God is at the centre of the Christian life. But it can be difficult and costly to love truly day after day. That's why Jesus says it's like taking up our cross to follow him.

✞ All make the Sign of the Cross.

Hymn

A Psalm for September

[Turn to page 174.]

Reading   Luke 14:25-29

Listen to the words of the holy gospel according to Luke:

Large crowds were walking along with Jesus, when he turned and said, "You cannot be my disciple, unless you love me more that you love your father and mother, your wife and children, and your brothers and sisters. You cannot come with me unless you love me more than you love your own life.

"You cannot be my disciple unless you carry your own cross and come with me. Suppose one of you wants to build a tower. What is the first thing you will do? Won't you sit down and figure out how much it will cost and if you have enough money to pay for it? Otherwise, you will start building the tower, but not be able to finish."

The gospel of the Lord.

Reflection

What kinds of 'crosses' do followers of Jesus carry today? What do you think Jesus means by his words about the tower? What does it 'cost' to be a Christian?

Closing

Let us bring our hopes and needs to God, as we pray: **God our companion, hear our prayer.**

Let us pray with the words that Jesus taught us:

Our Father …

God of love,
you call us to be followers of your Son, Jesus.
Help us to love you
with all our hearts.
Be with us at all times,
and keep us close to you.
We ask this through Christ our Lord. **Amen.**

[Sing 'alleluia'.]

✞ All make the Sign of the Cross.

September 6, 2019

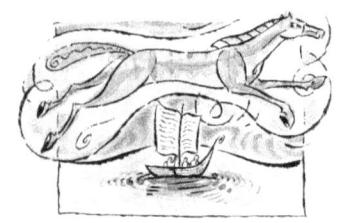

Monday Daily Prayer

Introduction

Today we have our one reading from a very unusual book of the Bible. It's a love poem called the Song of Songs (or sometimes the Song of Solomon). It seems to be a collection of songs in which a man and a woman speak like poets about their great love for each other. They use all sorts of amazing images to show how much in love they are.

✝ All make the Sign of the Cross.

Hymn

A Psalm for September

[Turn to page 174.]

Reading   Song of Songs 2:8-13

Listen to the words of the Song of Songs.

She speaks:
I hear the voice of the one I love,
as he comes leaping over mountains and hills
   like a deer or a gazelle.
Now he stands outside our wall,
   looking through the window and speaking to me.

He speaks:
My darling, I love you!
   Let's go away together.
Winter is past, the rain has stopped;
   flowers cover the earth, it's time to sing.
The cooing of doves is heard in our land.
Fig trees are bearing fruit,
   while blossoms on grapevines fill the air with perfume.
My darling, I love you!
   Let's go away together.

The word of the Lord.

Reflection

This is not the way we talk every day at school or at home. These are the words of two people deeply (even madly) in love. What images do they use to speak of their love? What are they trying to say?

Closing

Let us bring our hopes and needs to God, as we pray: **God of wisdom, hear our prayer.**

Let us pray with the words that Jesus taught us:

Our Father …

God of grace and wisdom,
you continually raise up good people
who show with their lives
that they follow a holy and loving God.
Let our lives be true to all that our faith teaches,
so that we will grow more and more
in your son's likeness.
We ask this through Christ our Lord. **Amen.**

[Sing 'alleluia'.]

✝ All make the Sign of the Cross.

September 9, 2019

Tuesday Daily Prayer

Introduction

Today we begin a short set of readings from a very long and important book in the Old Testament. It's called the book of Job (*JOHB*). It tells story of a rich and successful man who loses everything he has. He cannot understand why God has allowed this to happen to him. He has always been a good man. Even now we don't find it easy to understand why bad things happen to good people. Our reading for today begins the story.

✝ All make the Sign of the Cross.

Hymn

A Psalm for September

[Turn to page 174.]

Reading   Job 1:1.13.14.18.19-22

Listen to the words of the book of Job.

Many years ago, a man named Job lived in the land of Uz. He was a truly good person, who respected God and refused to do evil.
Someone rushed up to Job and said,
"Your children were having a feast and drinking wine at the home of your oldest son, when suddenly a windstorm from the desert blew the house down, crushing all of your children. I am the only one who escaped to tell you."
When Job heard this, he tore his clothes and shaved his head because of his great sorrow. He knelt on the ground, then worshiped God and said:
"We bring nothing at birth;
we take nothing
   with us at death.
The Lord alone gives and takes.
Praise the name of the Lord!"
In spite of everything, Job did not sin or accuse God of doing wrong.

The word of the Lord.

Reflection

How do you feel when things go wrong for you? What if it's nobody's fault? What do you do if there's no-one to blame?

Closing

Let us bring our hopes and needs to God, as we pray: **God of wisdom, hear our prayer.**

Let us pray with the words that Jesus taught us:

Our Father …

God of grace and wisdom,
you continually raise up good people
who show with their lives
that they follow a holy and loving God.
Let our lives be true to all that our faith teaches,
so that we will grow more and more
in your son's likeness.
We ask this through Christ our Lord. **Amen.**

[Sing 'alleluia'.]

✝ All make the Sign of the Cross.

September 10, 2019

Wednesday Daily Prayer

[Reminder: For tomorrow's prayer in honour of the Holy Cross, you may wish to have a special cross to place before the class.]

Introduction

In the story of Job (JOHB) a number of his friends try to explain why he is suffering so much. They want to tell him that he must have done something wrong and should admit it. Job refuses, because he knows he has always led a good life. In today's passage he admits he does not understand why God seems to be treating him badly. All he can do is trust in God's mysterious wisdom.

✢ All make the Sign of the Cross.

Hymn

A Psalm for September

[Turn to page 174.]

Reading   *Job 23:8-14*

Listen to the words of the book of Job.

Job said:
I cannot find God anywhere –
  in front or back of me, to my left or my right.
God is always at work, though I never see him.
But he knows what I am doing,
  and when he tests me, I will be pure as gold.
I have never refused to follow any of his commands,
  and I have always treasured his teachings.
But he alone is God, and who can oppose him?
God does as he pleases,
  and he will do exactly what he intends with me.

The word of the Lord.

Reflection

Many things happen to people that don't seem to be fair. It is a big challenge for us to understand this. How can we keep trusting in God's goodness? What can help us be strong?

Closing

Let us bring our hopes and needs to God, as we pray: **God of wisdom, hear our prayer.**

Let us pray with the words that Jesus taught us:

Our Father …

God of grace and wisdom,
you continually raise up good people
who show with their lives
that they follow a holy and loving God.
Let our lives be true to all that our faith teaches,
so that we will grow more and more
in your son's likeness.
We ask this through Christ our Lord. **Amen.**

[Sing 'alleluia'.]

✢ All make the Sign of the Cross.

September 11, 2019

Thursday Daily Prayer

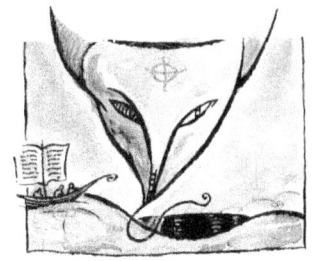

For today's prayer, place a cross in the prayer space.

Introduction

This coming Saturday is the feast of the Holy Cross. We remember it today. The cross is the symbol for the way Jesus defeated sin, hatred and death. Christians are signed with the cross when they are baptised and also when they are buried. Christians also mark themselves with the Sign of the Cross at the beginning and end of prayer. The Sign of the Cross shows our willingness to follow Jesus and our joy at being part of his family.

Today's reading comes from an ancient Christian hymn about Jesus' victory through the cross.

☩ All make the Sign of the Cross.

Hymn

A Psalm for September

[Turn to page 174.]

Reading *Philippians 2:8-11*

Listen to the words of the apostle Paul:

Christ was humble.
He obeyed God and even died on a cross.
Then God gave Christ the highest place
and honoured his name above all others.
So at the name of Jesus
everyone will bow down,
those in heaven, on earth,
and under the earth.
And to the glory of God the Father
everyone will openly agree,
"Jesus Christ is Lord!"

The word of the Lord.

Reflection

The Sign of the Cross is a very simple action but also a powerful prayer. What does it mean when I make the Sign of the Cross? How can I make it a real prayer?

Closing

Let us bring our hopes and needs to God, as we pray: **God of Jesus, hear our prayer.**

Let us pray with the words that Jesus taught us:

Our Father ...

On this feast of the Holy Cross,
let us look at the cross in this space
and think for a moment
about how much Jesus loves us.

[Pause and give the class a few moments to pray.]

Lord, we see in this cross
a sign of your great love.
May the cross be our comfort in trouble,
our shelter in the face of danger,
our safeguard on life's journey.
We ask this through Christ our Lord. **Amen.**
adapted from the *Book of Blessings*

[Sing 'alleluia'.]

☩ All make the Sign of the Cross.

September 12, 2019

Friday Daily Prayer

Introduction

Today's reading from the Sunday gospel is one of the most well-known and beautiful stories in the gospels. It's about a father and two sons, about the choices they make, and about love that forgives everything. It is a long reading, so we will begin it today and finish it next Friday.

✟ All make the Sign of the Cross.

Hymn

A Psalm for September

[Turn to page 174.]

Reading   Luke 15:11-16

Listen to the words of the holy gospel according to Luke:

Jesus told the people this story: "Once a man had two sons. The younger son said to his father, 'Give me my share of the property.' So the father divided his property between his two sons.

"Not long after that, the younger son packed up everything he owned and left for a foreign country, where he wasted all his money in wild living. He had spent everything, when a bad famine spread through that whole land. Soon he had nothing to eat.

"He went to work for a man in that country, and the man sent him out to take care of his pigs. He would have been glad to eat what the pigs were eating, but no one gave him a thing."

The gospel of the Lord.

Reflection

What might be some reasons why the young son left home? Do things like this really happen? What would I do if I were the son in this story? What would I do if I were the father?

Closing

Let us bring our hopes and needs to God, as we pray: **Forgiving God, hear our prayer.**

Let us pray with the words that Jesus taught us:

Our Father …

Forgiving Lord,
we have sinned against you
and against each other.
We have wasted the gifts you have given to us.
We don't deserve to be called your children.
But forgive us and open your arms
to welcome us.
We ask this through Christ our Lord. **Amen.**

[Sing 'alleluia'.]

✟ All make the Sign of the Cross.

September 13, 2019

Monday Daily Prayer

Introduction

Today we hear for the third and last time from the book of Job (JOHB). In this passage God puts Job to the test. He challenges Job to admit that he does not have the power and knowledge that God has. Job has no choice but to confess that he has no answers for God's questions. All he can do is to submit in silence.

✞ All make the Sign of the Cross.

Hymn

A Psalm for September

[Turn to page 174.]

Reading   *Job 38:1-3.33-36; 40:1-5*

Listen to the words of the book of Job.

From out of a storm, the Lord said to Job:
Why do you talk so much when you know so little?
Now get ready to face me!
Can you answer the questions I ask?
Do you know the laws that govern the heavens,
   and can you make them rule the earth?
Can you order the clouds to send a downpour,
   or will lightning flash at your command?
Did you teach birds to know
   that rain or floods are on their way?
I am the Lord All-Powerful,
   but you have argued that I am wrong.
Now you must answer me.

Job said to the Lord:
   Who am I to answer you?
I did speak once or twice, but never again.

The word of the Lord.

Reflection

Are we tempted to think we know better than God? Do we behave sometimes as if we were God? How can God help us in tough times?

Closing

Let us bring our hopes and needs to God, as we pray: **God of wisdom, hear our prayer.**

Let us pray with the words that Jesus taught us:

Our Father …

God of grace and wisdom,
you continually raise up good people
who show with their lives
that they follow a holy and loving God.
Let our lives be true to all that our faith teaches,
so that we will grow more and more
in your son's likeness.
We ask this through Christ our Lord. **Amen.**

[Sing 'alleluia'.]

✞ All make the Sign of the Cross.

[185]   September 16, 2019

Tuesday Daily Prayer

Introduction

Around this time we remember Karl Kulper, a homeless man who died in Sydney in 2002. For twenty-five years he lived in a bus shelter outside St Vincent's Hospital. He showed kindness to everyone and especially made sure the nurses got safely to their buses at night. On the wall of the bus stop now are the words: "A resident of St Vincent's bus stop for 25 years. Karl, in your bus stop in heaven may you rest in peace."

Today we have the first of two readings from an unusual book in the Old Testament called Ecclesiastes (ek-klee-zee-ASS-tees) after the author. He writes about his struggle to find meaning in life. It all seems to have no point. He feels that it's boring and makes no sense. We hear today how he makes his complaint.

✣ All make the Sign of the Cross.

Hymn

A Psalm for September

[Turn to page 174.]

Reading   *Ecclesiastes 1:1-4.8-9*

Listen to the words of the book of Ecclesiastes (ek-klee-zee-ASS-tees).

When the son of David was king in Jerusalem,
he was known to be very wise, and he said:
Nothing makes sense!
Everything is nonsense.
   I have seen it all—nothing makes sense!
What is there to show
   for all of our hard work here on this earth?
People come, and people go,
   but still the world never changes.
All of life is far more boring than words could ever say.
Our eyes and our ears are never satisfied
   with what we see and hear.
Everything that happens has happened before;
nothing is new, nothing under the sun.

The word of the Lord.

Reflection

Do you ever feel that life is dull and boring? That's how Ecclesiastes felt. Are you tempted to always look for something new and exciting? Are we sometimes blind to the good things of everyday life?

Closing

Let us bring our hopes and needs to God, as we pray: **God of wisdom, hear our prayer.**

Let us pray with the words that Jesus taught us:

Our Father …

God of grace and wisdom,
you continually raise up good people
who show with their lives
that they follow a holy and loving God.
Let our lives be true to all that our faith teaches,
so that we will grow more and more
in your son's likeness.
We ask this through Christ our Lord. **Amen.**

[Sing 'alleluia'.]

✣ All make the Sign of the Cross.

Wednesday Daily Prayer

Introduction

Today we remember the many Christians who were put to death in Korea over one hundred and fifty years ago. A lot of them were women. They bravely died for their faith between the years 1839 and 1867, trying to convince their rulers that the Catholic Church was not an enemy. Today many people in Korea are faithful Catholics. Let us give God thanks today for their steadfast courage.

Our second and last reading from the book of Ecclesiastes (*ek-klee-zee-ASS-tees*) may be familiar. It was once turned into a popular song. It's a poem about many of the different things that go together in life.

✞ All make the Sign of the Cross.

Hymn

A Psalm for September

[Turn to page 174.]

Reading *Ecclesiastes 3:1-8*

Listen to the words of the book of Ecclesiastes (*ek-klee-zee-ASS-tees*).

Everything on earth
   has its own time and its own season.
There is a time
   for birth and death, planting and reaping,
for killing and healing, destroying and building,
   for crying and laughing, weeping and dancing,
for throwing stones and gathering stones,
   embracing and parting.
There is a time
for finding and losing, keeping and giving,
   for tearing and sewing, listening and speaking.
There is also a time
   for love and hate, for war and peace.

The word of the Lord.

Reflection

Ecclesiastes doesn't tell us whether any of these things is good or bad, just that they are part of life. Is this helpful? How can we accept the world as it is? What should we try and change?

Closing

Let us bring our hopes and needs to God, as we pray: **God of wisdom, hear our prayer.**

Let us pray with the words that Jesus taught us:

Our Father …

God of grace and wisdom,
you continually raise up good people
who show with their lives
that they follow a holy and loving God.
Let our lives be true to all that our faith teaches,
so that we will grow more and more
in your son's likeness.
We ask this through Christ our Lord. **Amen.**

[Sing 'alleluia'.]

✞ All make the Sign of the Cross.

September 18, 2019

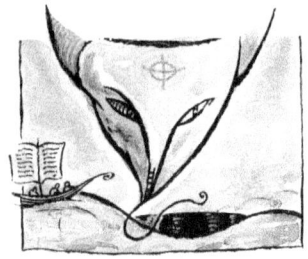

Thursday Daily Prayer

Introduction

Today is the International Day for World Peace. This was established by the United Nations in 1982. It is a day when individuals, communities, nations and governments highlight efforts to end conflict and promote peace. Many groups keep a 24-hour vigil on this day to pray for peace in our homes, in our communities and between nations.

Our final wisdom book from the Old Testament is the book of Proverbs. A proverb is a short saying that contains practical advice for living. Today we hear the first few verses that introduce the book.

✞ All make the Sign of the Cross.

Hymn

A Psalm for September

[Turn to page 174.]

Reading   Proverbs 1:1-7

Listen to the words of the book of Proverbs.

These are the proverbs of King Solomon of Israel, the son of David.
Proverbs will teach you wisdom and self-control
   and how to understand sayings with deep meanings.
You will learn what is right and honest and fair.
From these, an ordinary person can learn to be smart,
   and young people can gain knowledge and good sense.
If you are already wise, you will become even wiser.
And if you are smart, you will learn to understand proverbs and sayings,
   as well as words of wisdom and all kinds of riddles.
Respect and obey the Lord!
This is the beginning of knowledge.
Only a fool rejects wisdom and good advice.

The word of the Lord.

Reflection

Do you know any proverbs? What is their message? Are they always true or are they just a useful guide?

Closing

Let us bring our hopes and needs to God, as we pray: **God of wisdom, hear our prayer.**

Let us pray with the words that Jesus taught us:

Our Father ...

God of grace and wisdom,
you continually raise up good people
who show with their lives
that they follow a holy and loving God.
Let our lives be true to all that our faith teaches,
so that we will grow more and more
in your son's likeness.
We ask this through Christ our Lord. **Amen.**

[Sing 'alleluia'.]

✞ All make the Sign of the Cross.

September 19, 2019

Friday Daily Prayer

Introduction

Last Friday we read the first part of a parable that Jesus told. A young son wasted all that his father had given him and had to take a job feeding pigs. Things looked pretty bad for him. Today we read the second-last part of the story which tells what happened to him.

Parables can have many meanings. As we listen today to this part of the story, let us ask ourselves what it might mean.

Hymn

A Psalm for September

[Turn to page 174.]

Reading   Luke 15:17-24

Listen to the words of the holy gospel according to Luke:

Finally, the boy came to his senses and said, "My father's workers have plenty to eat, and here I am, starving to death! I will go to my father and say to him, 'Father, I have sinned against God in heaven and against you. I am no longer good enough to be called your son. Treat me like one of your workers.'"

The younger son got up and started back to his father. But when he was still a long way off, his father saw him and felt sorry for him. He ran to his son and hugged and kissed him.

The son said, "Father, I have sinned against God in heaven and against you. I am no longer good enough to be called your son."

But his father said to the servants, "Hurry and bring the best clothes and put them on him. Give him a ring for his finger and sandals for his feet. Get the best calf and prepare it, so we can eat and celebrate. This son of mine was dead, but has now come back to life. He was lost and has now been found." And they began to celebrate.

The gospel of the Lord.

Reflection

What is this parable usually called? What could it teach us today? What do you think of the father's action? Why is this a favourite gospel story of Christians everywhere?

Closing

Let us bring our hopes and needs to God, as we pray: **Forgiving God, hear our prayer.**

Let us pray with the words that Jesus taught us:

Our Father …

Forgiving Lord,
we sometimes sin against you
and against each other,
and sometimes we waste the gifts you have given to us.
But forgive us and open your arms
to welcome us.
We ask this through Christ our Lord. **Amen.**

[Sing 'alleluia'.]

✠ All make the Sign of the Cross.

September 20, 2019

Monday Daily Prayer

Introduction

Today is the feast of the apostle Matthew. He was working as a tax collector for the Romans when he met Jesus. The Jews did not like to give their money to pay the Roman tax, and so many people did not like Matthew. They were surprised that Jesus became his friend. Jesus made many friends among those who were rejected.

✝ All make the Sign of the Cross.

Hymn

A Psalm for September

[Turn to page 174.]

Reading   *Matthew 9:9-13*

Listen to the words of the holy gospel according to Matthew:

Jesus saw a tax collector named Matthew sitting at the place for paying taxes. Jesus said to him: "Come with me." Matthew got up and went with him.

   Later, Jesus and his disciples were having dinner at Matthew's house. Many tax collectors and other sinners were also there. Some people asked Jesus' disciples, "Why does your teacher eat with tax collectors and other sinners?"

   Jesus heard them and answered, "Healthy people don't need a doctor, but sick people do. Go and learn what the Scriptures mean when they say, 'Instead of offering sacrifices to me, I want you to be merciful to others.' I didn't come to invite good people to be my followers. I came to invite sinners."

The gospel of the Lord.

Reflection

Why did Jesus get into trouble for eating with tax collectors and sinners? Was Matthew a sinner before he followed Jesus? What difference does it make when I choose to follow Jesus? How do I encourage others?

Closing

Let us bring our hopes and needs to God, as we pray: **God of apostles, hear our prayer.**

Let us pray with the words that Jesus taught us:

Our Father …

Lord God,
we thank you for sending apostles
to the whole world.
We welcome those who bring your good news.
We pray for them and listen to their teaching.
Call on us, one day, to become apostles, too.
We ask this through Christ our Lord. **Amen.**

[Sing 'alleluia'.]

✝ All make the Sign of the Cross.

September 23, 2019

Tuesday Daily Prayer

Introduction

Today's reading from the book of Proverbs is different. Instead of short pieces of advice about everyday life, it is part of a speech that Wisdom makes. Wisdom speaks like a person, a woman who is a close friend of God and who helped God create everything. In some ways Wisdom is like the Holy Spirit who makes us friends of God.

✞ All make the Sign of the Cross.

Hymn

A Psalm for September

[Turn to page 174.]

Reading   *Proverbs 8:12.22-23.30-31*

Listen to the words of the book of Proverbs.

I am Wisdom—Common Sense is my closest friend;
   I possess knowledge and sound judgment.
From the beginning, I was with the Lord.
   I was there before he began to create the earth.
At the very first, the Lord gave life to me.
   I was right beside the Lord, helping him plan and build.
I made him happy each day, and I was happy at his side.
   I was pleased with his world and pleased with its people.

The word of the Lord.

Reflection

The whole Bible begins with a story of creation. It says that God was pleased with everything he made. Do we love the world as God loves it? Do we care for it as God's gift to us?

Closing

Let us bring our hopes and needs to God, as we pray: **God of wisdom, hear our prayer.**

Let us pray with the words that Jesus taught us:

Our Father …

God of grace and wisdom,
you continually raise up good people
who show with their lives
that they follow a holy and loving God.
Let our lives be true to all that our faith teaches,
so that we will grow more and more
in your son's likeness.
We ask this through Christ our Lord. **Amen.**

[Sing 'alleluia'.]

✞ All make the Sign of the Cross.

September 24, 2019

Wednesday Daily Prayer

Introduction

Today's reading is a set of four proverbs. Each one has some practical wisdom for us. They advise us to be honest and humble and respectful to God. The book of Proverbs has hundreds of sayings like these. They give us much food for thought.

☩ All make the Sign of the Cross.

Hymn

A Psalm for September

[Turn to page 174.]

Reading *Proverbs 11:1-4*

Listen to the words of the book of Proverbs.

The Lord hates anyone who cheats,
   but he likes everyone who is honest.
Too much pride can put you to shame.
   It's wiser to be humble.
If you do the right thing, honesty will be your guide.
   But if you are crooked, you will be trapped by your own dishonesty.
When God is angry, money won't help you.
   Obeying God is the only way to be saved from death.

The word of the Lord.

Reflection

Today's world tempts us to succeed by being dishonest and proud and by ignoring God. It takes courage to be honest, humble and obedient to God. Why should we try? How can we help each other?

Closing

Let us bring our hopes and needs to God, as we pray: **God of wisdom, hear our prayer.**

Let us pray with the words that Jesus taught us:

Our Father …

God of grace and wisdom,
you continually raise up good people
who show with their lives
that they follow a holy and loving God.
Let our lives be true to all that our faith teaches,
so that we will grow more and more
in your son's likeness.
We ask this through Christ our Lord. **Amen.**

[Sing 'alleluia'.]

☩ All make the Sign of the Cross.

Thursday Daily Prayer

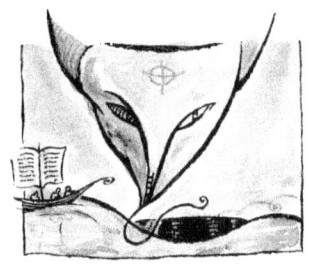

Introduction

Today we remember Saint Vincent de Paul. Vincent was born in France in the year 1580. When he moved to Paris as a young priest, he organised groups to help people to pray and to serve the needs of others. Vincent loved the sick and poor, especially children.

In our own day members of the Saint Vincent de Paul Society supply food, money and clothing to those in need. They visit the sick and the poor. There may be one of these societies in your parish.

Our last reading from the book of Proverbs is another set of wise sayings that give advice about how we can live good lives.

☙ All make the Sign of the Cross.

Hymn

A Psalm for September

[Turn to page 174.]

Reading *Proverbs 16:16-20*

Listen to the words of the book of Proverbs.

It's much better to be wise and sensible
 than to be rich.
God's people avoid evil ways,
 and they protect themselves by watching where they go.
Too much pride will destroy you.
You are better off to be humble and poor
 than to get rich from what you take by force.
If you know what you're doing, you will prosper.
 God blesses everyone who trusts him.

The word of the Lord.

Reflection

What are the main lessons that these proverbs teach us? Is it good advice? How can we put them into practice?

Closing

Let us bring our hopes and needs to God, as we pray: **God of wisdom, hear our prayer.**

Let us pray with the words that Jesus taught us:

Our Father ...

God of grace and wisdom,
you continually raise up good people
who show with their lives
that they follow a holy and loving God.
Let our lives be true to all that our faith teaches,
so that we will grow more and more
in your son's likeness.
We ask this through Christ our Lord. **Amen.**

[Sing 'alleluia'.]

☙ All make the Sign of the Cross.

September 26, 2019

Friday Daily Prayer

[Reminder: The Psalm for October is on page 198. Make a copy for each member of the class.]

Introduction

Sometimes the gospel readings are about the rewards we will be given when our lives are over. In today's reading from the Sunday gospel Jesus tells a story about two men and their very different rewards. The Jewish people imagined heaven as a great feast or banquet. So Jesus uses a feast as the setting for his story.

Hymn

A Psalm for September

[Turn to page 174.]

Reading   Luke 16:19-21, 22-25

Listen to the words of the holy gospel according to Luke:

Jesus told his disciples this story: "There was once a rich man who wore expensive clothes and every day ate the best food. But a poor beggar named Lazarus was brought to the gate of the rich man's house. He was happy just to eat the scraps that fell from the rich man's table. The poor man died, and angels took him to the place of honour next to Abraham.

"The rich man also died and was buried. He went to hell and was suffering terribly. When he looked up and saw Abraham far off and Lazarus at his side, he said to Abraham, 'Have pity on me! Send Lazarus to dip his finger in water and touch my tongue. I'm suffering terribly in this fire.'

"Abraham answered, 'My friend, remember that while you lived, you had everything good, and Lazarus had everything bad. Now he is happy, and you are in pain.'"

The gospel of the Lord.

Reflection

What could this story mean? Why didn't the rich man give Lazarus more than scraps to eat? How do I picture heaven?

Closing

Let us bring our hopes and needs to God, as we pray: **God of the poor, hear our prayer.**

Let us pray with the words that Jesus taught us:

Our Father …

God of the poor and powerless,
you are always present to us
in our sisters and brothers who are in need.
Open our eyes to see you.
May our hands be always ready to serve you
in everyone we meet.
We ask this through Christ our Lord. **Amen.**

[Sing 'alleluia'.]

✚ All make the Sign of the Cross.

September 27, 2019

October

Monday, October 14, to Thursday, October 31

Ordinary Time ~ October 2019
Looking Ahead

Note: Because of overlapping school holidays throughout Australia, there is a two-week gap in Daily Prayer from Monday, 30 September, to Friday, 11 October.

About the Month

Spring is a wonderful time of the year no matter where we live. It holds the promise of new life. Spring flowers, desert wildflowers, blossoms and bulbs all come into bloom. Throughout the country, many different kinds of golden wattle are at their most colourful. Their perfumes fill the air. Trees that have lost their leaves bud with new, spring green, leafy growth.

Days are getting longer and warmer as we come out of the longer nights and cooler days of winter. Winter sports have come to an end with Grand Finals and end of season celebrations. We will begin to spend more time outdoors. Sports such as cricket, tennis and, of course, swimming are signs that warmer days are not far off.

With all of these signs of new life, spring is a good time to think about our earth and what we have done to help or hurt it. We might put new energy into recycling newspapers and cans or into other projects we have begun; we might also be careful not to waste water.

Let us remember to give praise and thanks to God who has created the universe and all that is in it.

Daily Prayer for October begins in week Twenty-eight of Ordinary Time and takes us through to Week Thirty.

Readings

During October we will hear the story of how Jesus Christ was born. We will hear it again at Christmas time, but we are often very busy then. Now we can listen more carefully. We begin with God's message and promise to Mary. This is one of the Joyful Mysteries of the prayer we call the Holy Rosary. This is remembered especially during the month of October (see below).

Our readings for Fridays will anticipate the gospels of the Twenty-ninth and the Thirtieth Sundays of Ordinary Time.

Other Feasts

Across Australia, all schools are on holidays for some or all of the period from Monday, 30 September, to Friday, 11 October. Those who return to school on Monday, 7 October, may wish to pray a simple prayer on the feast of the Holy Rosary.

1. Begin with the Sign of the Cross
2. Read the passage about the feast
3. Pray the Psalm for October
4. Read the scripture passage indicated below.
5. Reflect in silence after the reading
6. Pray intercessions in the usual way
7. Use the Closing Prayer for October.

MONDAY, OCTOBER 7
FEAST OF THE HOLY ROSARY
Reading: Luke 1:35-38

Today we celebrate the feast of Our Lady of the Rosary. The Rosary is a prayer in which we remember events of Jesus' life and Mary's part in this. There are four groups of these events which are called mysteries. They are: the Joyful Mysteries which are about the incarnation and birth of Jesus; the Mysteries of Light, about the public life of Jesus; the Sorrowful Mysteries, about the suffering and death of Jesus; and the Glorious Mysteries, about Jesus' triumph over death through his resurrection.

We pray the Rosary by repeating the 'Hail Mary' many times; this is a way of joining Mary in prayer. We pray the 'Hail Mary' in sets of ten; each set is called a decade. When we say the Rosary, we pray five decades.

Feasts and Other Commemorations

- The feast of St Luke the Evangelist is on October 18; we will keep it on the 17th. Luke became a Christian after Jesus' resurrection and learned about Jesus from other Christians. He is named as the author of the third gospel and of the Acts of the Apostles. Luke became a missionary and travelled with Paul bringing the good news of Jesus to other nations.
- The feast of another two apostles, Simon and Jude, occurs on October 28. Simon, known as the Zealot was very enthusiastic about God's work. It is said that Jude did very brave things for Jesus.
- World Food Day (October 15) and the International Day for the Eradication of Poverty (October 17) call us to be mindful of the many in our world who are hungry and without adequate clothing. During this week we can bring tins or packets of food as gifts that can later be given to the Saint Vincent de Paul Society in the parish, or to some other charitable organization, for distribution to those in need of food.
- On October 22 the Jewish feast of Simkat Torah is celebrated. Simkat Torah means 'the rejoicing in the Torah.' Torah is the name for the first five books of the Bible – Genesis, Exodus, Leviticus, Numbers and Deuteronomy. In many Jewish meeting places on this day, the scrolls of the Torah are carried around the synagogue seven times. Jews begin reading from the book of Genesis on this day. Throughout the year they continue reading the Torah and finish with the book of Deuteronomy. They will finish the whole Torah by this time next year. Then they will begin again.
- United Nations Day is on October 24. Its purpose is to remind people everywhere of the need for peace between all people, races and nations.

Preparation for October

As we begin the new term, make sure that the prayer space still looks bright and fresh, and reflects the new life of spring.

The Psalm for October is on page 198. It is called the Canticle of Daniel and is full of images of nature and the earth. All creation cries out in praise of God. Copy the psalm for each member of the class.

Suggested Hymns

October is a month to rejoice in God's creation. The 'Prayer of Saint Francis', 'For the fruits of this creation', 'All creatures of our God and king', 'One great family' are all suitable.

Suitable songs while we are reading about the events leading up to the birth of Jesus are 'There is nothing told about this woman', 'Christ be our Light', 'He came down' (GA, 293) and 'Laudate Dominum'. If you have the little book *Come all you People: Shorter Songs for Worship* (John Bell. Wild Goose Publications, 1994) there is a very suitable round 'Now let us sing'. It is better not to sing Christmas carols at this time of the year. For further suggestions refer to the hymn chart on pages viii-ix

A Psalm for October

Daniel 3:56-57, 62-63, 66, 70, 72-73

LEADER
Bless God beyond the stars.
Give praise and glory.
ALL
Bless God, heaven and earth.
Give praise and glory for ever.

SIDE A
Bless God, sun and moon.
Give praise and glory.

SIDE B
Bless God, stars of heaven.
Give praise and glory for ever.

SIDE A
Bless God, fire and heat.
Give praise and glory.

SIDE B
Bless God, frost and sleet.
Give praise and glory for ever.

SIDE A

Bless God, light and darkness.
Give praise and glory.

SIDE B
Bless God, lightning and clouds.
Give praise and glory for ever.

LEADER
Bless God beyond the stars.
Give praise and glory.
ALL
Bless God, heaven and earth.
Give praise and glory for ever.

Glory be to the Father, and to the Son,
and to the Holy Spirit:
As it was in the beginning, is now,
and ever shall be,
world without end. **Amen.** Alleluia.

[Turn back to Daily Prayer for today.]

Monday Daily Prayer

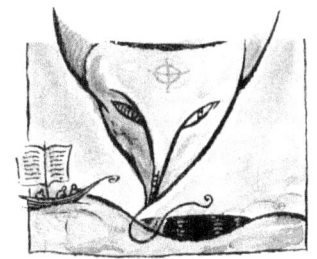

[Reminder: the Psalm for October is on page 198. Make a copy for each member of the class.]

Introduction

Last night Jewish people began celebrating the feast of Sukkot (*su-KOT*). They build tents and decorate them to recall God's protection for their ancestors when they wandered in the desert and lived in temporary shelters. The tents also remind them of shelters built in the fields at harvest time. For all these blessings they give God thanks.

During this month we will hear the story of how Jesus Christ was born. We will hear it again at Christmas time but we are often very busy then. Now we can listen more carefully. We begin with God's message and promise to Mary.

✝ All make the Sign of the Cross.

Hymn

A Psalm for October

[Turn to page 198.]

Reading   *Luke 1:26-32*

Listen to the words of the holy gospel according to Luke:

God sent the angel Gabriel to the town of Nazareth in Galilee with a message for a virgin named Mary. She was engaged to Joseph from the family of King David. The angel greeted Mary and said, "You are truly blessed! The Lord is with you."

   Mary was confused by the angel's words and wondered what they meant. Then the angel told Mary, "Don't be afraid! God is pleased with you, and you will have a son. His name will be Jesus. He will be great and will be called the Son of God the Most High."

The gospel of the Lord.

Reflection

Why was Mary confused and made afraid by what the angel was saying? How does this reading show that Jesus is truly human and truly divine?

Closing

Let us bring our hopes and needs to God, as we pray: **God of tender mercy, hear our prayer.**

Let us pray with the words that Jesus taught us:

Our Father …

Lord our God,
through the angel Gabriel
you prepared Mary
for the coming of Jesus, the Saviour.
Open our hearts to receive him.
Teach us to look for him each day,
and follow him with joy.
We ask this through Christ our Lord. **Amen.**

[Sing 'alleluia'.]

✝ All make the Sign of the Cross.

October 14, 2019

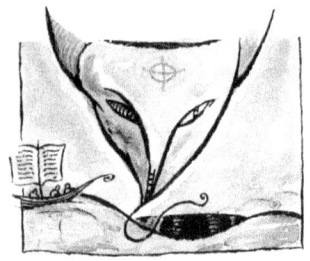

Tuesday Daily Prayer

Introduction

Today we remember Saint Teresa of Jesus, sometimes known as Teresa of Avila. Teresa of Jesus was a Carmelite (*KAR-muh-lite*) sister in the town of Avila in Spain. She wrote many excellent books about God and the life of prayer. She died in 1582. Four hundred years later, Teresa was named a Doctor of the church. The word doctor can mean 'wise teacher'. Teresa is one of only three women Doctors of the Church.

Today's reading reminds us that Mary was full of God's grace from the first moment of her life. Because of this honour, she would be invited to be the mother of the Saviour. Mary accepted this invitation with wonder and trust.

✞ All make the Sign of the Cross.

Hymn

A Psalm for October

[Turn to page 198.]

Reading   *Luke 1:26, 29, 34-38*

Listen to the words of the holy gospel according to Luke:

God sent the angel Gabriel to the town of Nazareth in Galilee with a message for a virgin named Mary.
   Mary was confused by the angel's words and wondered what they meant.
   Mary asked the angel, "How can this happen? I am not married!"
   The angel answered, "The Holy Spirit will come down to you, and God's power will come over you. So your child will be called the holy Son of God. Your relative Elizabeth is also going to have a son, even though she is old. Nothing is impossible for God."
   Mary said, "I am the Lord's servant! Let it happen as you have said." And the angel left her.

The gospel of the Lord.

Reflection

What is Mary's first response to God's plan? How does this change? How do I respond when I am afraid and confused? Can I say 'yes' to God like Mary?

Closing

Let us bring our hopes and needs to God, as we pray: **God of tender mercy, hear our prayer.**

Let us pray with the words that Jesus taught us:

Our Father …

Lord our God,
through the angel Gabriel
you prepared Mary
for the coming of Jesus, the Saviour.
Open our hearts to receive him.
Teach us to look for him each day,
and follow him with joy.
We ask this through Christ our Lord. **Amen.**

[Sing 'alleluia'.]

✞ All make the Sign of the Cross.

October 15, 2019

Wednesday Daily Prayer

Introduction

Today is World Food Day and tomorrow is the International Day for the Eradication of Poverty. These days call us to be mindful of the many in our world who are hungry and without adequate clothing or shelter.

Let us think about all that we have, all that we are, and all who love us. All good things come from God to share with those who are not as fortunate as ourselves.

Today's reading tells us what Mary did when she learned that her cousin Elizabeth was going to have a baby. Mary went to visit her. The happy meeting of these two pregnant women is our story today. Elizabeth's child was John the Baptist. Mary's child was Jesus. That is why Elizabeth told Mary she was so blessed.

✞ All make the Sign of the Cross.

Hymn

A Psalm for October

[Turn to page 198.]

Reading *Luke 1:39-42, 45-48*

Listen to the words of the holy gospel according to Luke.

Mary hurried to a town in the hill country of Judea (*joo-DEE-uh*). She went into Zechariah's (*zek-uh-RYE-uhz*) home, where she greeted Elizabeth. When Elizabeth heard Mary's greeting, her baby moved within her.

The Holy Spirit came upon Elizabeth. Then in a loud voice she said to Mary, "God has blessed you more than any other woman! He has also blessed the child you will have. The Lord has blessed you because you believed that he will keep his promise."
Mary said,
"With all my heart I praise the Lord,
   and I am glad because of God my Saviour.
God cares for me, his humble servant.
From now on, all people will say
   God has blessed me."

The gospel of the Lord.

Reflection

Why did Mary go to visit her cousin Elizabeth? Why were they both full of joy? What promise did God make to each of them? Do I bring joy to others?

Closing

Let us bring our hopes and needs to God, as we pray: **God of tender mercy, hear our prayer.**

Let us pray with the words that Jesus taught us:

Our Father …

Mary, our mother,
you sheltered Jesus in your own body.
You raised him with a mother's care
and followed him in faith.
Teach us all to celebrate God's saving love.
We ask this through Christ our Lord. **Amen.**

[Sing 'alleluia'.]

✞ All make the Sign of the Cross.

October 16, 2019

Thursday Daily Prayer

Introduction

Today is the feast of Luke the evangelist (*ee-VAN-jel-ist*). Luke wrote the third gospel and the Acts of the Apostles. He was a doctor, and some think he was also an artist. Luke became a Christian after Jesus' resurrection and had to learn about Jesus from other Christians. Luke became a missionary and travelled with Paul bringing the good news of Jesus to many nations.

✝ All make the Sign of the Cross.

Hymn

A Psalm for October

[Turn to page 198.]

Reading 2 Timothy 4:9-11, 13, 16-18

Let us listen to the words of the apostle Paul:

Come to see me as soon as you can. Demas loves the things of this world so much that he left me. Crescens (*KRESHs-ens*) has gone to Galatia (*guh-LAY-shuh*) and Titus has gone to Dalmatia (*dal-MAY-shuh*). Only Luke has stayed with me.

Mark can be very helpful to me, so please find him and bring him with you. When you come, bring the coat I left with Carpus. Don't forget to bring the scrolls, especially the ones made of leather.

When I was first put on trial, no one helped me. In fact, everyone deserted me. I hope it won't be held against them. But the Lord stood beside me. He gave me the strength to tell his full message, so that all Gentiles would hear it. The Lord will always keep me from being harmed by evil, and he will bring me safely into his heavenly kingdom. Praise him for ever and ever! **Amen.**

The word of the Lord.

Reflection

Do you think it was harder to be a Christian in the early days than it is now? Is there anyone who would stand by me the way Luke stood by Paul? Do I stand by my friends?

Closing

Let us bring our hopes and needs to God, as we pray: **God of strength, hear our prayer.**

Let us pray with the words that Jesus taught us:

Our Father ...

Divine Wisdom,
you led Saint Luke and other women and men,
to put into the holy Bible
words that would bring us closer to you.
Help us to understand the Bible
better and better each day.
Let your word, like good seed,
take root in our hearts
and bear fruit in our lives.
We ask this through Christ our Lord. **Amen.**

[Sing 'alleluia'.]

✝ All make the Sign of the Cross.

October 17, 2019

Friday Daily Prayer

Introduction

People sometimes get tired of each other. Parents get tired of children asking for things. Teachers and students get tired of the same old lessons. We sometimes get tired of friends who borrow our things. In today's reading Jesus tells us that God never gets tired of us. God is the one who will never say, "Stop bothering me!"

☦ All make the Sign of the Cross.

Hymn

A Psalm for October

[Turn to page 198.]

Reading   Luke 18:1-8

Listen to the words of the holy gospel according to Luke:

Jesus told his disciples a story about how they should keep on praying and never give up: In a town there was once a judge who didn't fear God or care about people. In that same town there was a widow who kept going to the judge and saying, "Make sure that I get fair treatment in court."
 For a while the judge refused to do anything. Finally he said to himself, "Even though I don't fear God or care about people, I will help this widow because she keeps on bothering me. If I don't help her, she will wear me out."
 The Lord said, "Think about what that crooked judge said. Won't God protect his chosen ones who pray to him day and night? Won't he be concerned for them? He will surely hurry and help them."

The gospel of the Lord.

Reflection

We often turn to God when we need help. Do I get discouraged when God does not seem to do what I ask in prayer? What is Jesus' advice to us?

Closing

Let us bring our hopes and needs to God, as we pray: **Patient God, hear our prayer.**

Let us pray with the words that Jesus taught us:

Our Father ...

Gracious God,
through the presence of your Spirit
and the unity of the church,
you hear and answer us.
Strengthen in us the gift of prayer
and deepen in us the gift of faith.
We ask this through Christ our Lord, **Amen.**

[Sing 'alleluia'.]

☦ All make the Sign of the Cross.

October 18, 2019

Monday Daily Prayer

Introduction

Last week we heard the beginning of Mary's song of praise for all that God has done for her and for all God's people. Today we hear more of it. Her song is called the "Magnificat" (*marn-YIFF-ee-cart*) because that is the song's first word in the Latin language. The church sings this great prayer of Mary every evening.

✝ All make the Sign of the Cross.

Hymn

A Psalm for October

[Turn to page 198.]

Reading *Luke 1:46-49, 53-55*

Listen to the words of the holy gospel according to Luke:

Mary spoke these words:
"With all my heart I praise the Lord,
   and I am glad because of God my Saviour.
God cares for me, his humble servant.
From now on, all people will say
   God has blessed me.
God All-Powerful has done great things for me,
   and his name is holy.
God gives the hungry good things to eat,
   and sends the rich away with nothing.
God helps his servant Israel
   and is always merciful to his people.
The Lord made this promise to our ancestors,
   to Abraham and his family forever!"

The gospel of the Lord.

Reflection

Like Mary, do I praise God with 'all my heart'? Does God turn the world upside down as Mary says? What promise did God make to Abraham? Am I part of his family?

Closing

Let us bring our hopes and needs to God, as we pray: **God of tender mercy, hear our prayer.**

Let us pray with the words that Jesus taught us:

Our Father …

Mary, our mother,
you sheltered Jesus in your own body.
You raised him with a mother's care
and followed him in faith.
Teach us all to celebrate God's saving love.
We ask this through Christ our Lord. **Amen.**

[Sing 'alleluia'.]

✝ All make the Sign of the Cross.

October 21, 2019

Tuesday Daily Prayer

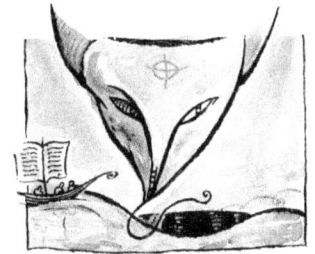

Introduction

At sundown last night, the Jewish festival of Simkat Torah (*SIM-hart TORE-uh*) began. Simkat Torah means 'the rejoicing in the Torah.' This is the first five books of the Bible – Genesis, Exodus, Leviticus, Numbers and Deuteronomy (*dew-ter-ON-uh-mee*). In many Jewish meeting places, the scrolls of the Torah are carried around seven times, perhaps with dancing. This shows the Jews' great love for the word of God. They read the whole Torah from start to finish each year.

Today's reading tells us about the birth of Jesus' cousin, John the Baptist, and how he came to be called John. When he was born, his parents Elizabeth and Zechariah (*zec-uh-RYE-uh*) and all their relatives and neighbours were very joyful and praised God. When he grew up John the Baptist made the way ready for Jesus.

✞ All make the Sign of the Cross.

Hymn

A Psalm for October

[Turn to page 198.]

Reading   Luke 1:57-64

Listen to the words of the holy gospel according to Luke:

When Elizabeth's son was born, her neighbours and relatives heard how kind the Lord had been to her, and they too were glad.

Eight days later they did for the child what the Law of Moses commands. They were going to name him Zechariah (*zec-uh-RYE-uh*) after his father. But Elizabeth said, "No! His name is John."

The people argued, "No one in your family has ever been named John." So they motioned to Zechariah to find out what he wanted to name his son.

Zechariah asked for a writing tablet. Then he wrote, "His name is John." Everyone was amazed. Right away Zechariah started speaking and praising God.

The gospel of the Lord.

Reflection

Why were people surprised when the baby was given the name 'John'? Are names often special in the Bible? What do they say? How was my name chosen?

Closing

Let us bring our hopes and needs to God, as we pray: **God of tender mercy, hear our prayer.**

Let us pray with the words that Jesus taught us:

Our Father …

Lord our God,
you prepared Zechariah and Elizabeth
for the birth of their son, John,
who would prepare the way for Jesus.
Open our hearts to receive Jesus, our Saviour.
Teach us to look for him each day,
and follow him with joy.
We ask this through Christ our Lord. **Amen.**

[Sing 'alleluia'.]

✞ All make the Sign of the Cross.

October 22, 2019

Wednesday Daily Prayer

Introduction

For some days we have been reading about how God prepared Mary to be the mother of Jesus, with Joseph by her side. Today we read the story of how Jesus was born. Those who go to the special Midnight Mass at Christmas will hear it again then.

☦ All make the Sign of the Cross.

Hymn

A Psalm for October

[Turn to page 198.]

Reading　　　　　　　　　Luke 2:5-14

Listen to the words of the holy gospel according to Luke:

Mary was engaged to Joseph and travelled with him to Bethlehem. She was soon going to have a baby, and while they were there, she gave birth to her first-born son. She dressed him in baby clothes and laid him in a manger, because there was no room for them in the inn.

That night in the fields near Bethlehem some shepherds were guarding their sheep. All at once an angel came down to them from the Lord, and the brightness of the Lord's glory flashed around them. The shepherds were frightened. But the angel said, "Don't be afraid! I have good news for you, which will make everyone happy. This very day in King David's hometown a Saviour was born for you. He is Christ the Lord. You will know who he is, because you will find him dressed in baby clothes and lying in a manger."

Suddenly many other angels came down from heaven and joined in praising God. They said: "Praise God in heaven! Peace on earth to everyone who pleases God."

The gospel of the Lord.

Reflection

Shepherds were dirty and poor. Why did the angel appear to them? What was the angel's message to them? How were they to recognise Jesus? How can I recognise Jesus today?

Closing

Let us bring our hopes and needs to God, as we pray: **God of tender mercy, hear our prayer.**

Let us pray with the words that Jesus taught us:

Our Father ...

Lord our God,
you prepared Mary and Joseph
for the birth of their son, Jesus.
Open our hearts to receive Jesus, our Saviour.
Teach us to look for him each day,
and follow him with joy.
We ask this through Christ our Lord. **Amen.**

[Sing 'alleluia'.]

☦ All make the Sign of the Cross.

October 23, 2019

Thursday Daily Prayer

Introduction

Today is United Nations Day. Australia played a key role in founding the United Nations Organisation in 1945. Its purpose is to remind people everywhere of the need for peace between all people, races and nations.
One person who worked with the United Nations for peace and human rights, especially in Kosovo, Rwanda and East Timor, was Sergio de Mello from Brazil. He gave his life for peace when he died in a bomb blast in Baghdad in 2003.

Today we continue the story of the birth of Jesus in Bethlehem. The shepherds hurry off to find the new-born child and they tell Mary and Joseph what the angels had said about him.

✝ All make the Sign of the Cross.

Hymn

A Psalm for October

[Turn to page 198.]

Reading   Luke 2:15-19

Listen to the words of the holy gospel according to Luke:

After the angels had left and gone back to heaven, the shepherds said to each other, "Let's go to Bethlehem and see what the Lord has told us about." They hurried off and found Mary and Joseph, and they saw the baby lying in a manger.
   When the shepherds saw Jesus, they told his parents what the angel had said about him. Everyone listened and was surprised. But Mary kept thinking about all this and wondering what it meant.

The gospel of the Lord.

Reflection

Mary was puzzled by the angel's words that her son was to be the Saviour, but quietly kept on thinking about it. Am I ever puzzled about God's ways? Are they different from what people expect? How can I get to know them?

Closing

Let us bring our hopes and needs to God, as we pray: **God of tender mercy, hear our prayer.**

Let us pray with the words that Jesus taught us:

Our Father ...

Lord our God,
you prepared Mary and Joseph
for the birth of their son, Jesus.
Open our hearts to receive Jesus, our Saviour.
Teach us to look for him each day,
and follow him with joy.
We ask this through Christ our Lord. **Amen.**

[Sing 'alleluia'.]

✝ All make the Sign of the Cross.

Friday Daily Prayer

Introduction

We have all met people who brag and show off. Jesus knows that we all act like that sometimes. In today's reading from the Sunday gospel Jesus tells us how important it is to be very simple and honest when we pray. We do not need to pretend with God, because God does not compare us with other people.

✝ All make the Sign of the Cross.

Hymn

A Psalm for October

[Turn to page 198.]

Reading   *Luke 18:9-14*

Listen to the words of the holy gospel according to Luke:

Jesus told a story to some people who thought they were better than others and who looked down on everyone else.
  "Two men went into the temple to pray. One was a Pharisee and the other a tax collector. The Pharisee stood over by himself and prayed, 'God, I thank you that I am not greedy, dishonest, and unfaithful in marriage like other people. And I am really glad that I am not like that tax collector over there. I go without eating for two days a week, and I give you one tenth of all I earn.'
  "The tax collector stood off at a distance and did not think he was good enough even to look up toward heaven. He was so sorry for what he had done that he pounded his chest and prayed, 'God, have pity on me! I am such a sinner.'"

Then Jesus said, "When the two men went home, it was the tax collector and not the Pharisee who was pleasing to God."

The gospel of the Lord.

Reflection

Why was the tax collector so pleasing to God? Do I sometimes look down on people? Why should we be honest when we pray?

Closing

Let us bring our hopes and needs to God, as we pray: **Just God, hear our prayer.**

Let us pray with the words that Jesus taught us:

Our Father …

Gracious God,
through the presence of your Spirit
and the unity of the church,
you hear and answer us.
Strengthen in us the gift of prayer
and deepen in us the gift of faith.
We ask this through Christ our Lord. **Amen**.

[Sing 'alleluia'.]

✝ All make the Sign of the Cross.

October 25, 2019

Monday Daily Prayer

Introduction

Today is the feast of two apostles, Simon the Zealot (ZELL-ut) or 'eager one,' and Jude Thaddaeus (th-DAY-us). Zealots work wildly for a cause. They have little balance and are not very cautious. Simon may have been called a zealot because he belonged to the political party called the Zealots, or maybe he was just enthusiastic about doing God's work.

Thaddaeus means 'brave.' This name tells us that Jude did brave things for Jesus. It also keeps us from mixing up Jude Thaddaeus with Judas Iscariot, the traitor.

✝ All make the Sign of the Cross.

Hymn

A Psalm for October

[Turn to page 198.]

Reading *Mark 3:13-19*

Listen to the words of the holy gospel according to Mark:

Jesus decided to ask some of his disciples to go up on a mountain with him, and they went. Then he chose twelve of them to be his apostles, so that they could be with him. Jesus also wanted to send them out to preach and to force out demons.

Simon was one of the twelve, and Jesus named him Peter. There were also James and John, the two sons of Zebedee. Jesus called them "Thunderbolts". Andrew, Bartholomew (bar-THOL-uh-mew), Matthew, Thomas, James son of Alphaeus (AL-fee-us), and Thaddaeus were also apostles. The others were Simon, known as the Eager One, and Judas Iscariot who later betrayed Jesus.

The gospel of the Lord.

Reflection

The word 'apostle' means 'someone sent on a mission.' Why is it important to know the names and stories of the apostles? Who are some people today who are like apostles? In what ways can I act like an apostle?

Closing

Let us bring our hopes and needs to God, as we pray: **God of apostles, hear our prayer.**

Let us pray with the words that Jesus taught us:

Our Father ...

Lord God, we thank you for sending apostles to the whole world.
We welcome those who bring your good news.
We pray for them and listen to their teaching.
Call on us, one day, to become apostles, too.
We ask this through Christ our Lord. **Amen.**

[Sing 'alleluia'.]

✝ All make the Sign of the Cross.

October 28, 2019

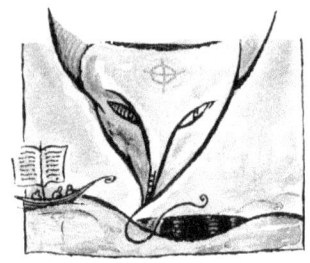

Tuesday Daily Prayer

Introduction

In today's reading, Mary and Joseph take Jesus to the Temple, forty days after he was born. This was to fulfil the law of Moses – mothers were to take their new-born babies to the temple to be presented to the Lord. On that occasion the parents are required to offer a special sacrifice.

✝ All make the Sign of the Cross.

Hymn

A Psalm for October

[Turn to page 198.]

Reading   *Luke 2:21-24*

Listen to the words of the holy gospel according to Luke:

Eight days later (after the birth of Jesus), Jesus' parents did for him what the Law of Moses commands. And they named him Jesus, just as the angel had told Mary when he promised she would have a baby.
The time came for Mary and Joseph to do what the law of Moses says a mother is supposed to do after her baby is born.
  They took Jesus to the temple in Jerusalem and presented him to the Lord, just as the Law of the Lord says, "Each first-born baby boy belongs to the Lord." The law of the Lord also says that parents have to offer a sacrifice, giving at least a pair of doves or two young pigeons. So that is what Mary and Joseph did.

The gospel of the Lord.

Reflection

Our practice today is different from the Jewish custom when Jesus was a baby. What do parents do today to make sure their baby is a child of God? What name does the church give to this special sacrament? Have you ever been to one of these celebrations?

Closing

Let us bring our hopes and needs to God, as we pray: **God of tender mercy, hear our prayer.**

Let us pray with the words that Jesus taught us:

Our Father ...

Lord our God,
you prepared Mary and Joseph
for the birth of their son, Jesus.
Open our hearts to receive Jesus, our Saviour.
Teach us to look for him each day,
and follow him with joy.
We ask this through Christ our Lord. **Amen.**

[Sing 'alleluia'.]

✝ All make the Sign of the Cross.

October 29, 2019

Wednesday Daily Prayer

Introduction

One of the people who was in the temple in Jerusalem when Mary and Joseph came with the baby Jesus was an old man named Simeon. He had been waiting all his life for God to send a Saviour to his people. When he saw that Jesus was the one whom God had promised, he broke out in a song of praise to God.

✣ All make the Sign of the Cross.

Hymn

A Psalm for October

[Turn to page 198.]

Reading   *Luke 2:25-27, 27-32*

Listen to the words of the holy gospel according to Luke:

Simeon (*SIM-ee-un*) was a good man. He loved God and was waiting for God to save the people of Israel. God's Spirit came to him and told him that he would not die until he had seen Christ the Lord.
When Mary and Joseph brought Jesus to the temple, the Spirit told Simeon to go into the temple. Simeon took the baby Jesus in his arms and praised God,
"Lord, I am your servant,
and now I can die in peace,
because you have kept your promise to me.
With my own eyes I have seen
what you have done to save your people,
  and foreign nations will also see this.
Your mighty power is a light for all nations,
and it will bring honour to your people Israel."

The gospel of the Lord.

Reflection

Simeon was a patient man, waiting a long time for God to act. What did he see when Mary and Joseph brought Jesus to the temple? How did he react? How can I see with eyes of faith like Simeon?

Closing

Let us bring our hopes and needs to God, as we pray: **God of tender mercy, hear our prayer.**

Let us pray with the words that Jesus taught us:

Our Father …

God of joy,
you prepared Simeon and Anna
for the birth of Jesus the Messiah.
Open our hearts to receive Jesus, our Saviour.
Teach us to look for him each day,
and follow him with joy.
We ask this through Christ our Lord. **Amen.**

[Sing 'alleluia'.]

✣ All make the Sign of the Cross.

October 30, 2019

Thursday Daily Prayer

[Reminder: The Psalm for November is on page 216. Make a copy for each member of the class.]

Introduction

Today we finish the story of Jesus' birth. Another person who was in the temple when Mary and Joseph brought Jesus was an elderly widow named Anna. Like Simeon, she saw that Jesus was the one whom God had promised to save his people. So she too praised God. Then Jesus' family took him home to Nazareth.

✞ All make the Sign of the Cross.

Hymn

A Psalm for October

[Turn to page 198.]

Reading   Luke 2:27, 36, 37, 38-40

Listen to the words of the holy gospel according to Luke:

When Mary and Joseph brought Jesus to the temple, the prophet Anna was also there. She was eighty-four years old. Night and day she served God in the temple by praying and often going without eating. She praised God and spoke about the child Jesus to everyone who hoped for Jerusalem to be set free.

After Joseph and Mary had done everything that the Law of the Lord commands, they returned home to Nazareth. Jesus became strong and wise, and God blessed him.

The gospel of the Lord.

Reflection

Anna was old and holy and wise. Do I know anyone like her? Do I listen to them? Am I like Jesus, growing strong and wise?

Closing

Let us bring our hopes and needs to God, as we pray: **God of tender mercy, hear our prayer.**

Let us pray with the words that Jesus taught us:

Our Father …

God of joy,
you prepared Simeon and Anna
for the birth of Jesus the Messiah.
Open our hearts to receive Jesus, our Saviour.
Teach us to look for him each day,
and follow him with joy.
We ask this through Christ our Lord. **Amen.**

[Sing 'alleluia'.]

✞ All make the Sign of the Cross.

October 31, 2019

November

Friday, November 1,
to Thursday, November 28

Ordinary Time ~ November 2019
Looking Ahead

About the Season

November is the last month of spring. It holds the promise of summer. Some parts of our country may already be quite hot.

In an earlier calendar that began in March, November was the ninth month of the year. This meant that September, October and December were the seventh, eighth and tenth months of the year. The Latin words for seven, eight, nine and ten were used to name these months. When two more months were added to the calendar, these names were retained.

November is the last month of the thirty-four weeks of Ordinary Time. We begin November in the thirty-first week. Sunday, November 24 is the Feast of Christ the King, the last Sunday of the Church year. A week later the new year for the church will begin with the First Sunday of Advent on December 1.

November begins with a double feast in remembrance of those who have died. Our Christian faith tells us that one day, we will all be reunited with God in heaven, because we share in the resurrection of Jesus. This belief is known as the 'Communion of Saints.'
All through the month, we offer prayers to remember the dead and to thank God for their lives.

Readings

During November our readings for Daily Prayer come from several books of the bible. In the early part of the month, we will read the story of the raising of Lazarus from the dead. Lazarus was a friend of Jesus and so this story is very suitable for a time of remembering our own relatives and friends who have died. It is a story that proclaims our faith in the power of Christ's resurrection.

For the remainder of November, we will hear a series of readings about women in the Hebrew Scriptures who were known to be holy and 'lovers of wisdom'. As we begin October we will read about women of the early church that were ordinary people who had to go to work, were married, or were leaders in their local churches. We will meet Mary, Dorcas, Lydia, Priscilla, Phoebe, Eunice and Lois. Because these women were baptised and followed Jesus faithfully, we can call them saints.

Feasts and Other Celebrations

- The feast of All Saints is celebrated on November 1. On that day we celebrate all the known and unknown saints and martyrs of the Christian faith.
- Many members of our own families have died and are now with God. We pray for them on November 2, All Souls Day. On both of these days, we are reminded of all who have lived as faithful Christians. They encourage us to grow in our own faith.

- The feast of the Presentation of the Blessed Virgin Mary is celebrated on November 21. The feast came from an ancient legend that Mary's parents, Anna and Joachim, had offered her to God when she was three years old, bringing her to the Temple to dedicate her to the service of God.
- Monday, November 11 is Remembrance Day. It is a special day for remembering those who have died in war. This day marks the end of World War II.

November 20 is observed as United Nations Children's Day. It helps us be aware of children around the world and to join together in improving their lives.

Preparation for November

The Psalm for November is on page 216. In this psalm, peoples, nations and the whole cosmos join to praise God. Copy the psalm for each member of the class.

In November, many people arrange a shrine to honour people who have died. In Japan, people burn incense at their shrines. The people of Mexico have a day called the Day of the Dead and decorate their shrines with symbols of death and resurrection.

You may wish to think about a shrine for your classroom. It can be as simple as a candle (perhaps a new and special one) and an attractively prepared list of people who have died whom you want to remember. You can bring photos or memorial cards of those you want to pray for. Discuss this with your teacher.

A well-known and ancient Prayer for the Dead is the 'Eternal Rest'. During this month the 'Eternal Rest' will often be used as part of our Closing.

Suggested Hymns

November is the last month of Ordinary Time. See the hymn chart on pages viii-ix for suitable Ordinary Time hymns. Also included in the November hymn selection are two suggestions for the last Sunday of Ordinary Time – the Feast of Christ the King – and those that can be sung when praying for our deceased family and friends.

A Psalm for November

Psalm 67:1-7

LEADER
Let all people sing your praises, Lord.
ALL
Let the nations celebrate with joyful songs.

SIDE A
Our God, be kind and bless us!
Be pleased and smile.
Then everyone on earth will learn to follow you,
and all nations will see your power to save us.

SIDE B
Make everyone praise you and shout your praises.
Let the nations celebrate with joyful songs,
   because you judge fairly and guide all nations.
Make everyone praise you and shout your praises.

SIDE A
Our God has blessed the earth
with a wonderful harvest!

SIDE B
Pray for his blessings to continue
and for everyone on earth to worship our God.

LEADER
Make everyone praise you and shout your praises.
ALL
Let the nations celebrate with joyful songs.

Glory be to the Father, and to the Son,
and to the Holy Spirit:
as it was in the beginning, is now,
and ever shall be
world without end. Amen. Alleluia.

[Turn back to Daily Prayer for today.]

Friday Daily Prayer

[Reminder: The Psalm for November is on page 216. Make a copy for each member of the class.]

Introduction

Today is All Saints' Day, the first of a two-day celebration of the saints and of all who have died. The second of these days is All Souls' Day.

During the month of November we turn our hearts to those who have fallen asleep in death. And so today we celebrate the communion of saints – the union of prayer and love between saints on earth (perhaps you and me) and the saints in heaven.

Some saints are famous. Their names are in prayer books and their pictures are in the newspaper or on the walls and windows of churches. Their stories teach us that there are many ways to follow Christ.

Today's reading is part of a vision of the saints in heaven praising God. We on earth join with them to sing one song of praise to God.

✞ All make the Sign of the Cross.

Hymn

A Psalm for November

[Turn to page 216.]

Reading   *Revelation 7:9–10, 13–14*

Listen to the words of the book of Revelation:

I saw a large crowd with more people than could be counted. They were from every race, tribe, nation, and language, and they stood before the throne and before the Lamb. They wore white robes and held palm branches in their hands, as they shouted,

"Our God, who sits upon the throne,
has the power to save his people,
and so does the Lamb."

One of the elders asked me, "Do you know who these people are that are dressed in white robes? Do you know where they come from?"

"Sir," I answered, "you must know."

Then he told me, "These are the ones who have gone through the great suffering. They have washed their robes in the blood of the Lamb and have made them white."

The word of the Lord.

Reflection

What might the white robes of the saints represent? Does your family have a baptismal robe? Which saints does my family honour? Which saints do I really admire and follow as an example?

Closing

Let us now keep silence,
and allow the word of God to sink into our hearts.

Let us pray with the words that Jesus taught us:

Our Father ...

God of grace and wisdom,
you continually raise up good people
who show with their lives
that they follow a holy and loving God.
Let our lives be true to all that our faith teaches,
so that we will grow more and more
  in your Son's likeness.
We ask this through Christ our Lord. **Amen**.

[Sing 'alleluia'.]

✞ All make the Sign of the Cross.

November 1, 2019

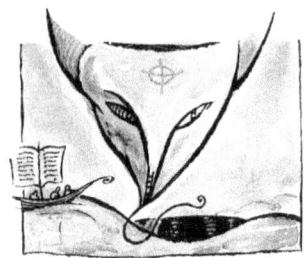

Monday Daily Prayer

Introduction

Saturday was All Souls' Day, the second day of our remembrance of those who have died. During this month we remember relatives and friends who have gone before us.

Many of them are not famous. Their statues are not in the church, but their pictures are in our homes. And their stories may be alive in our families. We know of their goodness and their struggles. We know that they were not perfect but they tried to do their best. We pray for them, and we remember them with love.

In today's reading we read how Jesus encouraged his disciples when they became afraid they were going to lose him.

✢ All make the Sign of the Cross.

Hymn

A Psalm for November

[Turn to page 216.]

Reading *John 14:1-6*

Listen to the words of the holy gospel according to John:

Jesus said to his disciples, "Don't be worried! Have faith in God and have faith in me. There are many rooms in my Father's house. I wouldn't tell you this unless it were true. I am going there to prepare a place for each of you. After I have done this, I will come back and take you with me. Then we will be together. You know the way to where I am going."

Thomas said, "Lord, we don't even know where you are going! So how can we know the way?"

"I am the way, the truth, and the life!" Jesus answered. "Without me, no one can go to the Father."

The gospel of the Lord.

Reflection

It can be very hard when someone important to us dies. Do Jesus' words help us? What is his message to us? How does he show us the way to our eternal home?

Closing

Blessed be God
who raised Jesus Christ from the dead.
Let us all say: Blessed be God forever.
Blessed be God forever.

Let us remember our relatives and friends who have died:

Eternal rest grant unto them, O Lord,
and let perpetual light shine upon them.
May they rest in peace. **Amen.**

May their souls
and the souls of all the faithful departed,
through the mercy of God, rest in peace.
Amen.

Let us pray with the words that Jesus taught us:

Our Father …

[Sing 'alleluia'.]

✢ All make the Sign of the Cross.

Tuesday Daily Prayer

Introduction

A holy hero we remember today is Mary Ward. She was born in England in 1585 when it was dangerous to be a Catholic. She pioneered a new form of life for women combining active service (especially the education of girls) and prayer. But she met with unjust opposition from church authorities and died before seeing her work approved.
In 1909 she was finally recognised as the founder of the Loreto Sisters and of the Congregation of Jesus. Mary was a woman of great courage, creativity, prayer and holiness, and an inspirational leader.

During this month we remember those who have fallen asleep in death and we reflect on our faith in the resurrection of Jesus. To help us do this, we will begin today to read the story of the raising of Lazarus to life.

✜ All make the Sign of the Cross.

Hymn

A Psalm for November

[Turn to page 216.]

Reading   *John 11:1-2, 3-7*

Listen to the words of the holy gospel according to John:

A man by the name of Lazarus was sick in the village of Bethany. He had two sisters, Mary and Martha. The sisters sent a message to the Lord and told him that his good friend Lazarus was sick.
   When Jesus heard this, he said, "His sickness won't end in death. It will bring glory to God and his Son."

   Jesus loved Martha and her sister and brother. But he stayed where he was for two more days. Then he said to his disciples, "Now we'll go back to Judea."

The gospel of the Lord.

Reflection

Jesus loved Martha and Mary and Lazarus. Do we think of Jesus having friends? What do you think Martha and Mary were expecting from Jesus?

Closing

Blessed be God
who raised Jesus Christ from the dead.
Let us all say: Blessed be God forever.
Blessed be God forever.

Let us remember our relatives and friends who have died:

Eternal rest grant unto them, O Lord,
and let perpetual light shine upon them.
May they rest in peace. **Amen**.

May their souls
and the souls of all the faithful departed,
through the mercy of God, rest in peace.
Amen.

Let us pray with the words that Jesus taught us:

Our Father ...

[Sing 'alleluia'.]

✜ All make the Sign of the Cross.

November 5, 2019

Wednesday Daily Prayer

Introduction

Today we continue to listen to the story of Lazarus, the brother of Martha and Mary. This story is taken from the gospel according to John, so we can expect that it will have many meanings for us. John calls each miracle of Jesus a 'sign.' People who believe in Jesus try to read these signs that have been left to us.

In yesterday's reading the two sisters of Lazarus ask Jesus to visit them because Lazarus is sick. So Jesus goes to Bethany and tells his disciples that Lazarus is dead. The disciples are puzzled by his words.

☦ All make the Sign of the Cross.

Hymn

A Psalm for November

[Turn to page 216.]

Reading   John 11:7, 11-15

Listen to the words of the holy gospel according to John:

Jesus said to his disciples, "Now we'll go back to Judea. Our friend Lazarus is asleep, and I'm going there to wake him up."

They replied, "Lord, if he's asleep, he'll get better." Jesus really meant that Lazarus was dead, but they thought he was talking only about sleep.

Then Jesus told them plainly, "Lazarus is dead! I'm glad that I wasn't there, because now you'll have a chance to put your faith in me. Let's go to him."

The gospel of the Lord.

Reflection

Would you have been puzzled about Jesus' words? Why do you think that death of someone we know and love is a time to put our faith in Jesus?

Closing

Blessed be God
who raised Jesus Christ from the dead.
Let us all say: Blessed be God forever.
Blessed be God forever.

Let us remember our relatives and friends who have died:

Eternal rest grant unto them, O Lord,
and let perpetual light shine upon them.
May they rest in peace. **Amen.**

May their souls
and the souls of all the faithful departed,
through the mercy of God, rest in peace. **Amen.**

Let us pray with the words that Jesus taught us:

Our Father …

[Sing 'alleluia'.]

☦ All make the Sign of the Cross.

November 6, 2019

Thursday Daily Prayer

Introduction

A great woman of spirit that we remember around this time is Oodgeroo Noonuccal (*OO-juh-ROO NOO-nuk-uhl*). Born in 1920 and given the name Kath Walker, she grew up on North Stradbroke Island near Brisbane. She became a poet, actress, writer, teacher, artist and campaigner (*kam-PAY-nuh*) for aboriginal rights. Her father taught her to be proud of her aboriginality.

In today's reading Jesus tells Mary and Martha that their brother Lazarus would live again. He tells them that he is the one who raises the dead to life. It is all very puzzling for them.

✞ All make the Sign of the Cross.

Hymn

A Psalm for November

[Turn to page 216.]

Reading   *John 11:1, 3, 20-27*

Listen to the words of the holy gospel according to John:

A man by the name of Lazarus was sick in the village of Bethany. He had two sisters, Mary and Martha. The sisters sent a message to the Lord and told him that his good friend Lazarus was sick.

When Martha heard that Jesus had arrived, she went out to meet him, but Mary stayed in the house. Martha said to Jesus, "Lord, if you'd been here, my brother wouldn't have died. Yet even now I know that God will do anything you ask."

Jesus told her, "Your brother will live again!"

Martha answered, "I know that he'll be raised to life on the last day, when all the dead are raised."

Jesus then said, "I am the one who raises the dead to life! Everyone who has faith in me will live, even if they die. And everyone who lives because of faith in me will never really die. Do you believe this?"

"Yes, Lord!" she replied. "I believe that you are the Christ, the Son of God. You are the one we hoped would come into the world."

The gospel of the Lord.

Reflection

Martha's faith is a model for every Christian. What helps me believe that Jesus is the Messiah, the Son of God? What do we mean when we say in the Creed that we look forward to the resurrection of the dead?

Closing

Blessed be God
who raised Jesus Christ from the dead.
Let us all say: Blessed be God forever.
Blessed be God forever.

Let us remember our relatives and friends who have died:

Eternal rest grant unto them, O Lord,
and let perpetual light shine upon them.
May they rest in peace. **Amen.**

May their souls
and the souls of all the faithful departed,
through the mercy of God, rest in peace.
Amen.

Let us pray with the words that Jesus taught us:

Our Father ...

[Sing 'alleluia'.]

✞ All make the Sign of the Cross.

November 7, 2019

Friday Daily Prayer

Introduction

As November continues, the church's year is coming to a close. At this time we think about the end of life, and even the end of the world. Jesus tells of those last days, and he urges us to live justly so that we will be ready when he comes in glory. Today's reading from the Sunday gospel helps us to imagine what those last days might be like.

☩ All make the Sign of the Cross.

Hymn

A Psalm for November

[Turn to page 216.]

Reading   Luke 21:25-26, 27-28, 34-35

Listen to the words of the holy gospel according to Luke:

Jesus told his disciples, "Strange things will happen to the sun, moon, and stars. The nations on earth will be afraid of the roaring sea and tides, and they won't know what to do. People will be so frightened that they will faint because of what is happening to the world. Then the Son of Man will be seen, coming in a cloud with great power and glory. When all of this starts happening, stand up straight and be brave. You will soon be set free.

"Don't spend all of your time thinking about eating or drinking or worrying about life. If you do, the final day will suddenly catch you like a trap. That day will surprise everyone on earth."

The gospel of the Lord.

Reflection

Can we tell when and how the world will come to an end? Does Jesus want us to be afraid or to be strong? What might it be like when Jesus comes 'in glory'?

Closing

Blessed be God
who raised Jesus Christ from the dead.
Let us all say: Blessed be God forever.
Blessed be God forever.

Let us remember our relatives and friends who have died.

Eternal rest grant unto them, O Lord,
and let perpetual light shine upon them.
May they rest in peace. **Amen**.

May their souls
and the souls of all the faithful departed,
through the mercy of God, rest in peace.
Amen.

Let us pray with the words that Jesus taught us:

Our Father …

[Sing 'alleluia'.]

☩ All make the Sign of the Cross.

November 8, 2019

Monday Daily Prayer

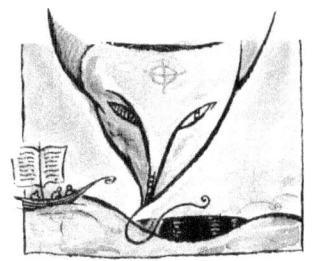

Introduction

Today is Remembrance Day, marking the end of World War I in 1918.

A hero from World War II is Sir Edward Dunlop. He was a surgeon in the Australian Army during the Second World War. His nickname was 'Weary' because he was tireless in his care of wounded soldiers.

They had been taken prisoner and forced build a railway from West Thailand into Burma, even though many were not fit for work. He is sometimes remembered as 'The Surgeon of the Railway' or 'The Christ of the Burma Railway'. He died in 1993.

Today's reading continues the story of Lazarus. When Jesus heard that his friend had died, he cried. It might be hard for us to think of Jesus feeling sad or worried. Even though Jesus had the power and glory of God, Jesus was also human, just as we are.

✞ All make the Sign of the Cross.

Hymn

A Psalm for November

[Turn to page 216.]

Reading *John 11:32-36, 38-40*

Listen to the words of the holy gospel according to John:

Mary went to where Jesus was. Then as soon as she saw him, she knelt at his feet and said, "Lord, if you'd been here, my brother wouldn't have died."

When Jesus saw that Mary and the people with her were crying, he was terribly upset and asked, "Where have you put his body?"

They replied, "Lord, come and you will see."

Jesus started crying, and the people said, "See how much he loved Lazarus."

Jesus was still terribly upset. So he went to the tomb, which was a cave with a stone rolled against the entrance. Then he told the people to roll the stone away. But Martha said, "Lord, you know that Lazarus has been dead for four days, and there will be a bad smell."

Jesus replied, "Didn't I tell you that if you had faith, you would see the glory of God?"

The gospel of the Lord.

Reflection

Is it hard to imagine Jesus crying? What does that tell us about his feelings for his friends? Is he by our side when we cry at the death of someone we know and love?

Closing

Blessed be God
who raised Jesus Christ from the dead.
Let us all say: Blessed be God forever.
Blessed be God forever.

Let us remember our relatives and friends who have died:

Eternal rest grant unto them, O Lord,
and let perpetual light shine upon them.
May they rest in peace. **Amen.**

May their souls
and the souls of all the faithful departed,
through the mercy of God, rest in peace. **Amen.**

Let us pray with the words that Jesus taught us:

Our Father ...

[Sing 'alleluia'.]

✞ All make the Sign of the Cross.

November 11, 2019

Tuesday Daily Prayer

Introduction

At this time we remember Catherine McAuley (*muh-KOR-lee*). She was born in Dublin in 1778 and died in 1841. In 1824 she built a house to serve poor women and children, and visited the sick in their homes and in hospital. Seven years later she and her co-workers founded the Sisters of Mercy.

There are many Sisters of Mercy in Australia and throughout the world, working in education, health care, welfare and justice ministries.

Today we come to the happy ending of the story of Lazarus. Jesus shows his divine power by calling Lazarus back from the dead and setting him free. Many of those who saw this great sign came to believe in Jesus.

✞ All make the Sign of the Cross.

Hymn

A Psalm for November

[Turn to page 216.]

Reading   John 11:41-45

Listen to the words of the holy gospel according to John:

After the stone had been rolled aside, Jesus looked up towards heaven and prayed, "Father, I thank you for answering my prayer. I know that you always answer my prayers. But I said this, so that the people here would believe that you sent me."

When Jesus had finished praying, he shouted, "Lazarus, come out!" The man who had been dead came out. His hands and feet were wrapped with strips of burial cloth, and a cloth covered his face.

Jesus then told the people, "Untie him and let him go."

Many of the people who had come to visit Mary saw the things that Jesus did, and they put their faith in him.

The gospel of the Lord.

Reflection

Sometimes this story is read at a Sunday Mass during the season of Easter. Why do you think that Easter is a good time to hear the story of Lazarus? Why is November also a good time to hear this story?

Closing

Blessed be God
who raised Jesus Christ from the dead.
Let us all say: Blessed be God forever.
Blessed be God forever.

Let us remember our relatives and friends who have died:

Eternal rest grant unto them, O Lord,
and let perpetual light shine upon them.
May they rest in peace. **Amen**.

May their souls
and the souls of all the faithful departed,
through the mercy of God, rest in peace.
Amen.

Let us pray with the words that Jesus taught us:

Our Father ...

[Sing 'alleluia'.]

✞ All make the Sign of the Cross.

November 12, 2019

Wednesday Daily Prayer

Introduction

In many of the stories in the Bible the main characters are men, but there are also good stories about women in both the Old and the New Testaments. In our readings over the two weeks we will hear about women who played important roles in the story of God's work in the world.

Today's reading tells us about Deborah, one of the judges of Israel. Before the Israelites were united under one king, they were ruled by judges. Judges settled disputes, gave sincere and honest leadership, and commanded armies when it was necessary.

✝ All make the Sign of the Cross.

Hymn

A Psalm for November

[Turn to page 216.]

Reading   *Judges 4:4–9*

Listen to the words of the book of Judges:

Deborah was a prophet and a leader of Israel during those days. She would sit under Deborah's Palm Tree in the hill country of Ephraim (EF–rum), where Israelites would come and ask her to settle their legal cases.

One day Deborah sent word for Barak to come and talk with her. When he arrived, she said, "I have a message for you from the Lord God of Israel! You are to get together an army of ten thousand men and lead them to Mount Tabor.

"The Lord will trick Sisera into coming out to fight you at the river. They will have their chariots, but the Lord has promised to help you defeat them."

"I'm not going unless you go!" Barak told her.

"All right, I'll go!" she replied. "But I'm warning you that the Lord is going to let a woman defeat Sisera, and no one will honour you for winning the battle."

The word of the Lord.

Reflection

How did Deborah show courage and wisdom? Why did Deborah think it might bother Barak when she got the honour for victory? Who did Deborah think should really get credit for the victory?

Closing

Let us bring our hopes and needs to God, as we pray: **God of prophets, hear our prayer.**

Let us pray with the words that Jesus taught us:

Our Father …

God of grace and wisdom,
you continually raise up good people
who show with their lives
that they follow a holy and loving God.
Let our lives be true to all that our faith teaches,
so that we will grow more and more
    in your son's likeness.
We ask this through Christ our Lord. **Amen.**

[Sing 'alleluia'.]

✝ All make the Sign of the Cross.

November 13, 2019

Thursday Daily Prayer

Introduction

In November 1989, six Jesuit priests with their housekeeper and her 15-year-old daughter were martyred in El Salvador, Central America. These men stood with the poor of this small country and with those who were unjustly and harshly treated by the government. They fearlessly preached the Gospel of Jesus Christ. They are models of faith and can be called modern peacemakers and prophets.

In today's reading we hear about another brave woman from long ago – Queen Esther. When her people were in danger of being killed, she prepared to beg her husband the king to spare them. To do this she had to be very brave. She had to risk her own life for the sake of her people. She made herself like a beggar and prayed hard for God's help.

✝ All make the Sign of the Cross.

Hymn

A Psalm for November

[Turn to page 216.]

Reading   *Esther 14:1-4, 12-14*

Listen to the words of the book of Esther:

Queen Esther was worried and upset, and she realised that only the Lord could save her people from being killed. So Esther took off her beautiful royal robes and put on clothes that showed this was a time of suffering and death. She put ashes and dirt all over her head rather than using any of her expensive lotions. And instead of doing everything she could do to look beautiful and dignified, Esther just let her long hair hand down in tangles. Then she prayed to the Lord God of Israel:

"You, Lord, are the only king we have. No one but you can help me now, because I am all alone."

The word of the Lord.

Reflection

How did Queen Esther prepare herself to pray for God's help? Why did she do these things? Do I pray for courage when I need to act boldly? Do I take a chance and speak up for others?

Closing

Let us bring our hopes and needs to God, as we pray: **Saving God, hear our prayer.**

Let us pray with the words that Jesus taught us:

Our Father …

God of grace and wisdom,
you continually raise up good people
who show with their lives
that they follow a holy and loving God.
Let our lives be true to all that our faith teaches,
so that we will grow more and more
   in your son's likeness.
We ask this through Christ our Lord. **Amen.**

[Sing 'alleluia'.]

✝ All make the Sign of the Cross.

November 14, 2019

Friday Daily Prayer

Introduction

As the end of the church's year comes near, we continue to think about the coming of Jesus at the end of time. In a sense, the end of the world comes for each person at death. But Jesus promises new life.

Jesus suffered before he died on the cross. In today's reading from Sunday's gospel, Jesus warns his followers that many of them will suffer too. Jesus knows that we will face difficult times. But we can be strong if Jesus is with us.

✞ All make the Sign of the Cross.

Hymn

A Psalm for November

[Turn to page 216.]

Reading　　　　　　　　　　Luke 21:12-19

Listen to the words of the holy gospel according to Luke:

Jesus said to his disciples, "Because of me you will be placed on trial before kings and governors. But this will be your chance to tell about your faith.

"Don't worry about what you will say to defend yourselves. I will give you the wisdom to know what to say. None of your enemies will be able to oppose you or to say that you are wrong. You will be betrayed by your own parents, brothers, family, and friends. Some of you will even be killed. Because of me, you will be hated by everyone. But don't worry! You will be saved by being faithful to me."

The gospel of the Lord.

Reflection

Do we know of saints who died because of their faith? Have I ever been made fun of because I was standing up for my beliefs? Do I turn to Jesus in prayer when I face difficulties?

Closing

Let us bring our hopes and needs to God, as we pray: **Saving God, hear our prayer.**

Let us pray with the words that Jesus taught us:

Our Father …

God of grace and wisdom,
you continually raise up good people
who show with their lives
that they follow a holy and loving God.
Let our lives be true to all that our faith teaches,
so that we will grow more and more
in your son's likeness.
We ask this through Christ our Lord. **Amen.**

[Sing 'alleluia'.]

✞ All make the Sign of the Cross.

November 15, 2019

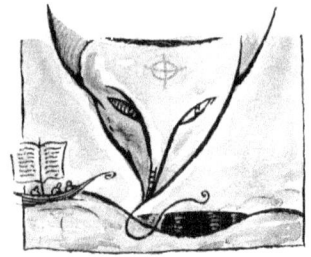

Monday Daily Prayer

Introduction

Our reading today is about a woman called Judith. It is the story of a victory won by the Jews through the actions of a woman.

An enemy has surrounded Judith's town and the people are starving. The elders of the town promise to surrender if, after five days, the Lord has not worked a miracle to save them. Judith gives the elders a lesson about courage and about the Lord.

☦ All make the Sign of the Cross.

Hymn

A Psalm for November

[Turn to page 216.]

Reading   Judith 8:10–12, 14, 15–17

Listen to the words of the book of Judith:

Judith said to the elders, "Listen to me, rulers of the people! What you have said to the people today is not right. You have promised to surrender the town to our enemies unless the Lord turns and helps us within so many days. Who are you to put God to the test today?

"You cannot plumb the depths of the human heart or understand the workings of the human mind. How do you expect to search out God, who made all these things, and find out his mind or comprehend his thoughts? No, my brothers, do not anger the Lord our God. For if he does not choose to help us within these five days, he has power to protect us within any time he pleases, or even to destroy us in the presence of our enemies.

"Do not try to bind the purposes of the Lord our God, for God is not like a human being, to be threatened. God is not like a mere mortal, to be won over by pleading. Therefore, while we wait for deliverance, let us call upon God to help us, and he will hear our voice, if it pleases him."

The word of the Lord.

Reflection

How did Judith show wisdom and courage? Have I ever tried to bargain with God? What does this story tell us about how we should pray?

Closing

Let us bring our hopes and needs to God, as we pray: **God of courage, hear our prayer.**

Let us pray with the words that Jesus taught us:

Our Father …

God of grace and wisdom,
you continually raise up good people
who show with their lives
that they follow a holy and loving God.
Let our lives be true to all that our faith teaches,
so that we will grow more and more
in your son's likeness.
We ask this through Christ our Lord. **Amen.**

[Sing 'alleluia'.]

☦ All make the Sign of the Cross.

November 18, 2019

Tuesday Daily Prayer

Introduction

In today's reading from the gospel of Mark, we hear about a woman who is not given a name. She was a widow and was poor. When rich people were making an offering in the temple, she not only gives the one coin which she has, but gives the second coin. She gives everything that she had.

✞ All make the Sign of the Cross.

Hymn

A Psalm for November

[Turn to page 216.]

Reading
Mark 12:41-44

Listen to the words of the holy gospel according to Mark:

Jesus was sitting in the temple near the offering box and watching people put in their gifts. He noticed that many rich people were giving a lot of money. Finally, a poor widow came up and put in two coins that were worth only a few pennies.

Jesus told his disciples to gather around him. Then he said, "I tell you that this poor widow has put in more than all the others. Everyone else gave what they didn't need. But she is very poor and gave everything she had. Now she doesn't have a cent to live on."

The gospel of the Lord.

Reflection

What did Jesus think of the poor widow's gift? What did he think of the rich people's large donations? How do the people of our parish help care for people who are poor? How does my family help?

Closing

Let us bring our hopes and needs to God, as we pray: **God of the poor, hear our prayer.**

Let us pray with the words that Jesus taught us:

Our Father ...

Loving God,
we thank you for all your gifts to us.
You have cared for and protected us.
You have healed and fed us.
Show us how to share what we have been given,
and to give with generous and loving hearts.
We ask this through Christ our Lord. **Amen.**

[Sing 'alleluia'.]

✞ All make the Sign of the Cross.

November 19, 2019

Wednesday Daily Prayer

Introduction

Today is Universal Children's Day. There are not many words about children in the gospels, but they are very wise. The teachings of Jesus are for everyone, young and old. They are good news for children as well as for adults.

We continue our readings about women in the Bible, turning now to women in the time of the early church. In many different ways women were faithful followers of the risen Jesus. We begin with Mary, the mother of Jesus, the first and most faithful of all disciples.

✢ All make the Sign of the Cross.

Hymn

A Psalm for November

[Turn to page 216.]

Reading   Acts 1:12-14

Listen to the words of the Acts of the Apostles:

The Mount of Olives was about half a mile from Jerusalem. The apostles who had gone there were Peter, John, James, Andrew, Philip, Thomas, Bartholomew (*bar-THOL-uh-mew*). Matthew, James the son of Alphaeus (*AL-fee-uss*), Simon, known as the Eager One, and Judas the son of James.
   After the apostles returned to the city they went upstairs to the room where they had been staying.
   The apostles often met together and prayed with a single purpose in mind. The women and Mary the mother of Jesus would meet with them, and so would the brothers.

The word of the Lord.

Reflection

Why would Mary's presence be important for the disciples after the death and resurrection of Jesus? Why do we call Mary the 'first and most faithful of all disciples'?

Closing

Let us bring our hopes and needs to God, as we pray: **Faithful God, hear our prayer.**

Let us pray with the words that Jesus taught us:

Our Father …

God of grace and wisdom,
you continually raise up good people
who show with their lives
that they follow a holy and loving God.
Let our lives be true to all that our faith teaches,
so that we will grow more and more
in your son's likeness.
We ask this through Christ our Lord. **Amen.**

[Sing 'alleluia'.]

✢ All make the Sign of the Cross.

Thursday Daily Prayer

Introduction

Today we celebrate the feast of the Presentation of Mary in the temple. This feast recalls a legend that Mary's parents dedicated her to God at the temple when she was three years old. With prayers and offerings they dedicated her to God's service.

In today's reading we meet another woman of the early church. Tabitha (or Dorcas) was very good at sewing and worked with other widows, doing many things for other people. There was great sadness when she died, but by God's power Peter the apostle restored her to life and returned her to her friends.

✚ All make the Sign of the Cross.

Hymn

A Psalm for November

[Turn to page 216.]

Reading   Acts 9:36-41

Listen to the words of the Acts of the Apostles:

In Joppa there was a follower named Tabitha. Her Greek name was Dorcas, which means "deer". She was always doing good things for people and had given much to the poor. But she got sick and died, and her body was washed and placed in an upstairs room. Joppa wasn't far from Lydda, and the followers heard that Peter was there. They sent two men to say to him, "Please come with us as quickly as you can!" Right away, Peter went with them.
 The men took Peter upstairs into the room. Many widows were there crying. They showed him the coats and clothes that Dorcas had made while she was still alive.

After Peter had sent everyone out of the room, he knelt down and prayed. Then he turned to the body of Dorcas and said, "Tabitha, get up!" The woman opened her eyes, and when she saw Peter, she sat up. He took her by the hand and helped her to her feet.

The word of the Lord.

Reflection

From where did Peter get his power to raise Dorcas to life again? Do I know people like Dorcas who help those in need? Does our parish have a special organisation that provides food and clothing for the poor? What can I do?

Closing

Let us bring our hopes and needs to God, as we pray: **God of the poor, hear our prayer.**

Let us pray with the words that Jesus taught us:

Our Father …

God of grace and wisdom,
you continually raise up good people
who show with their lives
that they follow a holy and loving God.
Let our lives be true to all that our faith teaches,
so that we will grow more and more
in your son's likeness.
We ask this through Christ our Lord. **Amen.**

[Sing 'alleluia'.]

✚ All make the Sign of the Cross.

November 21, 2019

Friday Daily Prayer

Introduction

Sunday is the feast of Christ the King. It is the last Sunday of the church's year.
Our reading on this day is about the crucifixion of Jesus, because the cross is the only throne that Jesus had on this earth. Jesus did not rule with armies but with truth and love. He was a different kind of king. He did not have a great palace but a great heart filled with love.

✢ All make the Sign of the Cross.

Hymn

A Psalm for November

[Turn to page 216.]

Reading   *Luke 23:36-43*

Listen to the words of the holy gospel according to Luke:

When Jesus had been crucified the soldiers made fun of him. They said, "If you are the king of the Jews, save yourself!"
   Above him was a sign that said, "This is the King of the Jews."
   One of the criminals hanging on the cross insulted Jesus by saying, "Aren't you the Messiah? Save yourself and save us."
   But the other criminal told the first one off, "Don't you fear God? Aren't you getting the same punishment as this man? We got what was coming to us, but he didn't do anything wrong." Then he said to Jesus, "Remember me when you come into power!"
   Jesus replied, "I promise that today you will be with me in paradise."

The gospel of the Lord.

Reflection

Many people wanted the Messiah to be a powerful ruler who would bring fame to their nation. How was Jesus a different kind of king? Why would people believe in a king who died powerless and like a criminal?

Closing

Let us bring our other hopes and needs to God, as we pray: **God of peace, hear our prayer.**

Let us pray with the words that Jesus taught us:

Our Father …

King of justice and compassion,
show us your face when we look at
the people around us.
Open our eyes to the needs of others.
Fill us with your grace,
so that our works and our words
may be signs of your coming.
We ask this through Christ our Lord. **Amen.**

[Sing 'alleluia'.]

✢ All make the Sign of the Cross.

November 22, 2019

Monday Daily Prayer

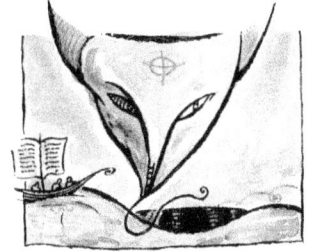

Introduction

Today we remember Saint Cecilia (*se-SEEL-yuh*), a Roman woman who died for her faith, and whose home later became a church. Cecilia is the patron of music and musicians. For centuries she has inspired people to write and sing music in praise of God.

In today's reading Paul and his companion, Silas (*SYE-lus*), were visiting the Greek city of Philippi (*FILL-uh-pye*). On the Sabbath they were walking along the riverside looking for a place to pray. They didn't find a building, but they found a group of women praying together. Paul and Silas joined them. One of the leaders of the women was called Lydia (*LID-ee-uh*). She was a strong believer.

☦ All make the Sign of the Cross.

Hymn

A Psalm for November

[Turn to page 216.]

Reading   Acts 16:12b-16

Listen to the words of the Acts of the Apostles:

We [Paul and Barnabas] spent several days in Philippi (*FILL-uh-pye*).
 Then on the Sabbath we went outside the city gate to a place by the river, where we thought there would be a Jewish meeting place for prayer. We sat down and talked with the women who came. One of them was Lydia, who was from the city of Thyatira (*thigh-uh-TEER-uh*), and sold expensive purple cloth. She was a worshipper of the Lord God, and he made her willing to accept what Paul was saying. Then after she and her family were baptised, she kept on begging us. "If you think I really do have faith in the Lord, come stay in my home." Finally Paul accepted her invitation.

The word of the Lord.

Reflection

What made the riverside a place for prayer? How did Lydia show that she really believed in the God that Paul and Silas spoke about?

Closing

In honour of Saint Cecilia, the patron of music, let us all respond, 'Bless the song we sing.'

God, whose song is deep in our hearts:
 Bless the song we sing.
God, whose song is heard in every language:
 Bless the song we sing.
God, whose song will last till the end of time:
 Bless the song we sing.

Let us pray with the words that Jesus taught us:

Our Father ...

God, you know the great joy and power of music.
Help us to sing your song each day.
Be with all who praise you through art and music.
We ask this through Christ our Lord. **Amen.**

[Sing 'alleluia'.]

☦ All make the Sign of the Cross.

November 25, 2019

Tuesday Daily Prayer

Introduction

Today we remember a most remarkable woman who was born in the United States and died around this time in 1980. Her name was Dorothy Day.

Dorothy led a pretty wild life as a young woman, but when she was 30, she joined the Catholic Church and dedicated her life to the service of others and the cause of peace and justice. She opened her home to poor people and to helpers. She even went to gaol for what she believed.

Today we read about another woman of the early church. Her name was Priscilla (*pr-SILL-uh*). She and her husband Aquila (*a-QUILL-uh*) worked with Paul and had a church in their own home. They helped Paul with his mission and seem to have been important people in the early church.

✞ All make the Sign of the Cross.

Hymn

A Psalm for November

[Turn to page 216.]

Reading   Acts 18:1-3

Listen to the words of the Acts of the Apostles:

Paul left Athens and went to Corinth where he met Aquila, a Jewish man from Pontus. Not long before this, Aquila had come from Italy with his wife Priscilla, because the Emperor Claudius (*CLAW-dee-uss*) had ordered the Jewish people to leave Rome. Paul went to see Aquila and Priscilla and found out that they were tent makers. Paul was a tent maker too. So he stayed with them, and they worked together.

The word of the Lord.

Reflection

How could Paul, Priscilla and Aquila have spread the good news about Jesus as they worked together? In what way might Priscilla and Aquila's home have become a church?

Closing

Let us bring our hopes and needs to God, as we pray: **God of wisdom, hear our prayer.**

Let us pray with the words that Jesus taught us:

Our Father …

God of grace and wisdom,
you continually raise up good people
who show with their lives
that they follow a holy and loving God.
Let our lives be true to all that our faith teaches,
so that we will grow more and more
   in your son's likeness.
We ask this through Christ our Lord. **Amen.**

[Sing 'alleluia'.]

✞ All make the Sign of the Cross.

November 26, 2019

Wednesday Daily Prayer

Introduction

We continue our readings about women in the Bible. Phoebe (*FEE-bee*) was a deacon of the early church. That means she was an officially recognised and respected leader in her church at Cenchreae (*SEN-cray*), a seaport of Corinth. Phoebe probably carried Paul's very important letter to the Christians who lived in Rome. This showed that Paul trusted her. She also helped Paul to spread the good news about Jesus.

✞ All make the Sign of the Cross.

Hymn

A Psalm for November

[Turn to page 216.]

Reading   *Romans 16:1-5*

Listen to the words of the apostle Paul:

I have good things to say about Phoebe, who is leader in the church at Cenchreae. Welcome her in a way that is proper for someone who has faith in the Lord and is one of God's own people. Help her in any way you can. After all, she has proved to be a respected leader for many others, including me.

Reflection

In what ways do you think Phoebe might have helped Paul at Cenchreae? Do you know any women who do important work in your parish? What do they do?

Closing

Let us bring our hopes and needs to God, as we pray: **Faithful God, hear our prayer.**

Let us pray with the words that Jesus taught us:

Our Father ...

God of grace and wisdom,
you continually raise up good people
who show with their lives
that they follow a holy and loving God.
Let our lives be true to all that our faith teaches,
so that we will grow more and more
in your son's likeness.
We ask this through Christ our Lord. **Amen.**

[Sing 'alleluia'.]

✞ All make the Sign of the Cross.

November 27, 2019

Thursday Daily Prayer

[Reminder: The season of Advent begins next Sunday but we will start our Advent prayer tomorrow. If you plan to have an Advent wreath for your classroom, you will need time to prepare it.
The Psalm for Advent is on page 240. Make a copy for each member of the class.]

Introduction

Today we read about another two women of faith. They were Eunice (*YOU-nuss*) and Lois (*LO-uss*) who were the mother and grandmother of Timothy. Paul encourages Timothy to have the same strong faith as they did.

☩ All make the Sign of the Cross.

Hymn

A Psalm for November

[Turn to page 216.]

Reading   2 Timothy 1:3, 5, 6a, 7

Listen to the words of the apostle Paul:

Night and day I mention you in my prayers. I am always grateful for you as I pray to the God my ancestors have served. I also remember the genuine faith of your mother Eunice (*YOU-nuss*). Your grandmother Lois (*LO-uss*) had the same sort of faith, and I am sure you have it as well. So I ask you to make full use of the gift that God gave you. Us it well. God's Spirit doesn't make cowards out of us. The Spirit gives us power, love and self-control

The word of the Lord.

Reflection

How is the faith passed on in families? Do I know older people who have great faith? How do they help me to have faith? Am I ever afraid to show my faith?

Closing

Let us bring our hopes and needs to God, as we pray: **Faithful God, hear our prayer.**

Let us pray with the words that Jesus taught us:

Our Father ...

God of grace and wisdom,
you continually raise up good people
who show with their lives
that they follow a holy and loving God.
Let our lives be true to all that our faith teaches,
so that we will grow more and more
in your son's likeness.
We ask this through Christ our Lord. **Amen.**

[Sing 'alleluia'.]

☩ All make the Sign of the Cross.

November 28, 2019

Advent

Friday, November 29, to Thursday, December 19

Advent 2019 Looking Ahead

About the Season

Advent heralds in the church's new year. This year it begins on Sunday, December 1.

Advent is a season of waiting. Many of the words we pray and sing are full of desire, hope and expectation. We wait as the days get warmer, and as the school year draws to a close. We look forward to the summer holidays. This 'waiting' can help us to celebrate Advent well.

Advent is a season to prepare for Christmas when Christ's first coming is remembered. It is not a penitential season like Lent but rather one of joyful expectation. We know that the first coming of Jesus at Bethlehem will not happen again, so during Advent, we prepare and long for a new coming of Jesus into our lives. We take this time every year to practise how to receive Jesus every day of our lives! We remember the call of Jesus to his followers to make our world a peaceful and loving place, and so, during Advent, we make special efforts to be signs that God is with us. This is what the word 'Emmanuel' means: God-with-us.

One of our Advent companions is Mary, and during these weeks we remember her as she waited for the birth of her child. During Advent we can try to wait, as the world waited long ago for the coming of Jesus, the 'Light of the world.' Over these last days of the school year, try to make the most of Advent with its many rich images.

Readings

Our readings for the first week of Advent come from the book of the prophet Isaiah who lived during a time of sadness among the people. A strong army was marching through the country, destroying everything on its way to the holy city of Jerusalem. Isaiah told the people that their troubles would not last forever. He told them to thank of the joy God would bring them

On the seven days before Christmas Eve, the church prays special prayers of longing called the 'O Antiphons.' They call Jesus by seven titles and all begin with 'O'. The verses of the song 'O Come, O Come, Emmanuel' are based on these prayers. Christ is named as: Wisdom, Great Lord, Flower of Jesse's Stem. Key of David, King of Nations, Rising Sun, Emmanuel. Although the church uses these special prayers from 17–23 December, we will pray them in these last days of the school year.

Our readings for Fridays will anticipate the gospels of all four Sundays of Advent.

Feasts and Other Commemorations

- The feast of the Immaculate Conception is celebrated on December 9 this year. We remember God's special love for Mary whom he chose to be the mother of Jesus.
- Beginning on the evening of December 22, Jewish people around the world will celebrate the festival of Hanukkah. It is an eight-day feast of lights in memory of when the Temple was restored for worship after a time when it was under attack by enemies.

Each night of the festival, Jewish people will light a new candle on a candlestand to remind them that God's presence is always with them.

Preparation for Advent

The Psalm for Advent on page 240 is part of the Song of Zechariah, the father of John the Baptist. This song celebrates the God who saves and proclaims God's love and kindness. God has given us a Saviour who will guide us into a life of peace.
Make copies for each member of the class.

Advent is a season with its own special mood, colours, sounds, words and joys. Make the classroom look and feel like Advent. Advent's colours are purple, mauve or magenta. Find a lovely cloth which is a blend of these colours. This will help our prayer space look and feel like Advent.

Each class could consider an Advent Wreath. An Advent Wreath is a circle, usually made of evergreen branches, with four candles placed in or around it (normally three purple and one rose-coloured), one for each of the four Sundays of the season. The circular wreath is a sign of God's never-ending and loving care.

An Advent Wreath is a good way to mark the weeks of Advent as we come closer to Christmas. We light one candle during the first week, two the second, three the third, and four the fourth week, although school will be finished by then. The rose candle is first lit on the third Sunday of Advent, called 'Gaudete Sunday.' 'Gaudete' is a word that means rejoice; we rejoice that the Lord is very near.

To make the wreath, try to find greenery that will last. Some native shrubs are good for this. Add some purple flowers to the greenery – maybe some jacaranda or agapanthus. Pink flowers could be added in the third week. You could decorate the wreath with ribbons of Advent colours. Whatever we use, the Advent Wreath needs to be kept fresh.

Suggested Hymns

See the hymn chart on pages viii-ix for a selection of Advent hymns. On the feast of the Immaculate Conception (December 8), select from the hymns for Feasts of Mary.

A Psalm for Advent

The Canticle of Zechariah
Luke 1:68-71, 78-79

Each day, light the correct number of candles of the Advent wreath:

November 29 to December 5:
  one purple candle
December 6 to December 12:
  two purple candles
December 13 to December 19:
  three candles – one rose and two purple candles

LEADER
Praise the Lord, the God of Israel!
He has come to save his people.
ALL
Our God has given us a mighty Saviour
from the family of David his servant.

SIDE A
Long ago the Lord promised
by the words of his holy prophet
to save us from our enemies
and from everyone who hates us.

SIDE B
God's love and kindness will shine upon us
like the sun that rises in the sky.
On us who live in the dark shadow of death
this light will shine
to guide us into a life of peace.

LEADER
Praise the Lord, the God of Israel!
He has come to save his people.
ALL
Our God has given us a mighty Saviour
from the family of David his servant.

Glory be to the Father, and to the Son,
and to the Holy Spirit:
as it was in the beginning, is now,
and ever shall be
world without end. Amen. Alleluia.

[Turn back to Daily Prayer for today.]

Friday Daily Prayer

[Daily Prayer for Advent includes lighting the candles of the Advent wreath. You can bless the wreath before you begin prayer today. Light one purple candle for today's prayer.]

Introduction

On Sunday, December 1, we begin the important and happy season of Advent. During these weeks we turn our thoughts to the coming of Jesus, who is the saviour of the world. Jesus is the Son of God, present among the people God loves. That is good news, and it makes us happy to remember that Jesus will come again in glory. During Advent we think about the many ways God comes to be with us. We try to make ourselves more ready to receive God in our day-to-day lives.

When Jesus comes again, we will see his work completed, and the rule of God will be made clear. In our reading today, Saint Paul reminds us to be ready for Jesus when he comes.

☩ All make the Sign of the Cross.

Hymn

A Psalm for Advent

[Turn to page 240.]

Reading   Romans 13:11-12

Listen to the words of the apostle Paul:

You know what sort of times we live in, and so you should live properly. It is time to wake up. You know that the day when we will be saved is nearer now than when we first put our faith in the Lord.

Night is almost over, and day will soon appear. We must stop behaving as people do in the dark and be ready to live in the light.

The word of the Lord.

Reflection

How would you describe the times we live in? What does Paul mean by the way people behave in darkness? What could Paul mean by being ready to live in the light?

Closing

Let us bring our hopes and needs to God as we pray: **God of hope, hear our prayer.**

Let us pray with the words that Jesus taught us:

Our Father …

[Sing 'O come, O Come Emmanuel' GA, 285, verse 1.]

God of hope, you bring light and joy
to the darkness of this world.
Let us carry your light in our hearts this day.

LEADER
Let us all say:
Come, Lord Jesus!
Come, Lord Jesus!

LEADER
Let us all say:
Come quickly!
Come quickly!

☩ All make the Sign of the Cross.

[Put out the candle of the Advent wreath.]

November 29, 2019

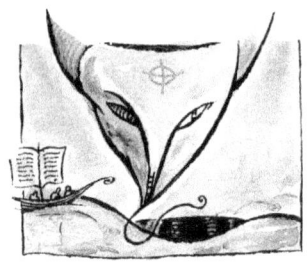

Monday Daily Prayer

[Reminder: If you are using an Advent wreath light one purple candle before the psalm.]

Introduction

Advent has begun! During this season we think about our need for Jesus, and we prepare to celebrate his birth at Christmas. We also think about the many ways God comes to be with us, and promises to be our light and strength.

This week we will read from the book of the prophet Isaiah (*eye-ZAY-uh*). He lived during a time of sadness among the people. A strong army was marching through the country, destroying everything on its way to the holy city of Jerusalem. Isaiah told the people their troubles would not last forever. He told them to think of the joy God would bring them.

Today we also remember four brave American women who were murdered in Advent 1980 because they were helping the poor people of El Salvador. Today let us pray that our Advent God will always be with the people of El Salvador and be their strength.

✞ All make the Sign of the Cross.

Hymn

A Psalm for Advent

[Turn to page 240.]

Reading   Isaiah 2:3-5

Listen to the words of the prophet Isaiah:

In the future, many people will come and say, "Let's go to the mountain of the Lord God of Jacob and worship in his temple." The Lord will teach us his Law from Jerusalem, and we will obey him. He will settle arguments between nations.

They will pound their swords and their spears into rakes and shovels; they will never make war or attack one another.

People of Israel, let's live by the light of the Lord.

The word of the Lord.

Reflection

What would a world without any guns or wars be like? What will it be like when no one attacks anyone else? How can we make our classroom a place like that?

Closing

Let us bring our hopes and needs to God, as we pray: **God of hope, hear our prayer.**

Let us pray with the words that Jesus taught us:

Our Father …

[Sing 'O Come, O Come Emmanuel' GA, 285, verse 1.]

God of hope, you bring light and joy
to the darkness of this world.
Let us carry your light in our hearts this day.

LEADER
Let us all say:
Come, Lord Jesus!
Come, Lord Jesus!

LEADER
Let us all say:
Come quickly!
Come quickly!

✞ All make the Sign of the Cross.

[Put out the candle of the Advent wreath.]

December 2, 2019

Tuesday Daily Prayer

[Reminder: If you are using an Advent wreath light one purple candle before the psalm.]

Introduction

Isaiah was one of the great prophets. He lived during wartime, when the people were nearly destroyed. Some people blamed God for their troubles, but Isaiah reminded them to trust God. He told them that one day death and suffering would come to an end. He encouraged them with a vision of a great banquet that God would give the people on his holy mountain.

☦ All make the Sign of the Cross.

Hymn

A Psalm for Advent

[Turn to page 240.]

Reading   *Isaiah 25:6, 8-10*

Listen to the words of the prophet Isaiah:

On this mountain the Lord All-Powerful
   will prepare for all nations
   a feast of finest foods.
Choice wines and the best meats will be served.
The Lord All-Powerful will destroy the power of death
   and wipe away all tears.
No longer will his people be insulted everywhere.
The Lord has spoken!
At that time, people will say,
   "The Lord has saved us!
Let's celebrate. We waited and hoped—
   now our God is here."
The powerful arm of the Lord
   will protect this mountain.

The word of the Lord.

Reflection

Why is a banquet such a strong image of hope and peace? In what ways does God give us comfort in times of trouble? How can I wipe away other people's tears?

Closing

Let us bring our hopes and needs to God, as we pray: **God of hope, hear our prayer.**

Let us pray with the words that Jesus taught us:

Our Father …

[Sing 'O Come, O Come Emmanuel' GA, 285, verse 1.]

God of hope, you bring light and joy
to the darkness of this world.
Let us carry your light in our hearts this day.

LEADER
Let us all say.
Come, Lord Jesus!
Come, Lord Jesus!

LEADER
Let us all say:
Come quickly!
Come quickly!

☦ All make the Sign of the Cross.

[Put out the candle of the Advent wreath.]

December 3, 2019

Wednesday Daily Prayer

[Reminder: If you are using an Advent wreath, light one purple candle before the psalm.]

Introduction

In ancient times it was important that cities be built safely on hill tops and have strong walls to protect it from enemies. In today's reading the prophet Isaiah teaches us that God is like a fortress in which we are safe and secure. God protects us and gives us peace.

✝ All make the Sign of the Cross.

Hymn

A Psalm for Advent

[Turn to page 240.]

Reading   Isaiah 26:1-4

Listen to the words of the prophet Isaiah:

The time is coming when the people of Judah
    will sing this song:
"Our city is protected. The Lord is our fortress,
    and he gives us victory.
Open the city gates for a law-abiding nation
    that is faithful to God.
The Lord gives perfect peace
to those whose faith is firm.
So always trust in the Lord
    because he is forever our mighty rock."

The word of the Lord.

Reflection

How is God like a fortress for me? Isaiah says that God gives peace "to those whose faith is firm". What does it mean to have firm faith? Do I trust God like a mighty rock? What other image of trustworthiness can we think of?

Closing

Let us bring our hopes and needs to God, as we pray: **God of hope, hear our prayer.**

Let us pray with the words that Jesus taught us:

Our Father …

[Sing 'O Come, O Come Emmanuel' GA, 285, verse 1.]

God of hope, you bring light and joy
to the darkness of this world.
Let us carry your light in our hearts this day.

LEADER
Let us all say:
Come, Lord Jesus!
Come, Lord Jesus!

LEADER
Let us all say:
Come quickly!
Come quickly!
✝ All make the Sign of the Cross.

[Put out the candle of the Advent wreath.]

December 4, 2019

Thursday Daily Prayer

[Reminder: If you are using an Advent wreath, light one purple candle before the psalm.]

Introduction

Can you guess the name of the saint we remember tomorrow? He was a bishop of the early church. People all over the world tell stories about him. He is the patron of sailors and sea travellers, and he is the protector of children. We call him Santa Claus. His real name is Saint Nicholas.

The word "advent" means "coming." During this season we prepare ourselves to welcome Jesus when he comes.

Of course, Jesus does not come just once a year. He comes when we are in trouble, when we rejoice, when we pray, when we celebrate and when we love one another in his name. We take this time every year to practise being ready so that we can learn how to receive Jesus every day of our lives!

✝ All make the Sign of the Cross.

Hymn

A Psalm for Advent

[Turn to page 240.]

Reading   Isaiah 29:18-19, 23-24

Listen to the words of the prophet Isaiah:

The Lord says this:
"In the future the deaf will be able to hear whatever is read to them;
　the blind will be freed from a life of darkness.
The poor and the needy will celebrate and shout
　because of the Lord, the holy God of Israel.
When they see how great I have made their nation,
　they will praise and honour me, the holy God of Israel.
Everyone who is confused will understand,
　and all who have complained will obey my teaching."

The word of the Lord.

Reflection

Isaiah says that there will be no disabilities or poverty in God's kingdom. There are no misunderstandings and no complaints. Does this sound like a kingdom worth living in? How do we live in this kingdom?

Closing

Let us bring our hopes and needs to God, as we pray: **Holy God, hear our prayer.**

Let us pray with the words that Jesus taught us:

Our Father …

[Sing 'O come, O Come Emmanuel' GA 285, verse 3.]

Lord our God, you bring light and joy
to the darkness of this world.
Let us carry your light in our hearts this day.

LEADER
Let us all say:
Come, Lord Jesus!
Come, Lord Jesus!

LEADER
Let us all say:
Come quickly!
Come quickly!

✝ All make the Sign of the Cross.

[Put out the candle of the Advent wreath.]

December 5, 2019

Friday Daily Prayer

[Reminder: If you are using an Advent wreath, light two purple candles before the psalm.]

Introduction

In today's reading from the Sunday gospel we hear about John the Baptist. He told people to prepare for God's coming. Long before him the prophet Isaiah (*eye-ZAY-uh*) told the people to wait patiently for God. Almost every day during the season of Advent, the church reads from the book of Isaiah. John lived hundreds of years after Isaiah. He was the last prophet to prepare the way for Jesus.

✞ All make the Sign of the Cross.

Hymn

A Psalm for Advent

[Turn to page 240.]

Reading   Matthew 3:1-3, 5-6, 11

Listen to the words of the holy gospel according to Matthew:

John the Baptist started preaching in the desert of Judea (*joo-DEE-uh*). He said, "Turn back to God! The kingdom of heaven will soon be here."

John was the one the prophet Isaiah was talking about, when he said,

"In the desert someone is shouting.
'Get the road ready for the Lord!
Make a straight path for him' "

From Jerusalem and all Judea and from the River Jordan Valley, crowds of people went to John. They told how sorry they were for their sins, and he baptised them in the river.

John said, "I baptise you with water so that you will give up your sins. But someone more powerful is going to come, and I am not good enough even to carry his sandals. He will baptise you with the Holy Spirit and with fire."

The gospel of the Lord.

Reflection

What would the world be like if it were really ready for Jesus? How can we and our friends do our part to help change the world?

Closing

Let us bring our hopes and needs to God as we pray: **God of hope, hear our prayer.**

Let us pray with the words that Jesus taught us:

Our Father …

[Sing 'O come, O Come Emmanuel' GA, 285, verse 1.]

God of hope, you bring light and joy
to the darkness of this world.
Let us carry your light in our hearts this day.

LEADER
Let us all say:
Come, Lord Jesus!
Come, Lord Jesus!

LEADER
Let us all say:
Come quickly!
Come quickly!

✞ All make the Sign of the Cross.

[Put out the candles of the Advent wreath.]

December 6, 2019

Monday Daily Prayer

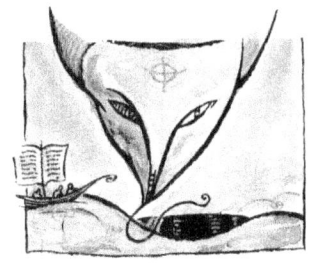

[Reminder: If you are using an Advent wreath, light two purple candles before the psalm.]

Introduction

Today's feast is called the Immaculate Conception (*ee-MAC-you-late con-SEP-shun*) of Mary. We celebrate our belief that Mary was full of God's grace from the first moment of her life. God gave Mary this honour because she would be invited to be the mother of the Saviour. In the reading today, we hear Mary's response.

☩ All make the Sign of the Cross.

Hymn

A Psalm for Advent

[Turn to page 240.]

Reading *Luke 1:26–32, 34–35, 38*

Listen to the words of the holy gospel according to Luke:

God sent the angel Gabriel to the town of Nazareth in Galilee (*GAL-uh-lee*) with a message for a virgin named Mary. She was engaged to Joseph from the family of King David. The angel greeted Mary and said, "You are truly blessed! The Lord is with you."

Mary was confused by the angel's words and wondered what they meant. Then the angel told Mary, "Don't be afraid! God is pleased with you, and you will have a son. His name will be Jesus. He will be great and will be called the Son of God Most High. The Lord God will make him king, as his ancestor David was."

Mary asked the angel, "How can this happen? I am not married!"

The angel answered, "The Holy Spirit will come down to you, and God's power will come over you. So your child will be called the holy Son of God."

Mary said, "I am the Lord's servant! Let it happen as you have said."

The gospel of the Lord.

Reflection

What words in this gospel tell us who Jesus is? What is Mary's response to God's plan? What can I do to say 'yes' to God's call in my life?

Closing

Let us bring our hopes and needs to God, as we pray: **God of all grace, hear our prayer.**

Let us pray with the words that Jesus taught us:

Our Father ...

[Sing 'O Come, O Come Emmanuel' GA, 285, verse 1.]

Lord our God, you bring light and joy
   to the darkness of this world.
Let us carry your light in our hearts this day.

LEADER
Let us all say:
Come, Lord Jesus!
Come, Lord Jesus!

LEADER
Let us all say:
Come quickly!
Come quickly!

☩ All make the Sign of the Cross.

[Put out the candles of the Advent wreath.]

December 9, 2019

Tuesday Daily Prayer

[Reminder: If you are using an Advent wreath, light two purple candles before the psalm.]

Introduction

Today we observe Human Rights Day. It commemorates the day when the United Nations adopted the Universal Declaration of Human Rights in 1948.

On the seven days before Christmas Eve the church prays special prayers of longing called "O Antiphons" (*AN-tee-fons*). They call Jesus by seven titles and all begin with "O". The verses of the song "O Come, O Come, Emmanuel" are based on these prayers. We will start praying them today. So far we have been calling Jesus "Emmanuel", which means "God is with us". Today we call him "Wisdom" and "holy Word of God."

✞ All make the Sign of the Cross.

Hymn

A Psalm for Advent

[Turn to page 240.]

Reading   Wisdom 9:9-11

Listen to the words of the book of Wisdom:

Wisdom has always been with you.
She knows your mighty deeds,
and she was there when you created the world.
Wisdom knows what pleased you,
and she knows what is right
according to your commands.
So from your glorious and holy
   throne in the heavens,
please send Wisdom to work beside me and teach me
what is pleasing to you.

The word of the Lord.

Reflection

Is it surprising that the Bible speaks of God's Wisdom as a woman? What do we learn about wisdom from this reading? What could it mean when we call Jesus God's 'Wisdom' and 'holy Word of God'?

Closing

Let us all say:
O Wisdom, O holy Word of God!
O Wisdom, O holy Word of God!

You govern all creation
with your strong yet tender care.
Come and show your people
   the way to salvation.

Let us bring our hopes and needs to God, as we pray: **God of wisdom, hear our prayer.**

Let us pray with the words that Jesus taught us:

Our Father ...

[Sing 'O come, O Come Emmanuel' AOV 1-174, verse 2.]

God of hope, you bring light and joy
to the darkness of this world.
Let us carry your light in our hearts this day.

LEADER
Let us all say:
Come, Lord Jesus!
Come, Lord Jesus!

LEADER
Let us all say:
Come quickly!
Come quickly!

✞ All make the Sign of the Cross.

[Put out the candles of the Advent wreath.]

December 10, 2019

Wednesday Daily Prayer

[Reminder: If you use an Advent wreath light two purple candles before the psalm.]

Introduction

The "O antiphon" for today calls Jesus the "Leader of the House of Israel." The prophet Jeremiah (*Je-re-MY-uh*) often had to speak hard words to the people at a time of great danger. But here he has a message of hope. God promises to give his people Israel a wise and just leader who will bring peace. We believe Jesus is our wise and just leader.

☩ All make the Sign of the Cross.

Hymn

A Psalm for Advent

[Turn to page 240.]

Reading   *Jeremiah 23:5-6*

Listen to the words of the prophet Jeremiah:

The Lord said:
Someday I will appoint
an honest king
   from the family of David,
a king who will be wise
   and rule with justice.
As long as he is king,
Israel will have peace,
   and Judah will be safe.
The name of this king will be
   "The Lord Gives Justice."

The word of the Lord.

Reflection

Jesus taught us to pray for God's kingdom to come. What kind of kingdom is God's kingdom? What kind of leader is Jesus? How can we follow him?

Closing

Let us all say:
O Leader of the House of Israel!
O Leader of the House of Israel!

You gave the Law to Moses on Sinai (*SYE-nye*):
Come, stretch out your hand to set us free.

Let us bring our hopes and needs to God, as we pray: **God of justice, hear our prayer.**

Let us pray with the words that Jesus taught us:

Our Father ...

[Sing 'O come, O Come Emmanuel' AOV 1-174, verse 3.]

God of hope, you bring light and joy
to the darkness of this world.
Let us carry your light in our hearts this day.

LEADER
Let us all say:
Come, Lord Jesus!
Come, Lord Jesus!

LEADER
Let us all say:
Come quickly!
Come quickly!

☩ All make the Sign of the Cross.

[Put out the candles of the Advent wreath.]

December 11, 2019

Thursday Daily Prayer

[Reminder: If you use an Advent wreath light two purple candles before the psalm.]

Introduction

In today's 'O Antiphon', we call Jesus the 'Flower of Jesse's stem'. Jesse was the father of David, Israel's greatest king. The people wanted another king like him. The prophets promised that a new king would, one day, spring from David's family.

In today's reading from the prophet Isaiah we hear about this promise. Isaiah uses the symbol of a family tree that has been cut down. Yet, he says, a new branch will grow from its stump. Christians call Jesus a flower blooming on Jesse's tree.

☧ All make the Sign of the Cross.

Hymn

A Psalm for Advent

[Turn to page 240.]

Reading   Isaiah 11:1–3

Listen to the words of the prophet Isaiah:

Like a branch that sprouts from a stump,
   someone from David's family
   will someday be king.
The Spirit of the Lord will be with him
   to give him understanding,
   wisdom, and insight.
He will be powerful,
   and he will know and honour the Lord.
His greatest joy will be to obey the Lord.
This king won't judge by appearances
   or listen to rumours.

The word of the Lord.

Reflection

How are we like branches on Jesus' family tree? Do I ever feel that the 'Spirit of the Lord' gives me understanding? Do I judge by appearances or listen to rumours?

Closing

Let us all say:
Flower of Jesse's stem!
Flower of Jesse's stem!

Sign of God's love for all his people:
Come to save us without delay.

Let us bring our hopes and needs to God, as we pray: **God of promise, hear our prayer.**

Let us pray with the words that Jesus taught us:

Our Father …

[Sing 'O Come, O Come, Emmanuel' AOV 1-174, verse 4]

Lord our God, you bring light and joy
to the darkness of this world.
Let us carry your light in our hearts this day.

LEADER
Let us all say:
Come, Lord Jesus!
Come, Lord Jesus!

LEADER
Let us all say:
Come quickly!
Come quickly!

☧ All make the Sign of the Cross.

[Put out the candles of the Advent wreath.]

December 12, 2019

Friday Daily Prayer

[Reminder: If you are using an Advent wreath, light two purple and one rose candle before the psalm.]

Introduction

During this season of Advent we remember that many people made ready for God to send the Saviour. But getting ready for the Saviour is hard and sometimes dangerous.

On Sunday we read how John the Baptist saw that his cousin Jesus was doing the work of God. Perhaps Jesus was the one they were all waiting for! But John was put into prison for suggesting this. From prison, John told his friends to go and find Jesus.

☩ All make the Sign of the Cross.

Hymn

A Psalm for Advent

[Turn to page 240.]

Reading   Matthew 11:2-6

Listen to the words of the holy gospel according to Matthew:

John sent some of his followers to ask Jesus, "Are you the one we should be looking for? Or must we wait for someone else?"

Jesus answered, "Go and tell John what you have heard and seen. The blind are now able to see, and the lame can walk. People with leprosy are being healed, and the deaf can hear. The dead are raised to life, and the poor are hearing the good news. God will bless everyone who does not reject me because of what I do."

The gospel of the Lord.

Reflection

Why do you think Jesus pointed to what he was doing instead of just telling people who he was? Do I know people whose 'good works' show that they are close to God?

Closing

Let us bring our hopes and needs to God, as we pray: **God of life, hear our prayer.**

Let us pray with the words that Jesus taught us:

Our Father ...

[Sing 'O come, O Come Emmanuel' GA 285, verse 1.]

Lord our God, you bring light and joy
   to the darkness of this world.
Let us carry your light in our hearts this day.

LEADER
Let us all say:
Come, Lord Jesus!
Come, Lord Jesus!

LEADER
Let us all say:
Come quickly!
Come quickly!

☩ All make the Sign of the Cross.

[Put out the candles of the Advent wreath.]

December 13, 2019

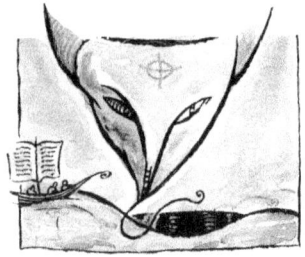

Monday Daily Prayer

[Reminder: If you are using an Advent wreath, light two purple and one rose candle before the psalm.]

Introduction

In today's 'O Antiphon', we call Jesus the 'Key of David.' People with keys are often people with authority. King David once held authority over the whole people of Israel. He united them and brought peace to the land.

We call Jesus a key. He will unlock the gate of God's kingdom for us.

✚ All make the Sign of the Cross.

Hymn

A Psalm for Advent

[Turn to page 240.]

Reading   *Revelation 3:7–8, 11*

Listen to the words of the book of Revelation:

The Lord says this: "I am the one who is holy and true, and I have the keys that belonged to David. When I open a door, no one can close it. And when I close a door, no one can open it. Listen to what I say.

'I know everything you have done. And I have placed before you an open door that no one can close. You were not very strong, but you obeyed my message and did not deny that you are my followers.

'I am coming soon. So hold firmly to what you have, and no one will take away the crown that you will be given as your reward."

The word of the Lord.

Reflection

What 'door' might Jesus be holding open for us? What do I have that Jesus wants me to 'hold firmly to'? Is there something I want Jesus to unlock?

Closing

Let us all say:
O Key of David!
O Key of David!

You open the gates of God's eternal Kingdom:
Come, free prisoners of darkness.

Let us bring our hopes and needs to God, as we pray: **God of freedom, hear our prayer.**

Let us pray with the words that Jesus taught us:

Our Father …

[Sing 'O Come, O Come, Emmanuel' AOV 1-174, verse 5]

Lord our God, you bring light and joy
to the darkness of this world.
Let us carry your light in our hearts this day.

LEADER
Let us all say:
Come, Lord Jesus!
Come, Lord Jesus!

LEADER
Let us all say:
Come quickly!
Come quickly!

✚ All make the Sign of the Cross.

[Put out the candles of the Advent wreath.]

December 16, 2019

Tuesday Daily Prayer

[Reminder: If you are using an Advent wreath, light two purple and one rose candle before the psalm.]

Introduction

For most of Advent we have been calling Jesus by the title 'Emmanuel' which means 'God is with us'. So far we have called Jesus by the names of 'Wisdom', 'Flower of Jesse', and 'Key of David'. They are all words of longing as we await the coming of the saviour. Today, after we have heard the prophet Isaiah speak of God as our everlasting light, we call Jesus 'Radiant Dawn'.

☩ All make the Sign of the Cross.

Hymn

A Psalm for Advent

[Turn to page 240.]

Reading *Isaiah 60:19–20, 22*

Listen to the words of the prophet Isaiah:

You won't need the light of the sun or the moon.
I, the Lord your God, will be your eternal light
    and bring you honour.
Your sun will never set or your moon go down.
I, the Lord, will be your everlasting light,
    and your days of sorrow will come to an end.
Even the smallest family will be a powerful nation.
I am the Lord, and when the time comes,
    I will quickly do all this.

The word of the Lord.

Reflection

What are some of the meanings light has for us? What are some of the ways we use lights in our celebration of Advent and Christmas? Do I know anyone who brings light and joy as soon as they come into a room?

Closing

Let us all say:
O Radiant Dawn!
O Radiant Dawn!

Splendour of eternal light and sun of justice:
**Come, shine on those you live in darkness
    and the shadow of death.**

Let us bring our hopes and needs to God, as we pray: **God of light, hear our prayer.**

Let us pray with the words that Jesus taught us:

Our Father …

[Sing 'O Come, O Come, Emmanuel' AOV 1-174, verse 6]

Lord our God, you bring light and joy
to the darkness of this world.
Let us carry your light in our hearts this day.

LEADER
Let us all say:
Come, Lord Jesus!
Come, Lord Jesus!

LEADER
Let us all say:
Come quickly!
Come quickly!

☩ All make the Sign of the Cross.

[Put out the candles of the Advent wreath.]

December 17, 2019

Wednesday Daily Prayer

[Reminder: If you have an Advent wreath light two purple and one rose candle before the psalm.]

Introduction

In today's 'O Antiphon' we call Jesus our keystone. The keystone is the stone in the middle of an arch. It supports the whole arch so it doesn't fall down and make the building or bridge collapse.

In the gospel of Matthew, Jesus is also called a cornerstone. The cornerstone of a building is like an anchor for the walls so they can be strong and true.

✞ All make the Sign of the Cross.

Hymn

A Psalm for Advent

[Turn to page 240.]

Reading   Isaiah 28:16-17

Listen to the words of the prophet Isaiah:

The Lord says this:
"I am laying a firm foundation for the city of Zion.
It's a valuable cornerstone proven to be trustworthy;
no one who trusts it will ever be disappointed.
Justice and fairness will be the measuring lines
    that help me build".

The word of the Lord.

Reflection

In what ways is Jesus like the keystone of my life? How is Jesus the cornerstone of the church? What other images suggest the strength and reliability of a building?

Closing

Let us all say:
O King of all nations and cornerstone of the Church!
O King of all nations and cornerstone of the Church!

You are the joy of every human heart:
Come and save your people whom you have formed from dust.

Let us bring our hopes and needs to God, as we pray: **God of strength, hear our prayer.**

Let us pray with the words that Jesus taught us:

Our Father …

[Sing 'O Come, O Come, Emmanuel' AOV 1-174, verse 7]

Lord our God, you bring light and joy
to the darkness of this world.
Let us carry your light in our hearts this day.

LEADER
Let us all say:
Come, Lord Jesus!
Come, Lord Jesus!

LEADER
Let us all say:
Come quickly!
Come quickly!
✞ All make the Sign of the Cross.

[Put out the candles of the Advent wreath.]

December 18, 2019

Thursday Daily Prayer

[Reminder: If you are using an Advent wreath, light two purple and one rose candle before the psalm.]

Introduction

The church's year began again this month with Advent, but the school year is coming to an end. Our prayer today is one that we have been preparing for. It is "O Emmanuel! O God with us!"

When we pray in the hymn for God to "ransom captive Israel" we remember the time when the people of God were taken as slaves to a far country. They longed for a time when they would be free to return to their homes. The prophets, like Isaiah, told them to have hope. God would send the messiah to rescue them. We have shared their hope during Advent. And so we, too, are ready to welcome the Saviour with great joy.

✛ All make the Sign of the Cross.

Hymn

A Psalm for Advent

[Turn to page 240.]

Reading   Isaiah 7:13-14

Listen to the words of the prophet Isaiah:

Then Isaiah said:
"Listen, every one of you in the royal family of David.
The Lord will give you a proof.
A virgin is with child;
she will have a son and will name him Immanuel."

The word of the Lord.

Reflection

Mary and Joseph are ready. Zechariah (*zek-uh-RYE-uh*) and Elizabeth are ready. They are prepared for the coming of the saving love of God. Are we prepared? Do we mean it when we pray, "Come, Lord Jesus"?

Closing

Let us all say:
O Emmanuel!
O Emmanuel!

You are the desire of all nations:
Come and set us free, Lord our God.

Let us bring our hopes and needs to God, as we pray: **God with us, hear our prayer.**

Let us pray with the words that Jesus taught us:

Our Father …

[Sing all verses of 'O Come, O Come, Emmanuel' AOV 1-174.]

Lord our God, you bring light and joy
to the darkness of our world.
Let us carry your light in our hearts this day.
May your light keep us safe from all harm.

LEADER
Let us all say:
Come, Lord Jesus!
Come, Lord Jesus!

LEADER
Let us all say:
Come quickly!
Come quickly!

✛ All make the Sign of the Cross.

[Put out the candles of the Advent wreath.]

December 19, 2019

Helpful Resources

Ritual Books, Prayer Texts and Other Liturgical Resources
Book of Blessings. Collegeville, MN: The Liturgical Press, 1988.
Catholic Household Blessings and Prayers. Publishing service, United States Catholic Conference, 1986. An invaluable resource for the classroom and home.
Lectionary for Masses With Children. Sunday volumes for Years A, B and C, and a volume for weekdays. Chicago: Liturgy Training Publications, 1993. The soft cover editions are good for classroom use. The hard cover Ritual editions could be used for more formal liturgical occasions.

General Reference
All Saints: Daily Reflections on Saints, Prophets and Witnesses for Our Time. Robert Ellsberg. New York: Crossroad Publishing Co., 1998.
Celebrating the Church Year with Young Children. Joan Halmo. Collegeville, MN: The Liturgical Press, 1988.
Companion to the Calendar. Mary Ellen Hynes. Chicago: Liturgy Training Publications, 1993.
The Folklore of World Holidays. Margaret Read McDonald, ed. Detroit: Gale Research, Inc., 1992.
A Pilgrim's Almanac. Edward Hays. Leavenworth, KS: Forest of Peace Books, Inc., 1989.
Saints Kit. Mary Kathleen Glavich. Chicago: Loyola University Press, 1994. Includes a Supplement that names some of the saints from the National Calendar for Australia.
Saints of the Seasons for Children. Ethel Pochocki. Ohio: St Anthony Messenger Press, 1989.
Sister Wendy's Book of Saints. Sister Wendy Beckett. London: Dorling Kindersley, 1998.
The Year of Grace: A Liturgical Calendar. Annual. A colourful poster of the liturgical year, which would be useful for each classroom. Chicago: Liturgy Training Publications

Materials Useful to Teachers
Blessings and Prayers through the Year: A Resource for School and Parish. Elizabeth McMahon Jeep. Chicago: Liturgy Training Publications & World Library Publications, 2004.
Break Open the Word. Annual. Brisbane: Liturgical Commission.
Children in the Assembly of the Church. Eleanor Bernstein, SCJ and John Brooks-Leonard, eds. Chicago: Liturgy Training Publications, 1993. Essays about liturgy with Children.
A Guide to the Lectionary for Masses with Children. Peter Mazar and Robert Piercy. Chicago: Liturgy Training Publications, 1994. Includes suggestions for weekday Masses during the school year.
Living Liturgy: Sundays and Solemnities. Years A, B, C. Joyce Zimmermann et al. Collegeville: Liturgical Press.
Preparing Liturgy for Children and Children for Liturgy. Gabe Huck et al. Chicago: Liturgy Training Publications, 1989. Valuable guide for those who work with children and worship.
Preparing Liturgies for the Classroom. Margaret Bick. Collegeville, MN: The Liturgical Press, 1998.
Sunday: Weekly Leader Guide: Sunday, Feast Days & Solemnities. Years A, B, C. Christiane Brusselmans, Paul Freeburg et al. Ohio: Treehaus Communications.

Music for the Liturgy
Hymn suggestions in the 'Looking Ahead' pages have been taken mainly from *As One Voice Vols 1 & 2* (Sydney: Willow Connections), with supplementary material from *Gather Australia* (Melbourne: NLMC Publications).
See also *Catholic Worship Book II* (Northcote, Vic., Morning Star Publishing).
Other:
Calling the Children. Christopher Walker. Portland, Oregon: Oregon Catholic Press Publications, 1992. Excellent liturgical and seasonal resource. Book and CD.
Come All You People: Shorter Songs for Worship. John Bell. Wild Goose Publications. book and CD.
Many and Great: Songs of the World Church. John Bell. Wild Goose Publications. Contains short refrains in different languages. Book and CD.
Music for Children's Liturgy of the Word — Cycles A, B & C. Christopher Walker. Portland, Oregon: Oregon Catholic Press Publications, 1988–1990. An invaluable resource for Weekly Prayer. Books and CDs.

Subject Index

This index covers the church festivals, saints' days, national days and other observances that are referred to in the Introductions to Daily or Weekly Prayer.

NB Please note that the date they are mentioned does not necessarily correspond to the actual day of observance.

*Days ranked as feasts and solemnities on the church's calendar are in **bold type**.*

Advent, season of, page 238 and November 29
All Saints Day, page 214 and November 1
All Souls Day, page 214 and November 4
Annunciation of the Lord, March 25
Ascension of the Lord, May 31
Ash Wednesday, March 6
Ashes, Preparation of, page 35
Assumption of the Virgin Mary, August 15
Aubert, Suzanne, June 19
Augustine, St, August 27

Bakhita, St Josephine, February 7
Body and Blood of Christ, June 21

Camara, Dom Helder, August 26
Cecilia, St, November 25
Charbel, St, July 24
Chardin, Teilhard de, May 1
Children's Day, United Nations, November 20
Chinese New Year, February 5
Chisholm, Caroline, May 29
Christ the King, November 22
Christian Unity, Week of Prayer for, May 31
Cooper, Whina, August 12
Creation, World Day of Prayer for Care of, page 172 and September 2
Cross, Triumph of the, September 12

Damien of Molokai, St, May 13
Day, Dorothy, November 26
Douglas, Francis, July 29
Dunlop, Sir Edward Weary, November 11

Eid al Fitr, June 5
El Salvador, Jesuit martyrs of, November 14
El Salvador, women martyrs of, December 2
Environment Day, World, June 5

Fathers Day, August 30
Flynn, John, May 15
Food Day, World, page 197 and October 16

Glowery, Mary, May 7

Hannukah, page 238
Harmony Day, March 21
Hollows, Fred, February 18
Holy Week, page 57
Human Rights Day, December 10

Immaculate Conception, December 9
Indigenous Peoples, International Day for the World's, page 147 and August 12
International Women's Day, March 7

James, St, page 128 and July 25
Joachim and Anne, Sts, page 128
John the Baptist, Birth of, June 24
Joseph, St, March 19

Kennedy, Ted, May 20
Kenny, Sr Elizabeth, May 16
Kolbe, St Maximilian, August 14
Kulper, Karl, September 17
Korean martyrs, September 18

Lawler, Kevin, June 25
Luke, St, page 197 and October 17

McAuley, Catherine, November 12
McCormack, Irene, May 21
Marcellin Champagnat, St, June 11
Mary Help of Christians, May 23
Mary MacKillop, St, page 146 and August 8
Mary Magdalene, St, page 128 and July 22
Matthew, St, September 23
Matthias, St, May 14

[257]

Miethke, Adelaide, June 12
Monica, St, August 27
Mother's Day, May 9

National Reconciliation Week, page 91
  and May 27
National Sorry Day, May 27
Nicholas, St, December 5
Nightingale, Florence, August 13
Noonuccal, Oodgeroo, November 7
Nurses, Australian War, August 21
Nurses, International Day for, May 16

O Antiphons, December 10
Ozanam, Frederic, Blessed, August 22

Palm/Passion Sunday, April 12
Patrick, St, March 18
Peace, United Nations Day for, September 19
Pentecost Sunday, page 90 and June 7
Peter, Chair of, February 21
Philip and James, Sts, May 2
Polding, Archbishop Bede, March 14
Poverty, United Nations Day for the
  Eradication of, page 197 and October 16
Presentation of the Lord, January 31
Presentation of Mary, page 215
  and November 21
Psalms
  • *Psalms are Prayers*, page 30
  • *Psalms are Poems*, page 54
  • *Psalms are Shouts*, page 88
  • *Psalms are Cries*, page 108
  • *Psalms are Cosmic Chants*, page 144
Purim, page 33 and March 20

Ramadan, page 71 and May 6
Refugee Day, World, June 20
Remembrance Day, November 11
Rice, Bl. Edmund, May 8
Rosh Hashanah, page 172

Sacred Heart, page 111 and June 27
Schütz, Bro Roger, August 19
Shrove Tuesday, March 5
Sick, World Day of Prayer for the, February 11
Simkat Torah, page 197 and October 22

Simon and Jude, Sts, October 28
Staines, Graham, May 21
Sukkot, October 14

Talbot, Matthew, June 6
Teresa of Calcutta, St, September 5
Teresa of Jesus, St, October 15
Thomas the Apostle, St, page 111
Transfiguration, page 146 and August 6
Trinity Sunday, Jun 14

United Nations Day, October 24

Valentine, St, February 14
Vincent de Paul, St, September 26
Visitation of the Blessed Virgin Mary, May 30

Waitangi Day, February 6
Ward, Mary, November 5

Yom Hashoah, May 2
Yom Kippur, page 173

www.ingramcontent.com/pod-product-compliance
Lightning Source LLC
Chambersburg PA
CBHW060510300426
44112CB00017B/2606